My Wandering Uterus

tales of traveling while female

Edited by K. A. Laity

Foreword by H. Byron Ballard

DEDICATION

For Margery Kempe
& all intrepid women who wander

CONTENTS

Acknowledgments   ix

Invocation: A Journey Charm — K. A. Laity   1

Foreword — H. Byron Ballard   3

Accidental Openings — Carolyn Coulson   5

Wearing the Shalwar Kameez — Dawn Reno Langley   17

Once Upon a Time in Mexico — Catherine Lundoff   37

Poems — Devon Balwit   46

In the Course of a Pilgrimage — Tahni J. Nikitins   52

The Five Dollar Car — Diane Payne   67

The Threshold of the Sheela — Amy J. Rio   77

Mexican Getaway — Tonja LH Vernazza   92

In Search of Sorrow — G. Clark Hellery   102

Freedom of Voice — Jessica Marie Baumgartner   114

How Could I Disappear? — Sandi Hoover   126

The Week I was Jodie Foster — Leanne Breiholz   136

The Time I Went to Malta — Holli Shan   148

Sally Lunn — H. Byron Ballard   158

Good Fortune — Ellen J. Perry   168

Five Poems — Miriam Sagan   177

From Warrior to Chaplain: Giving the Middle Finger to the Patriarchy — Tiffany Andes   182

Notes from Barakhamba — Kate Telma   190

Pilgrimages — Ginger Strivelli   200

Chasing Shadows — Tammy Conrad   213

Motosexual & Trains of Thought — Shannon McRae   221

Five Days in Sydney: Remembering Judy Garland — Joan Coulson   226

Journal of Drive Therapy — Clara Vann-Patterson   235

Get Miles — Susannah Blanchard   254

My Uterus Did Not Wander — Tamara Miles   260

Never Look at their Faces — Sonya M. Hamrick   263

Traveling the Crow Road with My Daughter — Sheri Barker   272

Freedom to Move About the Cabin — Angela Kunschmann   276

The Anniversary Train — Catherine Nurmepuu   285

The Beauty of Language and the Inadequacies of Standard Dictionaries — Ellen Sandberg   292

My Wandering Freedom — Lisa Wagoner   302

Walking Veiled through Khan el Kalili — Cynthia Talbot   312

Hotel Sheets – Victoria Squid   319

Across the Cerulean Sea: Woman on Water? — Jane Toswell   321

Colophon: Epilogue – K. A. Laity   344

Visit us!

KALaity.com

MyVillageWitch.com

Also on Facebook & Twitter

@katelaity

@byronballard

ACKNOWLEDGMENTS

Gracious thanks are due to so many people: first to my co-conspirator, Byron. It all kicked off on her Facebook page as random folks commented on a story about the medical condition known through the ages as the 'wandering uterus' and some bright soul suggested that it was a perfect title for a collection on travel writing by women. Somehow I agreed to edit the collection with Byron before I had a chance to say, 'Hang on—I'm too busy!'

Special thanks to the Queen of Everything, Stephanie Johnson for beautiful cover art that perfectly captures the adventurous spirit of this collection. I am always amazed at how you know just the thing to do. Flint & Steel always, my friend!

Thanks to the women who contributed: for some its their first publication, others are old hands, but all were willing to grab a seat on this journey.

Big grateful thanks to my world-wide web of support including the folks who've greeted me as a friend in strange cities across the globe, the SpeakEasy dames, and my family in Dundee. Wherever I am you are near.

K. A. Laity

Hudson NY

February 2018

INVOCATION
A JOURNEY CHARM
K. A. Laity (translator)

Here are some stanzas from an Old English charm meant to offer protection to one going on a journey. The manuscript dates to the eleventh century (MS CCCC 41). To modern readers it may seem rather pagan in form; the medieval Christians would have seen nothing perturbing about it. Casting spells was just the way divinity worked.

Ic me on þisse gyrde beluce
wið þane sara stice,
wið þane grymma gryre,
wið ðane micela egsa
and wið eal þæt lað
Sygegealdor ic begale,
wordsige and worcsige.
ne me mere ne gemyrre,
ne me næfre minum feore
Bidde ic nu sigeres god
siðfæt godne,
windas on waroþum.

and on godes helde bebeode
wið þane sara slege,
[...]
þe bið eghwam lað,
þe in to land fare.
sigegyrd ic me wege,
Se me dege;
ne me maga ne geswence,
forht ne gewurþe...
godes miltse,
smylte and lihte

I encircle myself with this safeguard
 and on god's protection call
Against the sore stitch
 against the slaying wound
Against the grim horror
 […]
Against the great terror
 that is everywhere loathed
And against all that is loathsome
 which travels through this land.
A victory-charm I invoke
 a triumphant rod I wield
Word-victory and work-victory:
 may they be mine.
May no nightmare oppress me
 nor the strongman afflict me
Nor never make me fear
 to lose my life…
I now beg the god of victories
 for divine mercy
For a good journey
 with calm and pleasant
Winds upon the shore.

FOREWORD
Byron Ballard

When I venture into the dynamic world of my state public television's "EX" channel, I often encounter travel programs. Generally speaking, they are peopled by dapper elder gents with antiquated travel guides and bright trousers or by barely-shaven extremists who can't wait to parasail over a minefield or a burbling caldera. The young ones have too little personality and the old ones far too much.

With some notable exceptions, this seems to be a format from which women travelers and women travel writers are excluded. How I dream of drinking an enormous glass of red wine while watching the adventures of a band of intrepid, middle-aged women in search of a pub or holy well or urban nightspot! Witty conversation, startling insights, self-deprecated humor— truly adult entertainment.

We have been harboring a notion for about a decade that no doubt fuels my fantasy television-watching. Kate (Laity), our friend Peg Aloi and I periodically revisit the notion of the three of us—Witches all!—walking the Ridgeway and filming it for posterity. The Ridgeway is one of the oldest tracks in Britain, beginning near High Wycombe and ending somewhere in the North Wessex Downs. It's about 87 miles altogether and there are pubs every fifteen feet or so. Perfect for the three of us, intrepid middle-aged women that we are.

Last April, Terri Kapsalis's excellent essay "Hysteria, Witches, and the Wandering Uterus: a Brief History" came across my Facebook newsfeed. It is a fascinating piece—I highly recommend it (lithub.com/hysteria-witches-and-the-wandering-uterus-a-brief-history/). I reposted it, as one does, and quipped, "Wouldn't it be fun to do an anthology of travel writing by women and call it 'My Wandering Uterus?'"

Kate, who is the most prolific writer I know, chimed in. "Why not?"

Why not, indeed?

This book is the answer to both questions. A decidedly quirky group of women responded with touching, funny and remarkable essays, and this book got birthed, largely due to the expertise of Madam Laity and our partner-in-art, Stephanie Johnson, the Queen of Everything.

Travel holds interesting challenges for women, challenges that most male travelers never consider. These challenges are the stuff of excellent tales in the pub and an expansion of the traveler's knowledge, as well as her courage and persistence.

Every pilgrim has a story and these pilgrims share theirs with us here. It is strange Chaucer and humble Froissart, but it is also a bold leap into a place that women too rarely occupy—the traveler's progress, annotated and lovingly described.

ACCIDENTAL OPENINGS
Carolyn Coulson

I expect I became a wandering woman in utero. My parents' rootlessness was certainly part of what brought them together. My father was a peripatetic foster child in England, later a sailor. Until he was in his 60s, the longest he had lived in one place was seven years. His sense of 'home' until he died lay in his belongings, not in a geographic place. When she was eighteen, my mother hitch-hiked around Europe and her life was changed. She is, and has always been, most happy when traveling. She despises nearly everything 'domestic,' but in a foreign country surrounded by people from other cultures, she is in heaven. This summer, at the age of 85 with a chronic disease, she is traveling to the UK, France, Spain, Albania and Sweden. While many women my age were taught by their mothers to keep a nice house and develop their mothering skills, I was taught to value travel and to shun domesticity. These days, I actually value them both equally, but I had to teach myself the domestic stuff.

I took my first trans-Atlantic flight before I can remember, and spent my first three years of school living in the UK. When we moved back to the States, I was tormented by taunting children who wanted to hear me talk in my funny accent. Like my parents, I have never felt that I belonged anywhere in particular. I have learned to belong to myself, no matter where I am, and travel has helped me to do so. Travel has helped me develop my independence and an ability to read people quickly; it has opened my eyes and taught me to embrace the adventures that present themselves.

My traveling shoes were polished early during journeys with my parents. When we moved to England, my mother chose to transport my brother and me via ship. With a five-year-old and a two-year-old, and without her husband, she boarded a ship called the *Arcadia* in San Francisco, and we spent two weeks traversing the Panama Canal, stopping at Caribbean islands, and crossing the Bermuda Triangle, where I got sick. Only after I had traveled with my own children at a similar age did I truly begin to appreciate my mother's adventuresome spirit. Some of that spirit must have rubbed off on me when I was very young, as I still have Bahamian money that a man gave me for singing in a bar on this trip....when I was five!

While we lived in England, my family went on holiday to Torremolinos, a beach town in Andalusia when I was about six or seven. I only remember a couple of experiences from that trip: an excursion to the Alhambra and, notably, being awoken in the night by my father who took me to see a late-night flamenco show. I had to swear that I would not tell my brother, and I never have, not that he would care now. The Taberna Flamenca Pepe Lopez has held such shows since 1965, originally under the name "El Jaleo." The videos on YouTube look the same as the movies in my mind of that hot, late, intoxicating night, when I was the only child in the room. These early experiences showcase the surprises that travel has always sprung on me, the unsought discoveries that become the hallmarks of each trip. Often these discoveries are about myself more than they are about the place I'm visiting. While abroad I learn what I am capable of and what I am not afraid of.

When we were in our early teens, my mother took my brother and me on a two-week coach trip of Europe, along the lines of the 1969 movie *If it's Tuesday, This Must be Belgium*. While the trip served to orient me to the major cities of Europe, my vibrant memories of the time are not of the tourist sites we visited, but instead of the people we met and the accidental discoveries we made: the couples from Texas and Illinois who alternately adopted my brother or me for days (the Hills from Chicago took me to the red-light district in Paris); the Indian family on the trip who responded to my question about the meaning of the bindi by applying one to my 'third eye' while we were on a water-taxi in Venice (my mother made me wear it all day in order to be respectful); the one afternoon we had in Florence when I realized Michaelangelo's *David* was in the Galleria dell'Accademia, and although my mother and I failed to get there before the gallery closed, we banged on the door until an employee opened it and we could briefly see the statue down the hall; the afternoon in Lucerne, Switzerland, when I dawdled on the Kapelbrücke and got separated from the group, but realized I would be okay by myself in a foreign place. It is almost impossible to convey how important this last discovery was: in a foreign country, at age fifteen, before I had learned any German, I knew I would be okay.

Throughout all of my subsequent travel experiences, that feeling of self-reliance and independence has been reinforced. At eighteen, I back-packed around Europe with two girlfriends and a Eurail pass. The most important day of that trip was when I got separated from them in Munich and I realized it didn't matter. I knew where they would be in the evening, and I would catch up with them then. That day was golden, and ultimately it led to my tendency to prefer traveling alone.

Traveling alone, however, has its own psychological challenges, and as I reflect on my peregrinations and reread the journals I've always kept while I travel, I realize that every trip is an exercise in balancing the tension between the beauty and loneliness of solitude and the camaraderie and irritations of fellow travelers. Where I go and what I see are the physical and sensory destinations, but the journey is internal, psychological and emotional.

When I travel alone, I make my own itinerary, spending my time as I wish to spend it, eating when and what I want to eat. I can sit in front of one painting for half an hour, or cruise through an entire museum in the same time; choose to walk five miles or learn how the local transit system works; splurge on a meal or buy food from a street vendor. I am an introvert and being alone is usually less stressful than being with other people. And yet…my travel journals are full of the names and details of people I have talked to in train stations, airports, bus stops, and hostels. I have no memory of most of those people, but in the moment, I have needed them. Sometimes I needed them to help me decide where to go or what to do. Sometimes I needed them to simply give me a reason to talk out loud. Often, I needed them to remind me that I wanted to be alone! Unlike my mother, who has formed lasting friendships with the strangers she has met in airports and museums, my strangers have served an immediate purpose and generally evaporated from my memory. But a few linger, having left their mark on me permanently. I like to think of them as my travel guardian angels, magically there when I needed them for one reason or another, and then just as magically gone.

In the summer 1986, I was studying in London and spent several weeks on either side of the summer session traveling by myself and visiting relatives. Early in the trip, after visiting my cousins, I set off for York in northern England. I had a ghastly train journey without a seat, stationed by the toilets and outside the smoking carriage (back when there were smoking carriages). When I reached the youth hostel in York, I was looking for a friendly face. The young women in my dorm room were all traveling with companions and, although pleasant, were not interested in more than a quick conversation. That has frequently been my experience in hostels: women travel with friends and therefore aren't looking for new friends, while men are more often alone and link up temporarily with other travelers. I spent some time in the evening with a couple of guys from New York, who actually irritated me as much as they entertained me. I truly believe that I only socialized with them because I didn't know how to make the transition to being by myself, and all-in-all, the evening left me feeling dispirited about the rest of my brief solitary sojourn. I was feeling so out of sorts that I was half-way planning to travel with them to Edinburgh the next day, just to avoid being alone. In the morning, I ate breakfast in the big dining hall across from another young man who was heading to London. His name was Jim, and he was a student at Stanford, not far from where I went to university. We had a wonderful conversation in which I revealed my anxiety about being alone and my feeling the need to find companions. I don't remember the details of that conversation, but I do remember feeling much calmer and more confident after it. I don't know what he said to me, but it helped set my head straight. As it happened, when I did meet up with the New Yorkers in Edinburgh, it didn't take me long to decide they were a waste of time. I shook them off and went on my way more comfortable with myself. Jim from Stanford was instrumental in my ability to do so.

Less than a week later, I met up with my mother in London to experience the excitement of the Royal Wedding of Prince Andrew to Sarah Ferguson. Neither of us was equipped for the chaos that such an event throws London into. We arrived outside Buckingham

Palace at 8:15 am and found a spot at the base of the Queen Victoria Memorial. Many of the people around us had camped out all night. Those people were stocked with food and drinks. We had arrived with nothing, not even a bottle of water. We had no idea that we would end up trapped in one place for nearly seven hours. The carriages with the royals left the Palace heading to Westminster Abbey at about 10:30, and we waited to listen to an audio broadcast of the wedding over loudspeakers throughout the crowds. The records say that Sarah Ferguson arrived at Westminster at 11:30, and the ceremony was about forty-five minutes long. By the time the ceremony was finished, we had been outside the Palace for four hours. Then the carriages and newlyweds rode back to the Palace, and all the people in London who were lining the streets along the carriage route came up the Mall to wait for the royal couple to emerge on the balcony for their first public kiss as man and wife. BBC News estimated that a crowd of 100,000 was outside the Palace to witness it. I suppose it would have all been very exciting if I had not been feeling ill, dehydrated, and hungry. I also suffer from panic attacks when I am caught in crowds, something I discovered on a crowded train platform in Munich. On the day of the Royal Wedding I had an additional challenge, which seems fitting to disclose given the title of this collection. I had that morning begun my menstrual period, two weeks late. Our position at the Victoria Memorial, which is in the center of the traffic circle outside the Palace, afforded us no access to toilets, and my desperation grew as the hordes of people streamed up the Mall. The press of 100,000 people prevented me from escaping or even searching for a porta-John.

I found an initial escape from the crowd by sitting in a deck chair on the side of the Memorial which afforded no view of the Palace balcony. In fact, a few days later, one of the major London papers ran a center photo in their Sunday magazine which was an aerial view of the crowd outside the Palace when the couple came out on the balcony. I could identify myself in that photo, because no one else was anywhere near me. By the time that photograph was taken, I was in a bad state, with blood soaked through my jeans halfway down my thighs. Shortly thereafter, I decided that I could not wait anymore and started to fight my way through the crowd, in tears. My mother was somewhere back in the throng, but all I could think of was getting to a bathroom. I was met with stares and looks of confusion, as no one could understand my anxiety and tears. In fact, the police from whom I asked for help rolled their eyes at me when I asked for a bathroom. Those police, both men and women, laughed at me saying I was 'hysterical' because I 'just needed a loo.' As a matter of fact, I was hemorrhaging. I don't remember much of the next half-hour or so, as I was more or less stumbling through London. I remember I found a bathroom somewhere but couldn't do much to help my situation, given the mess I was in. And then, outside Victoria Rail Station, I heard someone say my name. I turned around, and there was Jim from the York youth hostel! In a city the size of London, on a day with an unusually large crowd of visitors on the street, somehow I found a friend. He was astonished as I collapsed into his arms and babbled something about what was wrong. He said, "let's take you back to your hotel, get you cleaned up, and then go have some lunch." And that is what we did. My mother, in the meantime, was asking the police to call the hospitals, because she imagined I'd collapsed and been taken away! She was equal parts relieved and angry when she later found my note at the hotel: "I found a friend—gone to eat."

To this day, I do not understand how, at that moment of crisis, that "stranger-friend" found me. We had met once. What made him see me in the crowds on the street? How did we come to be in the same place at the same time? What would have been the outcome of my day if he hadn't called out to me? After we had something to eat, I was back on the street when the carriage taking the bride and groom to the airport to begin their honeymoon passed by. I stopped and waved to them, consciously thinking, "no hard feelings…you gave me one of the worst days of my life, but it turned out all right." Although I never saw Jim again, I did talk to him on the phone once. During the following fall, I was going through a particularly tumultuous time at college, feeling terribly depressed. Out of the blue one night, he called me, just to say hello and see how I was doing. Once again he saved me. Thank you, Jim from Stanford.

My experiences during the first two weeks of that trip in 1986 shaped the rest of my summer. Jim had taught me to trust my instincts about people. After the summer course was over, I headed out of London again with my BritRail pass. One of the towns I visited was Rochester, in Kent. My primary reason for going was that it was adjacent to the town where my father had been born. I arrived without much of an agenda or itinerary, feeling particularly philosophical, as a passage from *The Last Temptation of Christ* about the joy of arriving in a new town and being at the mercy of strangers for a meal had struck a chord in me. Rochester is not really a tourist destination; instead it is quite a sleepy town, especially on a late Sunday afternoon, which is when I arrived. The only person I saw on the street as I wandered around looking for a place to stay was an Anglo-Indian young man who said hello. After I had checked into my room, I walked to the closed Tourist Information Kiosk, because it had a map I wanted to look at. As I stood there reading the map, the same young man walked by and struck up a conversation with me. I suppose young women didn't backpack their way into Rochester very often in those days, as he was keen to know why I was there. After we spoke for about ten minutes, he said, "This is going to sound strange, but let me explain. When I was in Paris, the African vendors found out I had nowhere to stay and nothing to eat, and they took me in. Ever since, I have wanted to show someone else the same hospitality. Will you let me cook you dinner?"

Every shred of common sense says that I should have declined. I certainly would be concerned if my own daughter were to consider the same offer. But in that moment, next to that map of Rochester, I chose to follow the gut instinct that believed the young man's earnestness. I said, "Yes." He took me to his apartment, which turned out to be a 'squat,' meaning that he was occupying a vacant building. He had no electricity or running water. I did not ask why he was squatting—if it was due to financial need or a political statement. Instead, I realized that I was his guest, no matter how meager the abode, and I felt that to call attention to the abandoned building and lack of utilities would come off as criticism. He cooked up some curry on a camp stove, and it was delicious. After dinner, he asked if I'd like to go meet some of his friends at a pub, and off we trotted. I had a fabulous evening, and at the end of it, I arrived safely back at my hotel. Even thirty-one years later, the entire sequence of events seems surreal to me. What was I thinking? Why didn't I back out at some point, especially as I climbed the darkened stairwell in an abandoned building? I have no answer, except to say that my instinct told me he was genuine. He was so happy to show me the hospitality he had been shown in Paris. His friends seemed equally happy to host me at the pub. Nothing was expected of me in return. It was an evening that restored my belief in community and kindness. It was the best reason for traveling.

Thirty years later, in 2016, I was once again traveling solo while on sabbatical. When booking my train from London to Amsterdam, via Brussels, I discovered it was only €6 more to travel first class, so I decided to splurge.

I had an assigned seat, a single, with a table, facing another single. The carriage had a few other people in it, but lots of empty seats. Just before we pulled out of St. Pancras Station, a man sat down in the seat across from me. We both pulled out our laptops to work. About fifteen minutes into the trip, a light meal service began of a croissant, tea, and orange juice, and the woman serving the meal suggested that this man and I didn't need to sit facing each other, since there were lots of empty seats, and with our computers out, there was no room for the trays. In his totally London way, he rather charmingly said, "She's all right. She doesn't smell. In fact, she smells quite nice," suggesting we did not need to move. The rail lady said, "but there's no room," and I said I would take my meal tray to one of the empty seats.

After eating, I returned to my seat and worked on my computer for a while, with frequent breaks to stare dreamily out the window, wondering what Amsterdam would be like. I also spent some time looking at the man across from me, wondering what he was like and what he did for a living. I thought perhaps he was an actor. He looked like and had the carriage of an actor. But we shared no more words during the journey. Later, after some passengers had left, I moved to another seat across the aisle, took a little nap and stretched out my legs. When the train arrived in Brussels, my journey-mate and I finally had a little conversation which led to us finding out we were both bound for Amsterdam, and very quickly to the discovery that we both worked in entertainment fields. He was on a gig directing a commercial.

The speed at which one can find out things about strangers amazes me. In the amount of time it took for the train to pull into the station, for us to disembark and to get off the platform, he knew I was a theatre professor, director, and a medievalist, and I knew he was teaching and coaching actors and transitioning from directing commercials and video into feature films, after having a career in contemporary dance. How does that happen? How is it that we can be acquainted with people for years and know less about them (and disclose less about ourselves) than we can share with someone we meet while traveling? What is it about the mindset we get in when we travel?

This new friendship was useful to me in that I didn't know where I was going or what train I was supposed to get on for my change in Brussels, which is a huge, overwhelming station. My friend made the trip a lot, and escorted me to where he thought I should go, all the while madly discussing theatre, teaching, young actors, etc. There was some confusion about my ticket, and he took me to the information center and got me sorted out, then to the platform I needed. While we were waiting at the info center, I mentioned that I had just led a study abroad trip and seen a lot of shows in London. That led to a conversation about a particular actor whom I brought up as a stand-out and whom, it turns out, had repeatedly come up for him as a possible casting choice for an upcoming project. What are the odds that a random conversation would take this direction? What put us in seats directly across from each other when there were plenty of empty seats in the carriage?

We wrapped up the whirlwind conversation by introducing ourselves by name. Isn't that a funny thing? Names came last. He took my email and asked if I would give him my UK phone number, fearing that I might think he was stalking me. I said, "There aren't many things that scare me," as I typed my number and email into his phone. And that's the truth. There aren't many things that scare me, and I'm especially brave when I'm traveling. Perhaps that's why I love it so much. Some of my favorite memories in life are of the chance encounters I've had when my split-second decision to trust another human being has brought me face to face with the beauty of how kind and connected people can be.

These are my travel angels, a few of the hidden 'Easter egg' surprises of my journeys. This is my thank-you to them. They will never know their impact on me, but I am glad to have shared it with you. I hope we never stop traveling, encountering, and discovering new places in the world and new places in ourselves.

Travel. Smile. Open your mind. Open your heart. Stare dreamily out the train windows. Receive.

WEARING THE SHALWAR KAMEEZ
Dawn Reno Langley

-1-

The trip to Islamabad immerses you. Step by step. It starts in New York when you sit beside a woman in full-length black burkha that covers almost every inch of her body. You have something in common: you both hold tickets for Qatar. Beyond that, she is the most foreign person you've ever seen. She chats on the phone in another language, something Middle Eastern, her voice rising in excited octaves, her be-ringed fingers fluttering in ruby and emerald and diamond waves. You watch her fingers as she speaks, idly wondering exactly how much those rings are worth and whether she's part of a Saudi prince's harem. She finishes her conversation, snaps her phone shut, then turns to you and says, "Teenagers! Don't they ever stop eating junk food?" in a perfect English accent.

Your mouth moves but no words come out. The last thing you had expected was for this woman—dressed in black from head to toe, only her eyes showing through a thick piece of mesh—to connect with you on the most elemental level: motherhood.

A handsome, dark-haired boy wearing a red-and-white checked scarf haphazardly thrown around his neck hovers behind her, McDonald's bag in hand. She points a jeweled finger at him and says, "My son. Eighteen years old. Still asking me for money." She clucks her tongue and looks the other way, as though she is the one responsible for his neediness.

You commiserate about teenagers and their desire for fast food, cell phones and unsavory friends. Fifteen minutes later, you no longer register the full burkha but instead note her gorgeously smoky eyes, her hoarse laugh, and the way her hands flutter like purple and gold hummingbird's wings.

You and the woman fly to Qatar at opposite ends of the plane: she in first class; you doubled up and yearning for sleep near the rear of the plane. Nine hours later, you glance out the plane's window to see gleaming silver and glass skyscrapers. Qatar, home of the 'dallah' (the coffee pot monument), Al Jazeera TV, and some of the most incredible architecture in the world. The city rises into the sky like Coruscant, the Imperial Center from Star Wars, strange and post-modern and otherworldly, stretching toward the heavens, the lightning rod triumphantly reaching toward the solar system. If clouds littered the lavender ice-blue sky, Qatar would punctuate them, but this part of the world is dry.

Before you left North Carolina for the Fulbright fellowship you've been awarded to research creative women in education, you listened to warnings. Friends and family expressed their concern that you would be traveling to the part of the world where terrorism happens regularly. People blow themselves up in the Middle East, they said, often taking dozens with them. 'They' don't like Americans. 'They' burn effigies of 'us.' 'They' think 'we' are Satan incarnate. And 'we' think the same of 'them.' The basis of prejudice is stupidity and a lack of understanding, you tell them.

As you stand in line for customs, you gaze at the people around you. Dozens of languages float through the air, sounds that are hoarse and clacking, guttural and tinkling, sensual and raspy. Strange and unidentifiable. You search for something to understand.

Nothing.

Then, English. A couple traveling from England to India. "You put the fucking passport in the wrong blasted pouch!" She, gray haired and frazzled; he, tall and hook-nosed, his white hair in disarray, his eyes confused. How many others would understand their marital argument? You're mildly embarrassed by their confrontation.

But you're far more interested in those who are foreign to you, like the man in the next line. Hawk-faced, his brow tightly wrinkled, his small black eyes brought closer together by his frown. He wears a skull cap woven in oranges and browns and, like many others in line, his white Nehru-collared shirt hangs below his hips and is recently starched. You wonder where he lives, what his family is like, whether he is traveling home from work or to a funeral far away. He scans the crowd and his dusky eyes flitter by you, barely making contact, and you realize you are not as conspicuous as you feel.

-2-

On May 2, 2011, American news stations interrupted their regularly-scheduled programs to show a shadowy, tension-filled clip of Navy Seals descending from a helicopter to a rooftop in Abbottabad, Pakistan. Staccato gunshots split the black night air. Women screamed. Bodies fell. Then the cameras switched to President Obama, dressed in an open-necked shirt and light jacket, leaning forward, body taut, eyes intent, elbows on his knees, his chin cupped in his hands. He sat with his team, six people around a table, another group standing in the background. Secretary of State Hillary Clinton, one hand over her mouth, obviously amazed by the events she watched in real time, revealed a human fear repeated in the other faces around the room. Transfixed by the images of the daring infiltration of the terrorist Osama bin Laden's compound, everyone held their breath in the hope that the mission would be successful.

Mere moments later, the Navy Seals took the compound. Five people dead, including bin Laden himself, who had eluded capture for eleven years since masterminding the 9/11 attacks that had ended 2,996 lives. Since the attack against bin Laden took place on Pakistani soil, our tenuous friendship with that nation shivered.

While I watched the horrific scene like millions of others, I released a palpable sigh of relief. No dancing in the streets, as we had witnessed when Saddam Hussein was found burrowed like a crazy rat in an underground tunnel. Just relief. We'd cut off the cobra's head and terrorism as we knew it would now end, many believed.

But it didn't.

The cobra became a hydra and no amount of retaliation would sever the appropriate head.

I can understand the Pakistani people's Janus-faced opinion of Americans. Some hate us; some love us. Most know of someone (family member, friend, colleague) killed or injured by American drones patrolling the borders between their country and Afghanistan. Some know extremists who bomb Pakistani neighborhoods, targeting Westerners yet killing their own people. We have an alliance of sorts with their government, yet our border patrols do precious little to protect Pakistani lives. Instead, they threaten them.

News reports touted the compound where bin Laden lived as 'walled' and 'protected by barbed wire.' What the reporters failed to mention was that most homes in Pakistan's larger cities are 'walled' and 'protected.' The Fulbright house where I lived in Islamabad had a 7' high wall around its perimeter, painted to match the stucco exterior of the three-story house. Hot pink bougainvillea trailed merrily through coils of barbed wire atop the wall. A henna-haired guard patrolled the property's border 24/7. At the Fulbright offices less than ten kilometers away, guards checked each car entering the gates, running a long-handled mirror designed to spot bombs underneath each vehicle. It freaked me out a bit, but the Pakistanis said that the traffic stops and barbed wire and bomb checks had been part of their lives for decades. The only thing that had changed was that technology improved when the terrorist acts became more intense.

Yes, Osama bin Laden's compound was nothing unusual. What was strange was that Americans believed the news reports that his was the only building with such protection. No one questions the media.

How naïve, I thought.

-3-

The flight from Qatar to Islamabad lowers you further into the culture, bringing you literally and figuratively farther away from what you know of yourself. You willingly let that identity slide away, especially when you realize you are not only a woman traveling alone but also the only white woman on the plane. Everyone turns and stares. Hard.

Though you've been traveling alone for almost twenty hours, you feel more awake now than you had been in New York City. You want to miss nothing.

The man next to you fits the American stereotype of a terrorist: thick black hair, a full and unruly black beard, piercing eyes. He is dressed in a white tunic and loose pajama-style pants. He speaks with the flight attendant—in the gruffest voice you've ever heard—

when the food arrives. She waits on him attentively, answering his requests respectfully. You take for granted that he doesn't speak English nor does he want to be seated next to you. You don't glance in his direction, intimidated by his demeanor.

Then you hear his voice in your ear. "For why are you traveling to Pakistan?"

"Excuse me?"

"What is your purpose for visiting my country?"

You glance at him. He's smiling, but his black eyes still intimidate you. Stammering, you explain the Fulbright scholar program, how you will research creative women in education, and how your friend Shaheena, a Fulbright scholar and native Pakistani, talked you into coming to Islamabad. He listens, nodding, asking questions, making formal travel-talk.

The conversation shifts to him as filtered moonlight pours through the plane's small windows. He speaks of his work in Saudi Arabia's oil fields, talks of missing his children and his wife, of his home village in the mountains about an hour away from Islamabad, about the beauty of the land—especially at this time of year— and he invites you there to meet his seven children and the villagers, explains that his family are the leaders in the village, that his father and his grandfather and his great-grandfather have all been tribal chief during their lifetimes, and that the responsibility has been passed to him, and from him, will pass to his eldest son. Ibrahim is his name, he says, one hand on his heart, his head inclined reverently.

"A great responsibility," he looks to the heavens and whispers, "In'shallah," as a Christian might invoke an "amen" or a "praise Jesus."

You imagine his children rushing to meet him upon his arrival, wonder what his wife looks like.

He asks you about your family and you tell him about your husband and daughter, about your parents and how you were raised. By the time the plane begins its descent into Islamabad, you are old friends and it is 4 AM.

He begins pulling out many yards of white linen from his carry-on. Yards and yards of the cloth. Like a magician, he wraps the cloth around his head. Layer after layer. You are fascinated that it sits so perfectly on his head. Finally, he lifts the tail of the white linen to his lips and kisses it. Then he smiles at you.

The plane's landing gear lowers with a clunk.

"May I be the first to welcome you to Pakistan," he says.

-4-

In March, 2015, the terrorist group calling itself the Islamic State of ISIS murders 130 in Yemen. They bomb mosques where people come for their daily prayers, people who practice the same religion, yet do not believe in the ISIS vision of Islam. ISIS and their counterparts, al Qaeda and Houthis, target people they call infidels, choosing to bomb high-profile targets, getting the most 'bang for their buck,' as crass as that might sound. Choosing schools, shopping centers and mosques, the terrorist groups gain both attention and a death toll that moves them toward their goal. For al Qaeda, that goal is to establish an Islamic Caliphate, a government led by a religious leader believed to have a direct line to the prophet Muhammad. For ISIS, the goal is to gain territory. And the Houthis, a rebel group based in Yemen who originally fought for peace and were bent on changing things locally, have become a militia, chanting "Death to Israel, Death to Americans." They, too, bomb mosques.

In Islamabad, I loved the sounds of the call to prayer coming from mosques, but was warned again and again to be in a safe place during the call to prayer. Not a mosque. When the State Department reiterated that warning during our security briefing at the beginning of my stay in Pakistan, I thought that bombing churches—which is what a mosque is—would not be something we would tolerate. If one cannot practice one's own religion safely, what else is safe?

When some of the female students and I went shopping in a downtown area one day, my driver and I compared watches, agreeing that I would report back to the vehicle in a little over an hour. The girls and I, excited about getting to know each other, visited several boutiques where I bought two shalwar kameezes, the traditional Pakistani clothing. The three-piece outfit (long tunic, pajama-like pants, and scarf) became my dress for the rest of my visit, and I could see why everyone wore it. Not only was it comfortable, but it was perfect for the hot climate. I bought two: a sage green outfit and another in grey and pink.

As we shopped, I learned about the girls' families, the food they loved (chocolate is an international guilty pleasure), and their academic goals. We lost track of time, and entering the parking lot, I spotted my driver on his cell phone, spinning in agitated circles, talking loudly and gesturing wildly. When he sees us, he snaps the phone shut and moves forward, speaking rapidly in Urdu to the girls. They look properly chagrined and apologize for keeping me longer than they should have. In spite of the warnings at the Embassy, I have broken the rules and put myself—and the girls and my driver—in danger. It was prayer-time, and we were near a mosque. He berated me for being late when we got into the car, and I realized that my naiveté could have cost my life. The ride back to the Fulbright house became chillingly quiet.

-5-

When you arrive in Islamabad, you settle your suitcase on a double bed in the mahogany-paneled bedroom in the Fulbright house. Your chest thrums with your pulse. Your ears buzz as if you've had too much caffeine. You've been traveling for twenty-six hours, and if you don't sleep soon, you'll collapse, probably knocking your head on the large bureau. A vase filled with yellow and orange summer flowers sits on the bureau. It is the first of many bouquets you'll receive while in Islamabad, but you don't know that yet. There is much you don't know.

Moving to the tiny bathroom, you splash your face with tepid water, brush your teeth, trying to ignore the ringing in your ears then realize with a start that it is not ringing at all. Someone is singing. You turn off the water and move below the tiny window above your head. In the pre-dawn stillness, a deep voice intones the call to prayer. You've heard it before: in movies, on television, in news reports. It's always been foreign. Strange. Somewhat scary.

From a different direction, another voice chimes in. You stretch your neck to hear more clearly. Then another voice, a closer sound. And another. It is a symphony of prayers as if all the holy men timed their prayers to create a concert just for you. The sound mesmerizes and its beauty fills your eyes with tears. You stand there listening with every molecule in your body until the calls stop as they started: one at a time.

Over the next few days, you hear those prayers five times a day—before the sun comes up in the morning, at lunchtime, in the middle of the afternoon, near dinner, and at night—but the call to prayer is never more haunting and beautiful than it is during that quietest of time before dawn. You find yourself wandering to the roof to hear the call and gaze out over the dark shadows of Islamabad, spotting the silhouetted mosques and trying to match each call with the appropriate mosque.

Then one day during midday prayers, you have company.

The house next door is full of family members,

perhaps three generations, and some of the women appear on their rooftop in the middle of that sunny afternoon. Children laugh and chase each other, a mother hangs laundry out to dry, and on the bottom floor, yelling up at them occasionally, the bearded men sit in a half circle on old wooden chairs debating what appears to be something highly-charged.

A young girl, nine or ten years old, with long, glossy black hair and round dark eyes comes to the end of her roof, holding her hand up to wave to you. You wave back. She laughs and covers her mouth with her hand, then runs away to the other side of the flat rooftop. She returns moments later and lifts up something to show to you. The sun blinds you momentarily, but you use the book you've been reading to shade your eyes and see that what the girl is holding is wriggling. It's alive. You move to the end of the roof, the girl holds the animal up higher, and she's smiling as if proud to show you. A rabbit. She snuggles it tight to her face, then lifts it once again for you to see. You smile back, call out that the rabbit is beautiful, but it's unclear whether she's heard. Someone calls for her; she runs away. You never see her again.

-6-

Almost every day for at least a month after my return from Pakistan, one of the students I met at the universities where I spoke will friend me on Facebook. I don't remember most of them, so I accept all of their friendship requests, and we have wonderful conversations about university life or their families, about their upcoming weddings and the photos they post with their families. But there is one young man who wants a political discussion with me each time I log into my Facebook account. I wonder if he's always online because, inevitably, he is there on Facebook whenever I am.

He flirts mercilessly with me though there is at least forty years' age difference between us. At first, I joke with him, but after telling him nicely on at least five different occasions that I am married and uninterested in his advances, he becomes angry. His remarks become more sexual. He cyber stalks me on other websites, and finally, I block him.

For a couple of weeks afterward, I feel guilty. I must have given him reason to believe he could pursue me, I think. I wrack my brain trying to remember where I met him. Was it at the engineering university near the Khyber Pass? Was it at the lecture I gave on American education at the National University of Modern Languages? Was he the guy in the back of the room when we talked about creative writing? I can't place him. Finally, I ask my friend Shaheena, a professor in American Studies in Islamabad, whether she recognizes his name. She does and assures me he's harmless.

My husband wonders whether I've connected with someone who truly hates Americans and asks me to stop carrying on any kind of conversation with the students.

I refuse.

-7-

The U.S. Embassy in Islamabad is nestled behind some other official buildings in an enclave guarded by military police and surrounded by cement blockades topped with barbed wire. The driver brings you down a dirt road, driving very slowly as if maneuvering through a mine field, then leaves you at the entrance gate so you can attend the briefing every Fulbright recipient is given upon entering Pakistan. It's the first time you've been nervous in this country. Up until the moment when you leave your phone and purse in a steel box at the Embassy office, you've been fascinated but not afraid of anything.

Visiting the U.S. Embassy changes that completely.

For several hours, you watch videos on safety and attend lectures about international diplomacy with half a dozen other Americans. No one talks to each other, as if afraid they might be breaking the rules. And the rules are a long, long list.

- Don't travel with someone you don't know.
- Don't visit a private residence.
- Don't leave your driver.
- Don't visit tourist destinations.
- Don't linger on the street during prayer.
- Don't carry weapons.
- Don't share personal information with strangers.

Some of the rules resemble the ones my mother created for our family; some of the rules can only exist in Pakistan.

That afternoon, a suicide bomber rams the gates of the Pakistan Rangers office in Karachi, the largest city in Pakistan but hours away from Islamabad. One person is killed, dozens injured, and the bombed building sustains major damage. Your husband frantically calls you at 3 AM. You reassure him that you are nowhere near Karachi. Later that day, you talk to some of the students about the incident, but it's a minor one, they say, and conversation turns back to American education within moments.

You realize the incident is made larger by the media. In Pakistan, life goes on.

-8-

Almost a year after returning from Pakistan, I visited a charter school and spoke to 8th and 9th graders about my visit to Islamabad. I stumbled into the school lobby, arms full with the mugs and cups various universities had given me, a pair of tiny traditional Pakistani shoes, several silk scarves I'd bought in the local market, and even some of the tea biscuits some of the students bought for me when I confessed that I'd never tasted a more delicious cookie. I wore the sage green shalwar kameez I bought the day I went shopping with the group of female students. It took me more than a week to put together a PowerPoint presentation with almost 50 photographs from the visit, taking special care to include as much geographical and historical information as I could since the teachers who'd requested my visit suggested I offer as much educational info to their students as possible. I was happy to oblige.

"Did you see any bombs explode?" one precocious 13-year-old asked me. His teacher shushed him, but I told her I didn't mind answering the question. I wanted the kids to know what Pakistanis were really like, not the convoluted images they might have seen and heard from adults and convoluted news stories.

As I answered the question, I remembered Shaheena's visit to my college three years before. We had written a request for a Fulbright scholar to come to campus, and after interviewing three Muslims from various countries, we chose her to spend six weeks with us. She arrived with full knowledge that she'd be representing both her faith and her country.

During her time with us, I drove her to the college every day, becoming friends with her, and often squiring her to the various events we scheduled for her. I knew she was at her most comfortable with the children, especially the ones she met during a meeting with a group of young boys and girls being trained in the Southern cotillion tradition. She had patiently answered some of the same questions I was now answering, and her words now echoed in my memory.

"You're learning manners here, and we teach our children the same," she had said. Some of the kids turned and looked at each other as if surprised that kids across the world were taught how to say please and thank you, as they had been. "You will make your parents proud, won't you?"

That simple exchange resonated with the children so much that one of them had stopped me on campus the previous year during a school function, remembering that I'd been escorting Shaheena that day.

"Is that lady okay?" the girl asked me. A high schooler now, she told me she had gone home that day and educated her parents about Muslims in Pakistan. "My father always talked about Muslims as though they were criminals. He was pretty surprised that I knew more than he did."

I wondered if any of the other kids I talked with at the charter school might have taken my stories of Islamabad home with them. And if they did, how many had changed their parents' prejudices? Was it too much to hope that at least one person might think differently as a result of my experience?

-9-

You ask Zulfi, your host at the Fulbright office, whether you can visit Islamabad's museums and historical sites during the upcoming holiday. Not only does he tell you about the places you should visit, but he says he will take his day off and go to the sites with you.

The driver picks you up at 8 AM, and Zulfi announces the plan for the day. You'll visit the Pakistan memorial—"newly built," he says. "I haven't even been there yet."—and the Folk Art Museum, then you'll go to the Shah Faisal mosque, one of the largest in the world, and finally, you'll go to the ancient city and, "if we have enough time, we can travel to the Margalla Hills and to Daman-e-Koh, the mountain at the base of the Himalayas."

You wear the outfit purchased during the shopping spree with the female students: a light gray and pink shalwar kameez. In spite of the traditional clothing, you still stick out like a sore thumb. You are "the English," Zulfi says.

During that day, you learn more about the history of Pakistan than you learned while studying the dozens of books you bought during the months previous to this trip. No book could provide the empathy for the struggles this country has gone through while battling for its independence. You realize how many similarities there are between their history and America's: the need to independently govern (Pakistan had been part of India), the disagreements political leaders on both sides had (Gandhi and Muhammad Ali Jinnah had very different views about the partitioning of Pakistan), and the mistakes both young and newly-formed democracy made (the United States often stumbled in the early years, as did Pakistan). But, in spite of their struggles, both America and Pakistan have managed to carve out their own distinct identities, different from their origins, yet strongly influenced by them.

At the memorial, you're surrounded by groups of school children, all dressed in their school uniforms. Some groups of girls are in blue and white shalwar kameezes; boys in khaki pants, navy blue vests and ties; older kids in somber gray outfits. Each group moves like a school of fish, mingling with the other groups, then swarming back together. An aerial view of the groups would be akin to what you'd see snorkeling through a densely-populated coral reef.

Several girls walk up to talk to you. They haggle for photos, touch your hair, giggle. You giggle, too, and stand with them as their friends snap snots. They are sweet and shy, and you find yourself wanting to hug them.

The murals on the memorial depict various important moments in Pakistan's fifty-year history. Zulfi explains them to you, then you move toward the veranda overlooking the city. The mosque is in the distance, and Zulfi points out the Fulbright office's location, then he disappears to the rest room leaving you alone.

You gaze at the city skyline, committing the silhouetted buildings to memory, and spot another group of school children heading toward you. You watch them swarm around you, pleasantly confused by their curiosity, until one of the teenage boys touches you inappropriately, showing off for his friends. At that moment, you react like a mother, lashing out, rebuking him, then you realize you are on your own in this battle. The teenagers surround you, and the boy angrily spats out something in Urdu. If you call out, you will be misunderstood; besides, you are here as a representative of the United States. You don't want to call unwanted attention to yourself. This is what they warned you about at the U.S. Embassy.

You disentangle yourself and get back to the car, breathing hard and determined to forget the incident as the day moves on. You tell Zulfi about the incident, and he laughs. It's part of growing up, he points out. He did the same thing himself as a teenager. You want to rail about women's rights, but you can't change a culture in a couple of weeks. You seal your lips and look out the window as the driver maneuvers the car through disorganized traffic.

Next stop is the Faisal Mosque.

Even though you are the only "English" in the mosque, the atmosphere is different here. People are somber. Respectful. Reverent.

In bare feet, you walk on the polished marble floors, your scarf wrapped tightly around your head. No one speaks. No children run across the expansive outside court around the building. The prayer room holds thousands, the outside space holds thousands more, and the four minarets reach toward a sky where the mosque can be seen from space. You wonder how many Americans would find this spiritual place as peaceful as you have. How many would appreciate the serenity of the Bedouin-tent-shaped building?

The day ends overlooking that same mosque, but this time from the midpoint on Daman-e-Koh, the mountain at the base of the Himalayas that offers a panoramic view of the city of Islamabad. Monkeys swarm the mountain road, peacocks 'mew' in the distance, an old man in traditional dress plays a rubab, a stringed instrument shaped like a lute. Kids chase each other around the platform, families sit on the grass with their homemade picnics, lovers peer over the edge of the platform holding tightly to each other's hands. The sun sets against the dusty city as everyone releases a chorus of appreciation.

You reluctantly follow Zulfi back to the car, feeling like you've had a holiday, as Zulfi says. On the return ride to the Fulbright compound, he sings some Sufi music and you discuss poetry.

-10-

A couple of weeks before Christmas several years after my return, a horrible attack on school children innocently taking exams and listening to their instructors' lectures shook the world. The Army Public School and Degree College in Peshawar was under siege by the Taliban, and before that siege was over, one-hundred-forty-five innocent school children, staff members and soldiers, lay dead. Innocent children, like the ones I had seen and talked to the day Zulfi and I visited the museums and the mosque. One-hundred and thirty-five kids with families, sisters and brothers, friends, lives ahead of them. Children who had never done anything to warrant a brutal senseless death.

I sat in my living room, holding my dog on my lap, and I sobbed.

I thought of my friends in Islamabad: Shaheena, her daughter and son, her husband, sister-in-law, colleagues.

I had been invited to her home. They fed me and talked with me about the world around them, about my world, about our families and friends.

I thought about the students and teachers I had met at the National University of Modern Languages: Shazia, who had shared with me that she was Christian and celebrated Christmas even though most of her friends and family were Muslim. She brought me an intricately carved bowl for a going-home gift, and if I turned my head now, I could see it sitting on my dining room table filled with lemons for the holiday.

I thought about the women—students, faculty and administration—I had spent an afternoon with at Fatima Jinnah University. I thought about our discussions about female creativity in education. I thought about the young artist I saw there, a girl wearing Converse high top sneakers (one blue, the other red), her body covered in a full black burkha, her independent spirit showing through those sneakers. I thought about the beautiful art instructor, hair shorn above her ears, wearing a glorious gold and red kameez, particularly joyful because she'd married the man she loved, an anomaly in Pakistan where arranged marriages are the norm.

I wondered how many of those children were related to my friends. How many of them knew at least one of the families affected by the tragedy?

That night, the normally ebullient chatter from my Pakistani friends became subdued and angry. One by one, they changed their Facebook profile pictures and posted a completely black square to indicate their grief.

Pakistan's defense minister said, "The smaller the coffin, the heavier it is to carry." The weight on the people of Pakistan would not disappear, as the weight on New York City after September 11 did not.

Before I went to bed, I changed my profile picture to a black square.

-11-

You spend your last two days in Pakistan teasing the man who takes care of the Fulbright house, a short, thin guy with a Charlie Chaplin moustache. He does all the housecleaning and cooking, often joking with me that we are going to have yak for dinner. You talk about American food and print several recipes for him, finding a website that will translate the English version to Urdu. He promises to stay friends after you leave.

Another Fulbrighter arrives and she joins you in a couple of shopping excursions where you purchase more scarves and silver goblets from Iran, gifts for your secretary and the vice president who supported your visit. You talk about the possibility of returning, and she tells you she's been to Pakistan at least eight times, preferring to visit during the Fall when the weather is better.

You visit the National University of Modern Languages one more time to interview the dean about her views on creative women in education. She asks if you would be interested in evaluating some of the dissertations her students must complete before being awarded their doctorate degrees.

"I would be honored," you reply.

You talk to the women with whom you went shopping. They are students and adjunct instructors at Quaid-i-Azam University, the first school you visited, and as you sit in the tea room sipping sweet and hot tea and eating cinnamon-tinged cookies, you talk about literature and feel like you're with a group of old friends. Before you leave that balmy afternoon, they gift you with several packages of the cookies, as well as three novels, one of which you start as you sit in the airport waiting for the long flight home. You remember their warm hugs and their promises to keep in touch. No doubt one of them will be a Fulbrighter some day, as you are, and perhaps you will see them again.

As Zulfi accompanies you one last time, you journey to the airport past the hand-painted and colorfully-decorated trucks, the buses filled with so many passengers that they hang out the back door for the ride of their lives, the walled compounds that house the wealthy and near-wealthy, and the roadside beige tents that house everyone else. You feel somewhat nostalgic and totally changed, no longer the same woman you were when you arrived less than a month previous. The country is no longer a mystery. The people are not one step from terrorism.

In New York's LaGuardia Airport, you recognize the languages and the people. You are somewhat awed by the abundance of foods and goods for sale, though you have seen them a million times before. You are anxious to get home, though you are not quite sure if you feel worthy of all that belongs to you.

You acquiesce to a longing for a chocolate ice cream cone, and as you stand in line to order it, an American woman draws up behind you.

"I love your outfit," she says. "Where did you get it?"

You are taken off guard and glance down at yourself, wondering how she could possibly compliment you since you've traveled for more than twenty-six hours.

You are wearing your sage green shalwar kameez.

"Islamabad," you reply. "I've been to Pakistan."

ONCE UPON A TIME IN MEXICO
Catherine Lundoff

I spent two months of the summer after my junior year at Washington University in St. Louis studying in Guadalajara, Mexico while finishing up the requirements for my anthropology degree. It was the early 1980s and I lived with a Mexican family and several other American students in the family's home near the school. We all took classes in history, archeology and language immersion and attended cultural events like folkloric dances by way of class trips.

Guadalajara was beautiful, a city of wide boulevards, beautiful fountains and stunning museums. I can vividly recall the artwork and architecture, the lovely theaters and the magical moment when I discovered not-Americanized Mexican food in the little cafes. Not to mention the mariachis! I developed a lifelong enthusiasm for mariachi music from this particular trip.

The crafts and artwork of Jalisco was pretty spectacular. We took a road trip with our host family to the world-renowned craft markets in the nearby city of Tonala, and visited the pottery market. I still have one of the vases that I bought there and treasure it still. All the open-air markets were a revelation in their beauty and variety, as well as the staggering poverty they exposed. Up to that point I had never seen people begging on the streets for food.

It sounds so bland, benign and pleasant (except for the desperate begging part) when I describe it like this. And many parts of it were. I met some nice people, I enjoyed the folkloric dancing, the museums, the city, the folk arts, crafts and music. I enjoyed some of my classes (at 21, I enjoyed very few of my classes, as a rule).

Our host family was very kind and very interesting. They were retired Olympic athletes and found my stumbling Spanish and revolutionary partisanship for sundry movements in Nicaragua, El Salvador and Guatemala amusing. We had lively lunchtime discussions about the Sandinistas in Nicaragua and my Spanish improved by leaps and bounds with the practice.

I'm sure they found the sporadic drama and friction between the students staying in their home rather less amusing, but then they had daughters near our own ages living at home as well. They provided a buffer for some of the conflicts while coaching us in Spanish and giving us pointers about places to go and things to do. And they had their own drama: between the five of us, we were practically a performance troop unto ourselves.

But in between the bouts of interpersonal fallout at the house, I had my classes and trips around the city. And dating, more dating than I had done in awhile. It was a summer of wildness, of cutting loose, my first trip outside the country by myself. While I had been to several other countries with my mother, this was the first time I had to negotiate and navigate for myself in a language other than English, the first time I got to put my Brooklyn, New York-honed street smarts to the test and see how they worked outside my comfort zone.

I thought of myself of as tough and sophisticated, a product of a Brooklyn, N.Y. haunted by the attacks of Son of Sam and of a St. Louis, Missouri still divided and haunted by the ghosts of riots and urban decay. This was my outer shell, the armor I wore to fend off street harassment and come-ons, some of which I barely understood. Mexican slang is not something that gets taught much in earnest American language classes at the high school and college level. But I was fine and I could handle myself. That was what I told myself every day.

But emotionally, I was in pieces. One of my friends had committed suicide during our final exams week the month before I left for Guadalajara. She was my roommate during my sophomore year and I had seen her only a few days before she took a bunch of sleeping pills and didn't wake up for the finals that she was convinced she wouldn't be able to pass. The child of brilliant immigrant parents beset by the fear that she would never live up their expectations, she too was straddling multiple cultures, trying to find her way. But her battle was longer-term and more intense than any I would know.

Her ghost went with me everywhere I went for months afterward. I coped with the split between my tough exterior and my broken interior by drinking heavily. This didn't improve much once I was in Mexico, though I had been hoping that the trip would calm me down, help me find some level ground again. But there are few platitudes to be found about traveling when you're lost inside and out. A broadened mind isn't always enough. Level emotional ground eluded me even as I threw myself into new experiences with verve.

I have no idea why my original roommate loathed me (she likely had a perfectly good reason, given where I was at the time), but the upshot of a huge temper tantrum (hers) was that I got a change in roommates about three weeks into the trip. And that, in turn, brought some modifications to my social life since my new roommate came with a fuller social life. I began to hang around with some of the students who had been on the program the previous year, and they, in turn, introduced me to local nightclubbing and some serious bad boys.

During my first couple of weeks in the program, I had a fling with one of the other students and a flirtation with one or two others. My sexuality at the time was not something I questioned (I came out as bisexual a year later); men, flirtations and sex were a reasonably good distraction from the bleakness of my internal landscape. I was comparatively exotic because I had dark hair and eyes, a tan and passable Spanish, with an accent that was just good enough for many Mexicans to assume that I was from another Spanish speaking country. Once I explained that I was from the U.S. and wasn't Latina, a lot of the guys I met assumed that I was rich as well (alas, this part was not true, even by their standards).

Did I mind? Sometimes. But honestly, at the time, the attention was mostly welcome. The same couldn't be said of the street harassment that I experienced, of course; that was sometimes scary, sometimes just infuriating, even for a college student from my background. Still, being a center of attention at the local bars and cafes was kind of fun. I enjoyed being the 'pretty girl' as opposed to 'just' the smart one. Those spaces also felt safer to me than being out in the open on my own.

Once the over-the-top local nightclubs started giving the students free passes, I got to see a whole other side of Guadalajara nightlife. These nightspots were on a completely different planet from the places that we had frequented for the first month of our sojourn. The most popular one amongst the students was also the most popular for the local Mexican elite. It was a large Egyptian-themed club, with a gold pyramid inside it, and by my standards, pretty exotic.

My roommate knew a young Mexican man from a very well-to do and well-connected background from her previous year in the program. He was happy to introduce us to his friends. Things went 'send lawyers, drugs and money' very quickly. It was fairly obvious, even to me at the time, that these were rich and powerful young men, accustomed to getting what they wanted. Broken Me found this fairly intoxicating at the time.

One night, my roommate, a couple of other students and I all went to an impromptu house party, assuming we'd be safer if we went in a group. I was quite captivated by one of the young men, whom I'll call J for the purposes of this tale. J was model gorgeous, easily the most beautiful man I had ever seen up close. He was also charming and clever, and to my amazement, interested in me!

Given this, it wasn't too surprising that I agreed when he suggested we try some cocaine. I'd never done it before, but hey, I was embracing new experiences, and the pretty man didn't seem any the worse for the wear. I had reached the slight nosebleed and very hyper stage when my roomie appeared looking quite drunk and agitated. She pulled me aside and muttered, "There are guns all over the beds in the rooms upstairs. I think we need to get out of here right now."

That seemed a reasonable enough suggestion, under those circumstances. But what with all the competing chemicals then coursing through my system, it required some negotiation. Then, once I was clear on what the problem was and why we needed to go, we still had to convince the guys to give us a lift or call a taxi for us.

American girls had the reputation at the time of being easy and several of the guys we hung out with were optimistic about their chances of getting laid. Honestly, I would have considered it with J., but even as wasted as I was, I knew that the combination of cocaine and lots of guns did not bode well for us. In any case, neither he nor his buddies were pleased at our sudden desire to depart.

The guy who brought us to the party was eventually

persuaded to drive us home and we embarked on a truly terrifying coke-fueled drive home. By the time we got there, we were all pretty sober, if not exactly fun to be around. And the next morning, we all swore off going back to the club for the rest of our stay in Mexico, determined to lose ourselves in scholarship and cross-cultural understanding. From what I can remember, several of the other students left shortly after this, which made that particular decision at lot easier.

I, on the other hand, extended my stay a couple of weeks. I have vivid memories of several museum and other cultural trips during this later time period. I saw some fabulous artwork – Orozco's murals, a striking and somewhat ghastly painting of a crucified Virgin Mary (I never did find out who the artist was), the lovely statue of Minerva at the La Minerva fountain. And there were ongoing exotic side adventures, like learning to communicate with cab drivers in such a way that ensured that one got to the right place, and negotiating telephone conversations in Spanish. These can quite challenging at first because you can't see the other person's facial expressions or body language.

I think this was probably also when I finished reading *Yucatan Before and After the Conquest* by Diego de Landa, which was hands down the most horrifying book that I had ever read in my life up until that point. It is still one of the worst, depicting as it does the deliberate destruction of the Mayan civilization, along with a lot of murder and torture, accomplished with gleeful and fanatical enthusiasm. It was a good choice for this particular anthropology class because it forced a level of awareness that none of us previously had of early Mexican history. We read other books in the class, but that was the one that stuck with me, and I suspect, many of my compatriots.

Something else that stuck with me was the guy I had been flirting with at the guns-n-coke party. I know, you're thinking that I certainly would have had enough sense at the ripe old age of twenty-one to avoid getting involved with a guy who was clearly bad news. And you would be wrong about that.

I agreed to go over to J.'s house via taxi to 'hang out.' Because, really, what could go wrong? After all, I think it is safe to say that I had never before had a date that nearly ended in me being sold to drug dealers for my perceived worth in nose candy. See my previous comment about embracing new experiences.

Some of J.'s business associates stopped by, also to 'hang out.' One of them, clearly J.'s dealer, took an interest in me. This escalated to the point where he grabbed me by my chin and said, "I like her. Sell her to me." I will say that this moment was a wondrously clarifying experience for my young mind. Time did in fact stand still while I contemplated some things about the situation I was now in:

1. I was in seriously deep doo-doo.

2. My Spanish was decent for an English-speaking American college student but was not really up the challenge of getting myself rescued from really bad dudes who might actually own me in the very near future.

3. If I got out of this, I was never doing anything this stupid again.

As it happened, J. didn't think that the exchange was all that appealing (fortunately for me), and upon confirming that I did not, in fact, wish to be traded for my then current worth in coke, encouraged his business associates to wrap things up and depart. We hung out and I got to learn some interesting things about the effects of long-term cocaine use on the male anatomy. After that, I eventually made my way safely back to my temporary home via taxi and that was the last I saw of J.

Did this experience color my desire to embark on subsequent travels, perhaps feeling that there were insurmountable obstacles to my safety when traveling while unaccompanied and female? Eh, not really.

Honestly, it took a few days to really sink in. I did a couple more injudicious things on the fairly mild end of the scale before I left for home and ended my trip by spending the last of my available cash on a wool blanket and exchanging numerous protestations of lifelong friendship with my erstwhile companions and new friends before heading home.

I occasionally ran into some of the other students from the program (but only the ones at my own college) and we exchanged pleasantries and reminiscences. I don't believe that I ever told anyone on the program or my host family about what had happened to me. In the cold clear light of day, I felt like I'd been a naïve idiot and it took several years before the story moved into 'anecdotes about stupid things in our past' territory.

Would I have had the same kinds of experiences if I hadn't been a young, conventionally attractive Caucasian woman from a wealthy country? Almost certainly not. My circumstances made me desirable and 'exotic' in ways that I wouldn't have been back home, at least from my perspective. Some of the women I met on that summer program had similar experiences, some didn't, so I'm not inclined to universalize from it. That said, I'm fairly sure J.'s dealer wouldn't have offered that particular bargain had I been in a different demographic.

Did I learn much from this particular experience? I would say that I learned a bit about choosing better companions and being more cognizant of safety issues (like, hey, maybe don't hang out with guys who you know have their dealer on speed dial AND an arsenal upstairs). But considering that within a few years of my Mexican trip, I was hanging out with Sandinista combatants in Nicaragua, then a mere two years later, hanging out with FMLN combatants in El Salvador, I'd have to say that self-preservation was not always my take away from learning experiences in my younger years.

I will say, though, that spending several months in

Mexico helped me develop a greater appreciation for the culture than anything I had done previously. Prior to this trip, I had a sort of rosy romantic vision of Mexico and Mexican life brought on what I learned in my Spanish classes back home. I will also note that I continue to think that getting to live with a local family, even temporarily, in another country is an invaluable way to learn more about a language and culture, especially when supplemented with classes. I remain deeply grateful that the family I lived with was willing to open up their home to us and give us house keys so we weren't waking them up in the middle of the night.

Along with that, I learned a bit about aspects of Mexican history that I never would have explored in the U.S. These ranged from histories about the Mayan archeological past and anthropological present to the historical and artistic elements of the Mexican Revolution. What we didn't cover was the explosion of the drug trade between the U.S. and Mexico that would fuel growth of the drug cartels, the latest rendition of the War Against Drugs ("Just Say No!") and other subsequent 'fun.' Little did I realize that I was getting something of a front row seat to a soon-to-be launched series of historical events.

Of course, my immediate takeaway from the experience was that I was never trying coke again since it wasn't exactly fun, even on those very rare occasions that it was available to me. After several subsequent months of emotional crashing and burning, I did get into therapy to deal with a lot of things that had come up during the course of my trip. Thus, I had a personal happy(ier) ending than I might have had otherwise.

Overall, I think this trip helped inspire me to embrace my inner travel bug, risks and all. Admittedly, if I had been traded for cocaine, the rest of my life would have gone very differently, but now I have a bonus exciting cautionary tale to share with friends and really, who could ask for anything more than that?

POEMS
Devon Balwit

A Stubborn Country

The first thing I pack and the last I unpack
is always myself, the thing that I wear and
wring, then dry on a door handle, ever more
wrinkled and never quite right for the occasion.

Caelum non animum mutant qui trans mare currunt—
I sling myself over my shoulders to squares
and cathedrals, cafes and alleyways, project myself
onto those deftly going about their business:

crossing roads with no lights, bartering, balancing
baskets and babies, or elegantly wearing what
would make me clownish. I watch and wonder how
crazy I would be here, who my friends would be,

what my conveyance and who my lover, what my
job and what my view. I take no photos for my
inner voice puts a foot down, calls it intrusive,
tells me what I want to keep I'll have to remember.

MY WANDERING UTERUS

After I return, I wonder if I ever went, so clogged
is my head with myself, so loud with my own
clarion. I like to think I've crossed borders,
but ever I remain, a stubborn country of one.

Thanksgiving

The stiff breeze animates the drying clothes
draping tree branches and fence slats outside

the airbnb, limbless yet in motion, a Greek
chorus mocking my stress at *making do*,

calling me out as one who would not have
survived the trials of my ancestors. O woe,

no working dryer, no tub, no tweezers, no salt
for my Trader Joe eggs: how shall I cope?

My dead grandmother purses her lips at me
over her mustache, remembering the trains,

the sound of jackboots, the stink of relatives
lost to smoke, the ever-present need

for subterfuge. She wonders how two
generations have so softened her descendant's

spine that flapping shirts evoke suffering.
Shamed, I offer attenuated thanks, knowing

she deems me unworthy of her sacrifices.
Grandmother, perhaps this spindly fortitude is

what you fought for, children who know nothing
of bindles and jerry cans, chilblains and short

rations. I can manure the tree, but both of us
should hope no season forces it to blossom.

Better from Here

Drawn by the tiny terrier in her arms, my dog jumps up. Muddy paws streak white down. I see the faux pas coming, but do nothing, let the moment crest. *Bad dog*, I chide. *Now I'll have to go home and change*, she scolds. Change. Yes, she should, I should, something should. I missed the moment, missed the warning signs, my dog untrained. *Why the fuck did you let him jump up*, my husband yells. Why the fuck? I finish a different question sotto voce. Sometimes things happen in life, happen in a marriage. The muddy woman rolls her eyes. Her friend (and I) also. Oblivious, the dog pants.

Worship

(Oswald West State Park, Oregon)

Dead branches knob over the path,
lost wax castings of reaching hands.

Walking beneath them, I bow my head
as if in a cathedral choired by wrens,

the sun sinking and rising over the ocean
its eternal flame. There is no credo, only

one foot after the other, there and back,
my dog panting by my side, awed by

salt-breezes. I have come with too much
and will leave, I hope, with nothing,

spilling my overfull heart into sucking
shingle, wave after wave dragging away

grief and grievance. Like me,
everything on the tideline is broken.

A lone pelican skims the horizon.
Two supplicants, we await whatever is.

Piedad

Una caridad, por favor?
Coins rattle in outstretched hats,
in wrinkled hands under wizened faces.

Qué Dios le bendiga, Señora?
Small change clanks in the almost-empty bowls
of old men in wheelchairs, backs to the church wall.

Una moneda, por favor?
The murmur repeats,
a wave that crests as I pass.

Ayúdeme, Ayúdeme, Señora!
A woman perches on her single leg.
Another calls from a shop, shelves empty, bins
empty.

Por el amor de Dios!
Un peso, dos, cinco—
the price of the bathroom, a mango, a piece of
bread,

Una caridad, una caridad
the calls come from every well-traveled corner
from stoops, from scraps of shade.

Gracias a Dios, Qué Dios le bendiga, Señora?
Where are their people that they so need me,
and where will mine be when I, too, need?

MY WANDERING UTERUS

IN THE COURSE OF A
PILGRIMAGE Tahni J. Nikitins

I can't pronounce the name of the city, so I've already forgotten it. All I know about my location is that I'm somewhere between Berlin and Amsterdam, and somewhat certain I'm still in Germany. I'm not quite halfway to my journey's end—a pilgrimage in progress.

Huddled in a small glass shelter at the train station, my puffy blue jacket zipped and pulled up around my ears to keep out the chill, I try to keep my eyes open to read Cormac McCarthy's *Blood Meridian*. The night before, while waiting for my transfer after the ferry from Copenhagen, I blew through the first third of the book in the train station's McDonalds while listening to the man in the booth behind me mutter to himself under his breath. I could smell him, too—at least until the police came to fetch him after an hour or two. Even before the police came I kept my empty cup and burger wrapper on the table beside me, a left over American habit to prove I'd paid to be there.

At least the commotion helped keep me awake. It's hard to keep your eyes open through such a traumatic book when you're so sleep deprived you can't manage an emotional reaction to it. Tree decorated with dead babies? Whatever. I've only dozed a few times in the past forty-eight hours, I don't remember what emotions are.

I don't want to doze now. Alone in the train station, my only company is a group of young men—sometimes only two of them, sometimes three—who have been pacing the rails like hyenas for going on an hour now. They're typical young, white, wanna-be gangsters like you'd see wandering the streets in America—a little too thin, so their oversized clothes hang on them as though they're scarecrows, and looking too itchy to be sober. It's three-thirty in the morning, so even without the itchiness I'm already suspicious. I feel confident in the assumption that letting my guard down with them in the vicinity would result in having my one bag stolen— meaning goodbye change of clothes, goodbye wallet, goodbye laptop, goodbye phone—or, worse, being raped in a train station.

So I keep my back as straight as sleep deprivation allows, keep my head up, and keep reading. I pause only when they circle near to the little glass shelter, lifting my eyes from the book and fixing them firmly on the boys. I want them to know that I know they're there—that they won't get the jump on me. I'm grateful for the puffy blue jacket my sister leant me. Paired with my worn-out jeans it hides the most tellingly feminine traits of my body. The outfit, topped with a knitted hat pulled over my short hair, renders me nearly genderless. I put my hand in my bag to give off the impression I'm reaching for a weapon. In reality, I'm kicking myself for not thinking to bring a weapon (strangers have rarely posed any real threat to me—it's always been the people I thought I knew) and kicking myself even more for thinking this style of travel was a good idea.

I've been dozing on the trains and in the stations. The only place I have booked to sleep is in Amsterdam. I made this decision primarily due to paranoid thriftiness. The whole trip will cost a couple hundred

American dollars but at the end of it all I will also have the near existential revelation of just how easily I could have died.

Why? For a pilgrimage.

Ultimately I will find myself in a tiny village in Cumbria called Gosforth. There I will find a beautiful and fascinating relic of the Viking presence in Scotland and Britain, and the beginning of an era of conversion for Scandinavia. It is the only relic in existence that depicts the goddess Sigyn—the gentler wife of Loki, who comforts him where he was bound by the other gods.

But I am not there yet. In three more days I will arrive by train to a town called Seascale, discover that the busses aren't running regularly, it being New Years Eve, and walk three miles through rolling, impeccably green pasture spotted with wool-heavy, long-tailed sheep and hedgerows made haunting by the lack of leaf cover on their bristly, well-trimmed branches. I'll wind my way along the narrow road, keeping mostly to the ditch as there will be no shoulder to speak of and the few drivers I do see along that stretch of road will have no taste for caution. But the walk will give me time to breathe crisp country air, and despite the crazy drivers and shoulder-less road the familiar smells of grass, earth, sheep dung and fresh hay in the old stone barns will be comforting.

In three days.

For now I'm in gods-only-know-where Germany—or the Netherlands—pretending that I have a knife or a gun in my bag and hoping I'm projecting vicious, hostile vibes to keep the potential robbers/rapists at bay while wishing I actually did have a knife. In between these moments, I am reading Blood Meridian, the exhaustion, cold, and efforts to stay semi-conscious distracting me from the spiritual reverence I imagine good pilgrims maintain.

Two more folks arrive in the station, a man and a

woman both sporting bulky backpacks—the kind you might expect to see hikers on the Pacific Crest Trail packing. I perk up a little and watch them as they assess their surroundings. They notice me, but the prowling boys are, for the moment, nowhere to be seen. They make for a different shelter, go inside, and shuck their bags. I slouch back in my seat. At least I know I'm not the only traveler in the station, now.

It only takes about forty-five minutes for the prowlers to return, still itchy and jumpy and starting to weave and wobble a bit. I wonder if they've added alcohol to whatever else they've had tonight or are just experiencing some new symptoms.

From the corner of my eye I watch them as they make note of the travelers in the other shelter. They still haven't bothered to come into mine, but they approach the other shelter and poke their heads in. I wonder if they're more interested in these other travelers because they have bigger bags and, thus, more potential for loot than my one, pathetically small bag.

When the boys wander away again, the travelers get up and leave their shelter. They make their way over to mine and, once again, I perk up. I haven't had company since Copenhagen and though that's only been a few days, it has been a truly exhausting few days.

The travelers peek their heads in and the woman asks in heavily accented English, "Would you mind if we sat here?"

"Come in," I say, "please. I haven't had company for a while." As they come in and settle down on the bench across from me I ask where they're from. I don't recognize their accents.

"Argentina," the man says. He's tall and athletically thin with prominent and angular cheekbones and nose, dark hair, and a strong jawline and sharp chin. The type of person you can tell spends every iota of their free time trekking through the mountains. "We're on vacation, backpacking for a couple of weeks."

"We've backpacked everywhere there is to do so in Argentina," the woman chimes in. She's small and thin, wearing more athletic clothes than myself, but clothing that is still strictly practical for Europe in December. Her dark, curly hair is highlighted blonde in a way that seems to be natural and sun-kissed, and her eyes are crisp, clear, and blue. She has a tattoo on her right hand between her thumb and index finger—some kind of twirling symbol. She doesn't wear any makeup on her plain face, but she doesn't need to. She exudes a beautiful and admirable confidence. "And yourself?"

"From Oregon, in the United States," I say. "But I'm coming from Uppsala in Sweden. I'm doing a year of study abroad but I'm doing some traveling for winter break." I dart my eyes out of the shelter for a moment, looking for the boys. Nowhere to be seen, but still in the area I'm sure. "I've never done anything like this before. It's a little intimidating."

"After trekking back home," the woman says, "this is nothing."

"Right," I say, nodding as though I understand. "Are the cartels a thing in Argentina, or…" I'm not sure how to finish that sentence because I don't really know what I'm talking about, and I've already gotten enough shit in Sweden for not knowing certain details on what are, to me, foreign affairs. I don't want to come off any more American than I have to.

Luckily she picks up the end of the sentence and I don't have to worry about finishing it. "The drug trade is up," she says, "and with it the violence."

I try to chime in, but nothing I say can quite compare to Argentina's drugs wars. "I've felt so much safer in Sweden than in the United States. It's not the same thing you're talking about, but men here seem so much more content to leave you alone than in America. People generally are so much more content to leave you alone in Sweden," I say with a smile, "and I love it."

We chat a bit more about the states of our respective

nations and the relative safety we feel here, though we never do exchange names. The man nods along, but doesn't say much, and eventually the chit-chat dies down. I put my book away and lay down on the bench, tucking my bag under my head as a pillow. I feel much more comfortable taking a little doze now that I have company.

I must have slept for a little while, because voices disturb me and I stir out of a stiff, cold oblivion. I peel my eyes open and see one of the prowling boys from before has entered our little shelter. He's standing, talking to the woman from Argentina, making jittery little gestures with his long-fingered hands.

For her part, the woman looks entirely displeased. "I can't understand you," she says, her voice hard and forceful. "I do not speak German."

He glances at me, though I doubt it was intentional. It seems more a jerk of the head than anything, but I still muster a glare as he twitches his eyes back to the woman.

Grunting, I jam my bag a little more firmly under my head and roll onto my other side, the metal bars of the bench digging into my spine and ribs despite the puffy coat. I hope the grunt and my movement make clear that I am not any more interested in the boy's company than the woman from Argentina and, in fact, I cannot be bothered to give a single fuck about him. I feel much more comfortable turning my back on the boy now that I have company.

"You just seem like a good girl," the boy manages to say through a slur that overlays his thick accent. I hear his feet shuffling. "I wonder if you can help me out."

"No, I cannot," the woman says, her voice now taking on a sharp edge. "I am just waiting for my train and I want to be left alone."

"Why you taking a train so late at night?"

"Do not sit next to me." Her voice raises an octave

now, but the man she is with remains quiet.

I turn my head a little toward them, to better hear what is being said.

"Come on," he says, "I am just being friendly."

"I do not want you to sit next to me!"

I sit up and face them as the boy is standing and backing away with his hands in the air. "Okay, okay," he says, before reaching into his pocket and pulling out a pack of cigarettes and a lighter.

The woman's eyes narrow on the boy. Her thin lips are set in a hard line and her fine eyebrows come together in a frown.

"I just want to be a friend," the boy says, wobbling a little as he lights up a cigarette. Smoke coils off the ember into the shelter, with nowhere else to go and no way to escape the enclosed walls.

"Are you joking?" the woman snaps.

The boy looks at her, his dull eyes and expression making it quite clear he has no idea what she is referring to. The scent of the smoke has started to waft over to me and I curl my nose against it, my lips inadvertently pulling back from my teeth.

"Are you seriously smoking in here? We do not want to breathe your disgusting smoke!"

A second boy comes in. He says something to his buddy in German. The tension that had left my shoulders and spine when the travelers joined me is returning, making me grip the edge of the cold metal bench until my fingers go numb. Nonetheless, I don't say anything, just keep my eyes pinned on the boys.

"Get out of here with your stinky cigarettes!" The woman stands up, tossing her hand in a violent wave toward the door.

"Calm down," the boy says, "it is just a cigarette!"

"And we do not want it here. Leave! Go smoke outside, not in here with us!"

"C'mon," the boy's buddy says, patting him on the shoulder. "Let's go outside. It's okay, let's go outside."

Grumbling, the boy agrees and heads outside with his friend. The woman sits back down on the bench, her hackles still raised, and she looks at the man. "Can you believe that? Him just lighting a cigarette in here." She looks at me. "Can you believe that?"

I shake my head, but I'm looking through the glass, seeing if I can spot the third boy.

"Fucking inconsiderate. Ridiculous. Who does that? And was he drunk?"

"I think he might be high," the man says.

"Did you see the third one?" I ask, still scanning the station.

"No, but he is probably close by," the man answers.

We sit together for a while. The air between us tense, none of us saying anything further. Some silent minutes pass before I shake off as much of the tension in my shoulders as I can and lay back down and close my eyes. Once I do, the woman quietly starts talking to the man again about the rudeness of the boy lighting up a cigarette in the shelter.

It doesn't take long for the boy to come back. I hear the door open but I keep my eyes closed. I can smell that he has returned with a lit cigarette. The smoke quickly stretches to fill every corner with its stink. The woman, though, has kept her mouth shut, so I peel open an eye to assess the situation.

The boy is standing near my feet, one arm crossed over his chest and his other hand up by his face, lackadaisically holding the cigarette between his fore and middle fingers. He's looking at me. I open my other eye and turn my head just enough to draw his attention to my face and I lock my eyes on his. He turns away and strolls over to the other bench, where the woman and the man from Argentina are sitting. His gate is as loose as his grip on his cigarette, weaving back and forth. His eyes are once again fixed on the Argentinian woman and, once again, the man who is with her merely averts his eyes.

"I already told you," she said, "we do not want your stinking cigarette in here."

"I just want to ask you," he said, sliding onto the bench, leaving about a foot and a half between them. "Will you help us out? We need some money for the machine." He jerks his head toward a vending machine down the rail.

A few hours earlier I had put five euro into that machine and got two soup cups and a cup of hot cocoa. None of these things were high quality—the soup was a little short of what you would expect from that Maruchan Instant Lunch classic, Cup O' Noodles. A few stray noodles and a small handful of freeze-dried vegetable cubes in about ten ounces of hot water mixed with powdered chicken broth: I ate it less for the nutritious value and more for the feeling of having something warm in my belly. To be honest, the hot cocoa was probably heartier than the soup, but it, too, I drank mostly for the warmth.

In any case, I doubt the machine had anything of any interest to the prowling boys. I am even more confident that needing spare change for the machine is just an excuse to stay in the shelter with us—or rather, with the Argentinian woman—as I watch him scoot a couple inches toward her. My neck prickles when I wonder to what end.

"I am not giving you any money." The woman says this like she's spitting venom. Even as tensions continue to rise, I can't help but admire her.

"Just for the machine." He scoots closer. "Please?" And closer again. "We want something warm in our bellies."

"I am sure that between the three of you there is enough money for the machine. Do not come any closer to me." She jabs a sharp finger in his direction. She keeps her nails closely trimmed, like I keep mine, but carefully aimed fingers can still do plenty of damage, nails or no.

"I am just trying to be friendly," he says again, and scoots right up beside her.

The woman is on her feet and I sit up, leaning forward in my seat, like I'm readying myself to pounce. What good I think pouncing will do, I am entirely unsure. I have no doubt in my mind that if this boy doesn't have a knife on him then one of the others does, and they can't be too far away.

"I said to not sit next to me," the woman screams, jamming her finger toward the door. Her shrill voice reverberates off the glass and metal structure. The man beside her risks a glance up. "I told you to stay away from me and you did not. Now leave or I will call the police!"

Now the boy is on his feet, too, holding his hands out to the side like a rooster welcoming a fight. "You calm down, bitch!" he shouts, and I get to my feet, though no one notices me stand. "I come in asking for help and you are threatening me with police?"

"If you do not leave right now I will call the police," the woman shouts back at him. She's half a foot shorter than him but if she's intimidated at all, it doesn't show. She points at him again and follows through with her shoulder and hip, but her wide stance remains solid and unflinching. I wonder if she's a boxer. "I told you I did not want you to sit next to me! I told you to stay away from me! I told you no one here wants to smell your stinking cigarette! Do you hear me?"

"You think you can threaten me, bitch?"

"Do you hear me?" She surprises me again when her voice gets even louder, losing its shrillness and ballooning out like thunder, becoming a full-bodied, throaty shout. "We do not want you here! We do not want you in here! None of us! We all want you to leave—"

"You think you can tell me what to do?" He says it like a threat but doesn't move toward her. "Do you?"

A movement outside catches my attention. I glance

out the door. The two other boys are coming up quickly. They must have heard the shouting. I keep my eyes on them as they tentatively open the door and poke their heads in. Some of the cigarette smell rushes out and the icy December air rushes in to replace it. I don't know who to resent more, the boy with the cigarette or the boys letting in the cold.

"We want you to go and if you do not, I will call the police," the woman is shouting at him again.

The other boys come in. "Whoa," one of them says. "Whoa. Everyone can calm down."

"You take your friend and get him out of here," the woman says. "We do not want to be harassed by him. We do not want to smell his goddamn cigarettes!"

"Okay, okay," says one of the boys while the other mutters something in German, patting his agitated buddy's shoulder. "It is okay. We okay. We cool." He holds out his hands in a gesture of placation. He seems the most level headed of the three—seems to understand that the situation needs to deescalate, and quickly, if they are to avoid having the cops called. Judging by the jittery way they've been lurking from corner to corner all night, it seems a safe bet that having the cops called would be exceptionally bad news for these boys.

The level-headed one gestures to the other two and says something in German. Then he nods—first to the Argentinian woman, then to me. "We are going. You have a very good night. Safe travels." At last, he turns his back and ushers the group out of the shelter. They make a beeline for the end of the platform and descend the stairs that open onto the street below.

We let out a collective sigh. My shoulders relax and deflate and so do the woman's, even as she grabs her bag and hoists it onto her shoulders. "I cannot stay in here with this smoke smell."

Not wanting to be left alone, I pull my bag onto my back and the three of us make our way to the next shelter over. On the way I glance at the man, walking beside the woman, and see his head bowed just a fraction. He must feel ashamed for not piping up, I think, and it occurs to me that if he feels ashamed, then I probably ought to as well. I cast my eyes down, too, wishing I had gotten as loud and as aggressive as the woman from Argentina had. She, I think, is a badass. And me? I'm a bystander.

In the other shelter we sit together in the corner. I take the seat closest to the door and lay down again, with my head by the woman, separated from her only by a thin metal armrest. I close my eyes and listen to her as she speculates to her travel partner about what the boys had wanted: were they scoping out their bags? Had they been looking for an opportunity to mug us?

Whatever their motivation, the woman had done a damn good job of clearing them out. Every now and then I lift my head and open my eyes and do a scan, but they never do come back. At some point, though, the woman and the man doze off—she with her head on his shoulder, and he with his head on hers. It is comforting, somehow, that she doesn't seem to hold it against him that he hadn't gotten involved in the shouting. I hope she doesn't hold it against me, either.

She'd held her ground like a seasoned fighter. Maybe she wasn't a boxer at all, but had merely gotten used to having to hold her ground while trekking across Argentina? Maybe the people here in Europe really were nothing to be afraid of when compared with drug lords back home. But what do I know? She might have just been a boxer.

Dozing comes and goes, never staying for long. I'm antsy now, and keep lifting my head to scan the station. In America, whenever I'd seen something like that go down—usually from the window of an adjacent coffee shop or bar—the harasser would come back for round two, nine times out of ten. But here the boys don't return—they are gone and the incident has passed, and perhaps the risk of the moment is merely another offering in the course of a pilgrimage, like the exhaustion and the aches.

The rest of the morning passes without incident, and the train rolls up a little after six. We shake off our sleep and drag ourselves out of the shelter, and after a few minutes I realize they're going to be on the same train as me.

"Where are you going?" I ask.

"Amsterdam," the woman answers.

"Can I sit with you guys?"

"Of course." She smiles at me and her smile is warm. We still haven't exchanged names, but I think it's too late now to ask their names without it being a bit awkward.

I take a window seat and they sit in the seats beside me, sleeping fitfully against one another, while I watch reflections of the men in suits sitting across from me in the window. They chatter pleasantly and sip their coffee. The pungent smell of their drinks warms the air. Typically I don't like the smell of coffee, but after the long, cold, and sleepless night I just had, I don't mind it so much.

My temporary travel companions and I go our separate ways at the station in Amsterdam. I don't know where they're headed—I never did ask, just like I never asked their names. I find my way out of the station, though just barely. My exhaustion has left me confused and feeling more lost than ever.

Despite the exhaustion I persevere in obtaining a map of the city and taking advantage of my brief time here to explore. I spend too much time in the line to the Anne Frank House before realizing I'm wasting my short twenty-four hours here and getting on a canal boat that drops me off near enough to the Van Gogh museum to get there without getting too lost. I try a crêpe from a stand in a park along the way. It's not as good as my father's crêpes, but it is delicious, and as I order another I remember that the last thing I ate was two cups of soup and a cup of cocoa from the vending machine in the train station in that town whose name I don't know. I order a third crêpe for good measure.

The city is indescribably beautiful. Of the places I see on my short and frantic pilgrimage, it is one of the few I know I must return to someday. Amsterdam is a city worthy of more thorough exploration. There are too many museums to visit in one day and most of them have lines that circle a couple of blocks. Then there's all the back-alley nooks and crannies, the folks living in their little boats on the canals, the towering stone buildings.

I don't even have time to stop in one of the coffee shops, though I catch a whiff of the scent of marijuana wafting as I pass them. It's no matter; the hostel I booked for myself is a Christian establishment and strictly prohibits substances or the appearance of being intoxicated. After being in proximity to the boys in the station last night, it's a prohibition I welcome.

After days of changing my clothes in train car bathrooms and not having the chance to bathe, taking a shower in the Shelter City Hostel is damn near orgasmic. I let the hot water run through my hair and scrub my unshaven underarms. If I had become distracted from the spiritual nature of my journey, this hot shower reminds me. I scrub myself until I feel clean and because I don't have a towel I use my shirt to dry myself off. ·

Spreading my wet clothes on the end of my bed—a top bunk in the further corner of a room shared between a dozen traveling women, myself seeming the only stranger—I apply band-aids given to me by the front desk staff to the copious blisters on my feet. It is the first time in days they've been out of their shoes. Even though they're blistered, the cool air on my toes is delightful.

I'm already asleep as I tumble toward the pillow, all wrapped up in a blanket that's thick enough and more importantly warm. In eleven hours my alarm will go off, I will drag myself out of bed while everyone else is still sleeping, and I will make my way through the red light district to the train station. I'll become temporarily distracted by a woman in a window framed with red neon putting on her makeup and doing her long, thick, dyed-blonde hair. Two men walking ahead of me will stop to watch her and I will be tempted to stop too, but I'll make my way on past them while they consider entering the brothel. I'll get on the train to the airport and I'll fly to London, and two days from now I'll be walking to the tiny village of Gosforth, where everyone will know I'm a stranger, and I'll be pointed in the direction of the Gosforth Cross.

By then, my time in a train station somewhere in Germany with two travelers from Argentina will feel distant and far away. It'll only be a few days away but it'll feel like it's been months, and I will have largely forgotten how I lay beside those travelers in the station and half-dreamed about the vicious things I wish I had said to prowlers, instead of leaving the Argentinian woman to deal with it alone.

But for now, I'm in a bed that's heavenly. For now, I'm sleeping for the first time in days—sleeping through the whispers of the other girls in the hostel, sleeping with my bag under my pillow because I still don't trust them to not steal my computer or my wallet, but at least I trust them enough to sleep beside them. For now, I'm enjoying eleven hours of uninterrupted sleep.

For now.

THE FIVE DOLLAR CAR
Diane Payne

Soon it will be dark and I stand here on this deserted road wondering why that generous couple, who insisted on bringing me along to their ghost town picnic, left me stranded in the middle of nowhere.

Before they picked me up, I was heading west to Washington. I can still hear the driver asking if I had visited the ghost town, while he pointed upwards towards another Idaho range I knew nothing about. When I admitted I hadn't made it to those mountains, he said, "Then you ain't heading west quite yet." Still pointing, he added, "That's the reason mountains are called purple mountains majesty. Climb in the back of the truck and make yourself comfortable. We have plenty of food. You're going to see a ghost town like no other. And you've got the best guides in Idaho. That's Jane and I'm Jim."

After putting on an extra shirt, I opened their cooler, passed a couple of beers up front, and drank mine while taking in the majesty of purple mountains.

Jim and Jane turned out to be worth the detour. They were just the diversion I needed. We yukked it up imagining how it would have been had we lived in this mining town during its hey day. Everything we said seemed hilarious, yet believable. We felt more like old friends than strangers. Or maybe it just felt like that to me because I was feeling so damn lonely.

What they probably found most hilarious was that I believed them that someone would offer me a ride on this deserted road. I can just hear them laughing now, driving down the road, eager to get home so they can tell their friends about the hitch-hiker who drank all their beer and ate all their food, babbling on for hours pretending she lived in that ghost town, the crazy hippie-chick they ended up leaving on this dusty road miles from nowhere.

Just as I'm off the road relieving myself for the umpteenth time this evening, I hear my first car since I was abandoned. I yank up my shorts cursing all those afternoon beers, and run to the road. The car doesn't even slow down, though I'm sure that family sees me waving at them in their rear view mirror. I keep thinking Jane and Joe will return saying this was just a little more of that good humor we were spreading around this afternoon. But they don't come back for me, nor does anyone else, not even this family who is going out of their way to make sure they don't turn around for a quick look. I wonder if a young woman killed someone and they think I'm her. That'd be just my luck.

I'm down to my last few drops of water and think about setting up camp. Might as well make do with a lousy situation. But the situation improves. I hear a car in dire need of a muffler and hope they'll recognize that I'm in dire need of a ride. I wave frantically. The beat-up car passes me. I keep waving. It looks like someone in the front seat is flipping me off. I'm beginning to feel rather vulnerable out here.

The car backs up. The woman sitting in the middle of the two men leans over the passenger and tells me to get on in.

I'm not sure this is the right thing to do, but I'm not sure I want to be standing along this road another hour. I can't imagine a more motley crew driving a more ruined car, but also know this ride may be as good as it gets.

"George was just funning with you, weren't you, George?" she asks. I figure George must be the person with the long middle finger.

"Not really," he says. "You want a beer?"

I take one and ask where they're heading.

"West," Mikey, the driver says, laughing. "How 'bout you?"

"West," I say, relieved to be sitting in a car, even if it's this one.

"Then you're in the right car," he laughs. This gets them all laughing, so I try to laugh, but it comes off sounding just like that—a forced laugh—which makes everyone quiet. All three of them turn around and look at me, obviously disappointed that I'm not laughing as freely as they are. They don't know how much I laughed this afternoon, and look where all that laughter got me. It landed me in this filthy car with the ripped up back seat, and three nasty people giving me a look that would frighten a guard dog.

"You don't like my car?" Mikey asks.

"I like your car just fine," I fib.

"Bet you ain't never been in a five dollar car before, have you?" Mikey laughs.

I remember our thirty-dollar family car, the '62 Buick, but don't tell him about it "Nope, can't say I have."

"Well, you are now. This is something you'll have to tell your friends about. This is a five dollar car," he says, tossing his empty beer can out the window.

"This is definitely something to write home about," I agree.

We drive down the road in an uncomfortable silence, until the woman, Corina, starts crying. I overhear parts of their conversation, and don't like what I hear. It sounds like they killed an ex-boyfriend of Corina's, but she's screaming so much, I'm not exactly sure what they're saying. I'm ready to offer them my last forty-two dollars to buy the car and be off on my own.

"Shut up, Corina!" George yells. He's had it with her wailing, which is probably the only thing George and I have in common.

Once again we drive in silence and I pretend to sleep. It's late, and I'm not even sure we're heading west. "You said you were just going to get my shit and leave. Not kill him!" Corina yells, breaking the silence again.

"It was an accident. That fucker had a gun. He would've blown your fuckin' brains out if we left you there. You know that," George argues. "Anyhow, we don't know he's dead."

"Honey, I'm sorry it happened that way. Wait till you see my cabin," Mikey explains. He seems to be Corina's boyfriend, but I can't figure out how George fits in with these people. He could be Corina's brother. He could be another hitchhiker like myself, simply heading west at the wrong time. "You all right back there?" Mikey asks.

"Oh yeah, just fine," I lie, wondering when we'll come to a town.

No one says anything for a long time. Then I hear them celebrating that we've crossed into Washington. If I was a fugitive crossing a state line, I'd probably be whooping it up too, but all I'm trying to do is get to the

Greyhound bus station in Seattle and pick up my bike—
the bike I was supposed to ride down Highway 101
while admiring the coast. The coast I still haven't seen
because when the bus reached Montana, I became
restless and wanted to sleep in the mountains. When I
put the panniers on my head and started hitchhiking to
Yellowstone, I felt giddy with freedom, certain I was
doing the right thing. Now, I wonder if I'll ever see
Michigan again. Or a Greyhound bus. Or that old '62
Buick.

Finally, we stop for gas. I've never been so happy to
see a Circle K. "I can get out here," I say while grabbing
my panniers from the back seat.

"Not here you don't," Mikey hisses, while slamming
my door shut so I can't get out. And once again we
drive off into the darkness.

After a few more hours, we make it to Mikey's
decrepit cabin. He bolts the door, then piles chairs and
tables in front of it. "Don't want anyone breaking in,"
he laughs, as if I can't figure out that he doesn't want
me breaking out.

The three of them go into what must be the
bedroom, and I unroll my sleeping bag and lie on the
dirty floor, listening to them argue. After awhile the
fighting stops and it sounds like they're making love.
Someone farts and they all laugh. In some ways, they
remind me of my own bickering family, and in strange
ways, I begin to miss them.

The windows are boarded up, but I can still hear the
silence of the forest. I listen, hoping to hear familiar
remnants of my life. I'm not sure, but I think today's
laughter from our picnic is still reverberating from the
mountains, still laughing at me.

Suddenly I miss our family's old '62 Buick, and
remember the stories that go with that car. It dawns on
me that the five-dollar car may be like the old Buick and

won't require a key to start it. Could a five-dollar car that only needs a knob turned to have it start just be sitting there in the woods, ready to take off, ready to collect new stories? I could leave a twenty so it won't feel like I'm stealing, and Mikey will feel like he got a deal, except that he'll wake up carless in the middle of this forest. If they hear the car start, I'll end up like Corina's old boyfriend, who, if I'm lucky, is still alive. But if he isn't...

There's also the chance I could just move the furniture and slip away, ever so quietly, like tonight's breeze, leaving nothing but my footprints behind.

Lying here, I wonder if I'm the only one listening to the sounds of the night, immersed in memories, driven by possibilities, silently waiting for something to happen.

Ever so quietly, I move the table and chairs away from the door, listening to the sound of snoring coming from the other room. I stuff my things into the panniers and slip out the door. The Five Dollar Car sits there with the automatic starter just waiting for someone to turn it, but I've had enough memories with that car and decide it's time to give my feet some memories, and begin walking down the dirt road.

It's pitch black. Smells like rain. No moon. Between the clouds, a few stars shine. I seriously think about sleeping, but know I must walk away from here. Once again, I wear the panniers on my head and notice how good it feels to be on the road again.

Unfortunately, that good feeling doesn't last long, and I start envying my bike that is hopefully in Seattle, safely tucked in a box at the Greyhound station, while I'm out here on this dark, forest road, uncertain when Corina and the boys will awaken and come looking for me.

Just keep walking, I tell myself over and over. Walk

fast. Walk faster. Think about other things. Anything. Keep thinking. Keep walking. Think about Jack Kerouac. Seems to me he traveled by car, but I may be wrong. Remember sitting on a rickety old chair with a fifth of Jack Daniels one cold winter afternoon, surrounded by snow while I watched the dogs chase squirrels, whiskey bottle still in the paper bag, as I sat on that old chair drinking, pretending I was in the car with Kerouac, even though I was just on a rickety old chair in my backyard near the ninth hole of a funky golf course reading *On the Road*, wishing I was on the road.

And look at me now. On the road and wishing I was reading a book on that rickety old chair. Or at someone's house being treated like a guest. Or at least having permission to sleep in someone's backyard. But what kind of adventure would that be? Now I have to worry about three crazy people tracking me down, and it smells like rain, and I don't even know where I am, except that I'm in Washington, and everything seems so far away.

It starts raining and I sit beneath a tree watching for car lights. There's no reason they need to come after me; but there's no reason most people need to go after anyone, and it still doesn't stop them. What do they need me for? Always so much running. Don't dare sleep. I should have kept making cream puffs at Paul's house. Just because he said fucking me was like fucking an iron board, I could have given it another try. Maybe Günter would have been more instructive. At least he would have said the ironing board comment in German, blowing it as a romantic whisper into my ear, same way he said those other things on the bus, and I would have smiled foolishly, and on the train in Germany, he'd tell his friends about the time he broke in a virgin in Wyoming, and they'd all gave a good laugh. Enough thinking about sex. One less thing to worry about on my list.

Instead I think about catechism. Every Wednesday night I walked to church. Never by choice. Always by force. Mom didn't go to church, she liked watching it on TV.After catechism, I looked for my brother or sister, wanting to walk home with them. Figured they were either hiding from me or walking home with the neighbor kids in a group. Being safe. For some reason, by the time I left the classroom and climbed the stairs, the church was always dark and deserted. Everyone was gone.

I'd looked down a few basement hallways and open the doors of empty rooms, certain I'd find my brother and sister giggling in their hiding spot. When they didn't appear, I'd go to the closed library and hide a few books I'd check out later.

Never finding anyone to walk home with, I'd end up running home. Every tree had a shadow. Every shadow had a bogeyman. Neighbors said I ran like a bat out of hell and always wanted to know who I had made mad and was trying to out-run.

Behind the trees, arms grabbed for me. I heard panting. When I opened our kitchen door and ran inside the house, then held the door shut, my mom would yell, "Let go of that door!"

"I can't! Someone's out there!"

"Let go now!"

I'd let go, step back, and couldn't believe that no one pushed the door open. The bogeyman wasn't going to chase me inside the house. He wasn't after anyone but me. I knew he'd get me later.

I must think of something else. Too many shadows behind the trees. Usually the woods are the only place I feel safe, but not these woods so close to that cabin. It starts lightning and I decide to set up my tent. How could I be so unprepared? I can't believe my bike is wrapped in my sleeping bag while I'm out here wet and cold.

A night of thinking is exhausting, but I know I must get moving. No time to watch the sun rise. Today's the day I reach the Greyhound station.

I walk down the forest road. The flowers are covered with dew. Everything glistens. I've lost track of time but know I've been on the road a couple of weeks. Long enough to travel from Michigan to Washington alone. To have sex. And to get from one place to the other, only without a road map, since I just have those fancy topo maps for the coast. Still, I'm figuring out road signs and heading west. Last thing on my To Learn list is to learn how to read a road map, but I don't have one.

Was easy leaving Wyoming without a map. Hitch north to Montana. Hitch east to Idaho. Idaho where the friendly people with the warped sense of humor roam. Where the five-dollar cars stop for hitchhikers. All this thinking. But what else is there to do out here?

My hair is gritty. I feel dirty. I look ridiculous with panniers on my head. I finally reach a paved road. I look at the sun and try to figure out which direction to go. Who will offer me a ride? I hope it's someone with a car that costs more than five bucks.

A vehicle slows down and my thumb isn't even out. I turn around and see a Winnebago. A woman leans out the passenger's side and asks if I need a ride. I can't believe my luck. It's a retired couple. A normal looking retired couple with Minnesota license plates. Good ol' normal, kind Midwesterners.

I race to their Winnebago and the man directs me to the back, pointing to the blue plush recliner. "Looks like you could use a rest," he chuckles.

"Why are you out here all alone?" the woman asks.

"It's a long story but I'm on my way to Seattle to get my bike from the bus station. I should be pedaling but I took a little hitchhiking detour."

She leans over with her journal and asks me to

autograph it. "My grandkids won't believe we picked up a hitch-hiker. Please sign your name and beneath it write "hitch-hiker.""

It's one of the strangest requests I've ever heard, but I do it and feel rather second-rate, like they've picked up a whore and offered her a ride.

"Alice, don't embarrass our hitch-hiker or we won't be able to tell our grandkids we gave her a ride."

Alice feels uncomfortable and offers me her homemade chocolate chip cookies. Eating them I realize how hungry I am. Alice seems to notice and offers the entire bag. "Eat up, I need to make a new batch today."

I sit on their blue reclining chair, swiveling to the left, then to the right, watching the miles float by, wondering if I'll get on my bike now that I know I can ride like this. Maybe I'll ride my bike south as planned or head north to Alaska. One part of me wants to trade my bike in for a backpack and explore the mountains. Another wants to sit on a ferry and visit Vancouver and Victoria.

After I buy a road map, I'll just leave the topographical maps on a restaurant table for a hiker. Even hiking, I'll never figure out the meaning behind all those circles. All those circles won't make one iota of a difference if I'm riding down the highway or following a trail.

Maybe Alice will want me to meet her grandchildren when they visit them in the Cascades. Now there's a range I know nothing about. Why bother learning to read a road map if it really doesn't matter which way I go? For now I'll just swivel a little to the east, then west, stretch toward the north, lean back a little watching those purple mountains majesty, and fall safely asleep.

THE THRESHOLD OF THE SHEELA
Amy J. Rio

The roughened, worn stone sparkled in the rare sunlight. I wondered if its form would be more apparent in the typical spitting rain for which Scotland was better known. The spirits seemed to smile on me during my days visiting my ancestors' homeland. I even had to remove the red LL Bean rain jacket on occasion when the sun warmed my body. The figure before me certainly had seen more water than warmth over the 700 years it hung over the southerly facing window. Or was it actually older than that? Had the women placed it here from another location? The tiny island on which I stood was almost literally a stone's throw from a much larger island, and then other islands and the mainland beyond. Boats had ferried people from this island to various parts of Britain and Ireland well before the Middle Ages. Certainly a stone carving could have been brought from just about anywhere.

As the sunlight disappeared behind a cloud, the carving became more nuanced. The crone-like head almost grimaced, while stick arms and large fingers held open the generous, round womb edges. Too many years of exposure made it impossible to tell if anything issued forth from the womb. Regardless, the womb was the focal point. There was absolutely no mistaking that.

I had journeyed to Iona with several other clergywomen on a pilgrimage to worship at the Iona Abbey and to immerse ourselves in Celtic Spirituality. For almost 1500 years, Iona had been recognized as a holy site. A 'thin place' is a location where the veil between this world and some other world—the afterlife, a parallel world, the realm of the supernatural, etc.—is thin. Experiences can be strange, spiritual, seismic. For centuries, travelers have made their way to recognized thin places, where they experienced something beyond the tangible. Altars, sacred circles, wells, and even cathedrals were built on such locations so pilgrims could have a place to honor these holy spaces. Throughout the centuries, many of these sacred places have been held as holy by different religions. Even Jerusalem was a hallowed site for those who honored the divine in nature, especially as seen with the Mother Goddess, before the Hebrews settled there.

Iona was claimed by Christianity in the 6th century, when St. Columba founded a monastery on the tiny island. The land was well-situated to become a focal point in the Celtic Church. This tiny island, about 1.5 by 3 miles in size, became the principal point of Celtic Christianity when the Irish monk reportedly journeyed 80 miles from northeast Ireland—possibly as a fugitive from justice—and founded a small wooden monastery. The island was not uninhabited, but it was the monks who soon gave great fame to the location. The monastery survived Viking raids, even though a number of the monks and others on the land did not. Some scholars believe the breathtaking Book of Kells—a vividly illuminated manuscript of the Gospels—was created on Iona, and only taken to Ireland for safekeeping from the berserker Norseman.

By 1300, a beehive of activity filled Iona, with a large

red stone Abbey and adjacent buildings dominating the landscape. Intricately carved Celtic stone crosses, stretching several feet above the average person, marked the path pilgrims would take from the dock to the Abbey, providing an opportunity for penitents to kneel in prayer as they wandered the last few steps towards the holy site. Monks and laymen fished, cared for the ever present sheep, and encouraged gardens to grow out of rocks and sparse dirt. Boats continuously crossed the small strait to the much larger island of Mull, carting workers, merchants, and the countless pilgrims to the Holy Isle. I once heard someone call Iona of that time period the New York City of its day. I don't quite know how accurate that descriptor was, but regardless, the island was important in terms of business and the business of spirituality.

Then Henry VIII came to power and wreaked havoc on the church during his reign. While people often attributed his seizure of the Catholic Church properties to an unquenchable desire for an heir—possible only after a divorce and remarriage—gaining the immense wealth of the church was perhaps his primary goal. Once he became the head of the church in his realm, not only could he once again marry, even more importantly he could fund a lavish lifestyle and multiple wars. Many more Abbeys than Iona's were ransacked and left to ruin.

In 1899, key individuals begun the tedious and lengthy process of rebuilding the Abbey, an effort which took decades. Rev. George MacLeod, a Presbyterian minister, felt called in the late 1930s to form the 'Iona Community,' a modern version of a religious group housed in the Abbey, worshipping together, and welcoming pilgrims and visitors. By the time of my visit decades later, the Iona Community was well-established with volunteers from all over the world, and supported daily activities and programs in the Abbey itself. A publishing house had even been created to produce volumes about Celtic Spirituality and worship. Visitors today flock from all over the world to experience the divine, seemingly so effortlessly accessible on this tiny island.

As enthralling as I found the Abbey, I kept finding myself drawn to the ruins of the Nunnery, and the mysterious carving above the window of a partial wall. This neglected site, less than 500 steps from the much larger reconstruction, had been left to the elements over the years. Without the historical marker indicating the layout of the small convent, it would have been impossible for the average person to discover what the tumbled stone walls designated. I had read everything I could find about Iona before our journey, but no book had more than a few sentences about the Nunnery, established once the Abbey came into its height of building and power. Not one book, article, or website mentioned the Sheela-na-gig boldly facing the Pilgrims' Walkway over the main south window of the structure. I had discovered this unique feature from reading the welcome folder at the B & B where we were staying.

I wish I could have been surprised that this great expression of the feminine, the Sheela-na-gig, had been overlooked in the innumerous words written on the topic of the holy isle. But history, and especially religious history, has been dominated by men. A woman's uterus, exposed to the elements for hundreds of years, was just too easy for most men to ignore.

As I first gazed upon the Sheela, snippets of information floated back to me. Little had been written about the topic, but these designs and the mystery surrounding them had fascinated me for years. The stone carvings known as Sheela-na-gigs are found throughout the British Isles, and even a few locations in Western Europe. They are normally seen over doors or windows of religious buildings, like convents or churches, marking a threshold to another space. Others are located near wells or other sacred spaces. Most of the images seemed to have been placed on these structures during the religious building boom of the Middle Ages, although it appears that some Sheelas were added to construction as late as the 18th century. The face of the figure is normally a crone, an older wise woman past the age of childbearing, but commonly acknowledged as a wise elder. The aged head is juxtaposed with the large womb opening, held apart by enlarged hands, and oftentimes revealing an object just birthed.

The first question most people have about these carvings is the name. In seminary, when confronted with something to which we didn't know the answer, we would respond "It's a mystery." It was a total cop-out, but we precocious religious scholars thought it nicely covered any unknown. With the naming of the Sheela-na-gigs, it really is a mystery. Was this a medieval, or even pre-medieval name? Was it a name that emerged in 19th century Ireland, when some people began to ponder these carvings? Does it have something to do with the Irish tendency to call women "Sheelas"? It's a mystery.

The presence of Sheela-na-gigs themselves is also puzzling. Theories abound as to the existence, meaning, and placement of these stone carvings. Perhaps they represent the pre-Christian Divine Feminine, so important in Celtic Christianity but almost vanquished by the patriarchal and misogynistic Roman Catholic Church. Some insist they are a Goddess figure, giving birth to creation. Others see a Trinity, in the representation of the Crone, Mother, and Maiden. Most appear to have been created during the time the buildings were erected, but there is also the question if any were carved during an earlier period and simply incorporated with the church building boom.

The placement of the majority of Sheelas on religious buildings makes many uncomfortable. Since St. Augustine appeared on the scene in the late 4th/early

5th centuries, a great preponderance of Christian men have felt compelled to control the dangerous and voracious uterus. A woman's sexual appetite was believed to lead good men away from their desire for God. The temptation offered was seen as being of the Devil. St. Augustine even felt compelled to coin the concept of 'original sin,' a state in which all people find themselves because they are born from the sex act and via the womb. To be a woman was to be lesser. The insatiable womb represented all that was sinful in the world.

If one reads Augustine's Confessions, it becomes quite clear that he had issues. His mother, Monica, converted him to Christianity as an adult. Upon his conversion, he brought with him his education in Greek philosophy and its dualistic and hierarchical world view. Men were associated with reason, intellect, and the spirit. Women were lesser than men, and were seen as irrational, controlled and confined by their bodies. They could not attain the higher spiritual planes that men could due to their physical form.

Prior to Augustine's conversion, he kept a mistress for many years, and even shared a son with her. He bragged of his sexual exploits. While he migrated his intellectual ideals to his new faith, he rid himself of his mistress and insisted on a life of celibacy. He kept his son while exiling his son's mother. This man, so immersed in the concepts of Platonic dualism that he couldn't see its conflict with the message of Jesus, shaped the whole of Western Christianity.

It could have gone quite differently. Augustine's main rival was the first British theologian, Pelagius. It is only in recent years that this early scholar and religious leader has begun to come out of the stain of heresy that Augustine, and subsequently the Roman Catholic Church, placed on him. Pelagius believed that each child was born in grace and goodness. He encouraged women to listen to their instinct, knowing that God spoke to them, and that a man's approval was not necessary for understanding God's will for their lives. Each person, female and male, was made in God's image, and all creation was good.

Pelagius and Augustine had a rather public disagreement over these key theological issues, but Pelagius didn't seem to care too much about what Augustine thought. He concluded his life in Britain, quite unaware that Augustine and his zealous fervor would condemn women in the West, and their bodies, to the lower realm of sin. Augustine's views have been used as justification for almost 1700 years as to why men should make decisions about women's bodies, and why the uterus must be controlled by men.

Yet, no idea ever really completely dies. It might go underground for a while, but history in the West is filled with women and beliefs that would have horrified Augustine. The presence and preponderance of the Sheelas in the British Isles makes it clear that the concepts about humanity and creation held dear by Pelagius never really disappeared, even when the Roman Catholic Church imposed their theology on the land. The feminine—in its divine and physical form—could not be quelled.

The Sheela spoke to me during my week on the island—not literally, though many have experienced mystical occurrences at such a 'thin place' like Iona. At age 39, I found myself at a threshold. I wasn't certain where I was headed professionally in my career as a college minister, my children were growing up, and our family had moved from my beloved mountains of North Carolina the year before. I had spent months feeling as though I were in exile in the god-forsaken flatlands.

I read somewhere that there is a mineral found in the Scottish Highlands that is also found in the Southern Appalachian Mountain range in the eastern part of the

United States, primarily in the states of Virginia, North Carolina, and Tennessee. This particular mineral is found nowhere else in the world. Geologists explain it with the continental drift theory. Pictures of the Highlands certainly reminded me of my native North Carolina mountains, a place largely settled by the Scots during European immigration. The Scots reportedly enjoyed the similar climate, and were reminded of their own homeland—one most of them would never see again. The glimpse I gained of the Southern Highlands on my journey from Glasgow to Iona had felt like a homecoming.

As I came home to familiar mountains, I witnessed a homecoming with the Sheela. No longer a Maiden, fully engaged with the Mother phase of my life, and looking towards the wisdom of the Crone with my life transition, the Sheela on the Nunnery represented a coming home to who I am as a woman. I'm not just a body, a mother, a dispenser of wisdom. I am creativity itself, giving life to all creation. As my womb had given life, my soul and my heart were giving life. In fact, they were just starting to give birth to creation. I am the threshold.

Iona was absolutely glorious in late October. I spent each day hiking around the island, perching on various rocks or hills just to sit and contemplate. Sometimes I walked with my sister travelers, but often I journeyed alone. Even when I walked by myself, I felt surrounded by a cloud of witnesses. I never felt alone. I always felt safe and comforted. No doubt about it, this was sacred ground. And wherever I journeyed, the Sheela provided a comforting presence to my pilgrimage.

A good portion of the first day was spent on the northwestern coast, a beach bordering the Atlantic overflowing with tiny rocks of rich colors and striations. I marveled at the stunning stones, the most glorious assortment I had ever seen anywhere. I glanced occasionally at the multi-shaded blue ocean gently crashing on the shore, but most the day was spent squatting on the ground, sifting through the various nuggets. I eventually shoved a couple dozen in a side pocket of my pack. My selections were based on color, shape, feel. The rich blues and greens always attracted my eyes first, but a striated black rock, as well as a few others which resembled champagne, gray slate, sunflower yellow, and a robin's egg also caught my attention. I didn't want to claim too many of the jewels—I mean, if every visitor did that, then Iona would be barren of this amazing natural beauty.

Towards the end of the afternoon, as I mentally began to prepare myself to leave this isolated spot, I finally found what I didn't realize I had been looking for. That old U2 song began to thrum through my mind: "And I still...haven't found...what I'm looking for." A deep burgundy peeked from underneath another of the countless shades of blues and greens which always immediately appealed to me. My fingers gingerly uncovered the striking red. I had seen no other stone near that color. Faint snowy cracks flowed over the edge, so tiny they could only be seen at closer sight. As I cradled the stone in my palm, a heart shape began to emerge. Not a fake heart shape, like I always drew as a young girl. It was a true heart shape, one more easily recognized by someone in the medical field. Tears stung my eyes as I tried to hold them back. Here on the edge of the Southern Highland mountain range, I had discovered my heart. It revealed a few cracks, looked a touch rough for the wear, and was hidden under items more flashy—but there it was. I was surrounded by the spirits of Iona, and someone from perhaps long ago understood my feelings of loss, grief, and uncertainty during this transitory stage of my life. Someone made certain my heart made a new appearance—whole and ready for what lay next. The Sheela was at work, creating a new space for my heart.

With my heart safely tucked in the change pocket of my jeans, I continued my excursions around the small island in the coming days. My favorite spot was the Machair, a large grassy slope that descended into rocky black juts scattered along the west coast. Rolling waves broke against these volcanic formations, occasionally spewing water upwards fifteen or twenty feet, especially when it hit one of the little caves scattered along the short border with the water. The green plane hosted part of Scotland's only free golf course. Two hours might slip by before a lone golfer or two would stroll by, hitting the ball towards the next of the nine holes. It wasn't the threat of a golf ball that led me to balance my way over the risers protruding into the ocean. I was a bit more keen to avoid the cows that wandered around the area, and the deposits they sometimes left in their wake. When it was not misting, I folded my trusty raincoat underneath my bottom to ease the hardness of the uneven rocky seat. The salty mist filled my mouth and nostrils, cleansing my lungs. Most of my days included at least a couple hours spent resting in this spot. Sometimes I journaled, writing whatever my pop into my mind. I found myself recording random thoughts on loss, grief, my heart, and a new life.

Staring out at the Atlantic, I pictured Ireland in the distance. And beyond that – the end of the world. Celts imagined they lived at the edge of the world, the ocean stretching out for untold miles until it dropped off into an abyss. One of the best loved Celtic saints was Brendan the Navigator, a contemporary and friend of St. Columba. Ancient legend relates the voyage of Brendan, who reportedly travelled with 16 pilgrims through the dangers and adventures of the Atlantic until he reached the Garden of Eden. While a great deal of evidence confirms the actual life of Columba, probably embellished by sainthood nonetheless, far less exists confirming Brendan. His journey was filled with stories which would impress Sinbad the Sailor.

Journeying with Brendan certainly never appealed to me, but I could understand the desire to sail into the horizon. I knew North America—probably Canada—lay in that direction, but for so many countless centuries others had rested in this same spot believing they were at the edge of creation. I could imagine it filled them with a sense of security, wonder, perhaps even power, to know they sat at the threshold of the world. I personally felt like I could see forever, just like when I stood on a mountain peak surveying the rolling mounds before me. It provided perspective. The vastness of the blue/gray ocean, waves rolling and thundering around me, was far more massive than I could ever hope or want to be. I was a tiny speck in creation. The difficulties in my life were but a blip in the ages of the world, in the untold numbers who had walked the earth. My heart might have broken at being torn from my beloved mountains—my home—but it would heal, given time.

The last full day, our entire group decided to hike to the south end of the island, the location where Columba first arrived in a currach, a small boat encased in tightly drawn animal skins. After wandering through a herd of sheep, then a field of brown heather, a twisting and narrow gravelly trail descended deeply to waves crashing upon a small beach of the same kind of rocks that inhabited the northwestern shore we visited the first day. Tufts of scattered sea grass filled an area about the size of a basketball court before the stones began in earnest. A small, jagged cliff emerged on the eastern side of the area. It was hard to imagine that Columba found this a welcoming place. Yet, if he truly had run from imprisonment or punishment, I suppose any land—no matter how inhospitable it appeared—would be appreciated. It was a good thing he and his fellow travelers kept walking upwards to the main part of the island, which was as lovely as an Irish rose.

My companions quickly fanned out to the far reaches of the area, some walking along the coast until they were lost to sight. I slowly made my way to the beach, glancing at the wide variety of colors and shapes of the tiny rocks. Some larger rocks could be found further away from the water, and then I noticed a small labyrinth created out of the biggest rocks.

Labyrinths have existed since pre-Christian times. They are not mazes, even though often mistaken for them. A labyrinth is a circular design that forms a path for one to walk towards the center. There is only one path to take, but people may walk it any way they choose. After arriving at the center, one journeys the same path back to the beginning. It mirrors the journey of our life, walking towards the heart of the matter and then extending it out to the world around us. It is also a symbol for the womb, for the heart of life—much like the Sheela on the other side of the island. It was evident that someone had taken the larger rocks to create this small formation on the rocky beach of Iona. I guessed it had been there for a decade or more.

A lone goose rested next to the labyrinth. Geese filled the ground and skies around Iona, but this one was isolated. Honking sounds could be heard throughout the day, and long necks stretched to investigate various movements by other creatures, human and non-human. When Rev. George MacLeod had formed The Iona Community at the Abbey, he hoped to revitalize the island as a spiritual center. One of the many foresighted things MacLeod did was to take the great preponderance of geese and turn them into the major symbol for Iona. Geese posters, bookmarks, and drawings filled the Abbey bookstore. They symbolize the Spirit—the Holy Spirit, the spirit of life, the spirit of love.

It didn't surprise me that a symbol of the spirit rested beside a symbol of life's journey. I stood at the opening to the labyrinth, all my companions far out of sight by this time. As I waited for the spirit to move my right foot, I inhaled the clear air and concentrated on my heart. With the next beat, my foot slowly stepped forward. I had walked various labyrinths throughout the years—some outdoors made of rocks or cut into the grass, some painted on canvas and housed in a church fellowship hall. Each time I walked a labyrinth, the trek was different. It could only be what the spirit led.

I walked perhaps a third of the path when I came near the goose, still as a statue. He convulsed once, then again. I paused, staring at the animal I had assumed was sleeping. The tiny seizures continued. I quickly stepped outside the labyrinth—something I had never done before—and knelt down next to the animal. His black and gray markings were perfect. There were no cuts or abrasions I could see. But as I leaned closer, a sickly smell came upon me quickly. The goose was dying, and I was completely helpless.

I leaned back, resting on my bottom to settle in for however long it took. The day was cooler than previously, thus navy leather gloves covered my hands. I gently stroked the bird, smoothing back the feathers as he collapsed onto his side. I continually talked to him in a low voice. I later could not recall one word I spoke. I imagine I offered prayers for him, or perhaps words of comfort. No creature should be alone to die in pain. I have no idea how long I sat there, sounds coming from my lips and gloved hand softly covering the silky feathers.

I remembered the first time a creature died in front of me. I was in 7th grade, volunteering at the nursing home my mother ran. I wheeled around the residents, helped them with activities, and sometimes even fed someone who was unable to feed herself anymore. I practically grew up in the nursing home, so all these things seemed normal to me. Yet, one day as I waited to wheel a man from physical therapy back to his room, the world changed. He had a massive heart attack, dying immediately despite the best efforts of the staff. I spent the rest of the afternoon on the couch in my mom's office, reading Jane Austen once again. I refused to come back for two days, until Mom reassured me that the chances of someone else dying in front of me were pretty slim. She was right.

As an adult, my career would lead me to encounter many more people in the last days or moments of death. They were usually surrounded by loved ones or skilled hospital professionals. I was all this goose had. The afternoon stretched for an infinity. The goose eventually lay still, his spirit having flowed away from his body. I cried. I sobbed. My nose ran, and I removed my gloves so I could find a napkin in my coat pocket to wipe my face. The tears eventually dried, and still I remained beside the body of this lone goose. I simply could not move. Eventually my companions began to return. I must have been a magnet, because each one joined me. Astonishment filled their faces as I related my tale.

"I can't just leave him here, and I don't know what to do!" I sobbed once again. All the women behaved quite sensibly, finally deciding that the best thing would be to place him on the one of the ledges of the cliff near us. I could tell they were relieved I had worn gloves when touching the animal, so I donned them once again to carry him gently to his "burial site." We all spoke a few phrases, offering up his spirit.

Later that day, I relayed my story to the manager of the small inn where we were staying. He was an American who had lived on Iona for a number of years. Stunned at what had occurred, he admitted that he had never heard of such a thing happening to the many geese who called Iona home. We finally agreed that he must have ingested something which poisoned him. He also found it strange that not one other goose was nearby—they tended to stay in flocks.

"Seems like you were meant to find him, sounds like." I nodded my head in agreement.

I spent the rest of the evening, even in the company of my friends, contemplating death, creation, the release of the spirit, thresholds, and what it means to have a heart.

Our group left very early the next morning. I had said my good-bye to the Sheela the evening before. I tightened my grip on the dark ruby heart shaped stone in my palm, knowing that my heart would always be with me. I imagined the Sheela giving birth to the goose, flying forth from her womb to bring life to the world. Death and birth appeared one and the same. The spirit of the goose and of the Sheela had filled my heart, reminding me that new life comes with death, saying good-bye comes with new hellos, and with endings comes new beginnings.

Recommended Sources

Freitag, Barbara. Sheela-na-Gigs: Unravelling an Enigma. New York: Abingdon, 2004.

Marshall, Rosalind K. Columba's Iona: A New History. Rossland, Scotland: Sandstone Press, 2014.

Millar, Peter. Iona: A Pilgrim's Guide. Norwich, England: Canterbury Press, 2007.

Stark, Judith, editor. Feminist Interpretations of Augustine. Philadelphia: Penn State University Press, 2007.

MEXICAN GETAWAY
Tonja LH Vernazza

It was an unusually sunny day when my husband of nearly eight years asked me for a divorce. I was taken by surprise. Three weeks later, my beloved dog was dead. Gutted, I walked around in a daze for months, too numb to do more than attempt to contemplate a different life.

Early in my marriage, when the Internet was still new, I was a member of an online community devoted to marriage. The community was founded by a popular relationship counselor and author who wrote a series of books on maintaining a happy marriage and recovering a failing one, even after an affair. I spent hours offering support to dozens of people looking for comfort and advice. This community became my lifeline while I was embroiled in my own split.

Eventually, I met a few local community members; we all gathered at the Metreon Center in San Francisco. Over food and gallons of coffee, we spent hours telling each other our stories and bonding over our shared pain. Soon, we were meeting regularly for meals, movies or dancing.

To keep myself busy, I took classes at the local

community college. I hadn't worked since the dot com bust in late 2001, and it gave me something to do. I took beginning guitar, piano, and conversational Spanish. My Spanish instructors traveled frequently and I listened intently as they shared stories and tips for staying in Mexico, Spain, or Latin America.

International travel: it was always so romantic to me. I wistfully looked at postcards, photographs and shows about visiting other countries. As much as I longed to sip espresso in Rome, or stand atop the Eiffel Tower in Paris, or scale the pyramids of Egypt, the thought of travel was troubling. My mother discouraged my interest, afraid for my safety, and wouldn't hear of my studying abroad. I was taught that travel was risky and best avoided.

On a whim, I walked into a Walgreen's for a set of passport photos. I didn't have a trip planned, but I felt giddy when several weeks later, I slid out the dark blue passport from the envelope.

Henry and I became fast friends. He divorced his wife a year earlier when she left him for a coworker. They were still wrestling with child custody issues when we met at our first group meeting. We would sometimes do things by ourselves because our schedules often lined up. Henry was interested in a woman from his church and I would often dispense advice for gauging her interest. So it was a surprise when he mentioned going to Mexico together.

The prospect of traveling internationally was too enticing, so I leapt at the opportunity. Henry made the arrangements for an all-inclusive resort on the small island of Cozumel. I knew from my Spanish instructors that Mexico was very formal compared to the US. I used the little bit of money I had to purchase some skirts and dresses, and a pair of good walking shoes.

He picked me up and we drove to the airport on an April morning. I kept checking my carry-on bag to touch my passport. It was finally going to be stamped!

The flight was easy and we touched down in Cancun six hours later. We had to walk out to the small plane that was our connecting flight to Cozumel. I watched with curiosity as other passengers boarded a flight to forbidden Cuba.

It was almost dark when we landed in Cozumel, so it was impossible to enjoy the scenery as the shuttle dropped passengers off at the various resorts around the island. When we arrived at our hotel, we made our way to the front desk. It was warm and humid out with a soft breeze. We checked in and an employee guided us to our room. When they opened the door, I was shocked to see only one bed. Panicked I said no, and shook my head. The bellhop was confused by my reaction. I took a deep breath, here we go.

"Necessito dos camas, por favor." I need two beds.

Our bellhop took us back to the front desk and I did my best to explain in Spanish that we required separate beds. Everyone at the front desk laughed at first, especially after Henry looked a little crestfallen, but soon they found a replacement. Our bellhop showed us to our new room with two beds. I slipped him a $10 bill and thanked him for his help.

After we settled in, we went down to the buffet and had a light dinner. Over salads, we discussed the brochure of activities the resort offered, debating the various tours and other offerings. After dinner, we retired to our room and got ready for bed.

The next morning we had breakfast and met with our assigned concierge. We discussed with her the various offerings. After nixing scuba diving, we settled on horseback riding to see the Mayan ruins on Cozumel, taking a submarine tour of the coral reefs, renting a car to tour the island, and a day trip to Chichen Itza—the large Mayan pyramid complex about three hours away.

We got the keys to an old VW bug and immediately set out to drive around the island. We stopped at a beachside restaurant—really a beach shack that sold beer and tacos—and sat by the ocean. I was fascinated with things that were both familiar and new. Driving the manual transmission was easy, but the gauges and signs were in kilometers, not miles.

When we got back to the resort later that afternoon, we went back to our room. I thought to set out my clothes for the next day's trip to Chichen Itza. I settled on a modest skirt, blouse and my new sneakers. Something caught my eye and I looked more closely at my new shoes, realizing they were both left feet. Somehow, between taking off the shoes I had tried on and checking out, two left shoes ended up in my shoebox.

Once Henry was out of the bathroom, I showed him my shoes and told him I had to try and find a shoe store in San Miguel, the largest urban area on Cozumel. Luckily, Henry too had forgotten some things and wanted to find a drug store. We hopped back in our rented VW and headed to town.

We found parking in the small urban center and walked past dozens of little household compounds. Each house was surrounded by a tall fence—a mixture of cement blocks and wrought iron, with gates that allowed cars to be parked within the protective perimeter. Dogs barked at us as we walked past the homes decorated with colorful tiles and tropical plants. Soon we were seeing more businesses, shops, and cafes.

Even though Henry and I were walking together, men still called out to us. They tried a few words in various languages, but when my ears pricked up at Spanish, they asked where we were from. When I nodded my head no, they decided to guess. Australia? England? Germany? Canada? I laughed and shouted, "Estados Unidos!" Henry and I laughed and walked on.

When I spotted a shoe store, Henry left me there to go look for a drugstore. As I approached, I realized buying shoes in Mexico was a little different. Entering from the sidewalk, a long, tiled hallway was flanked by two large walls of glass cases. The walls were lined with shelves holding shoes and next to each shoe was a number. At the end of the little hallway was a glass door. Inside the store, there were a few upholstered chairs and a tall counter where the register was located. A salesperson approached me and asked which shoes I'd like to try. I hoped that my two classes of conversational Spanish would be good enough to get me some shoes.

I told the saleslady that I'd like to try on veintenueve—number 29—and she directed me to sit in one of the plain tan chairs before going to find my shoes. She asked my size, and I wasn't sure if Mexican sizing was different from European sizing. So I asked, "Cuarenta y dos?" before she cocked her head to the side, looked at my feet and nodded.

I could see partially into the large storage room beyond the doors and all the boxes stacked almost to the ceiling. The woman sitting next to me must have seen the curiosity in my eyes because she commented, "It's a little different, isn't it?" As we began to talk, I learned that she was from the United States and that she and her husband ran a business importing jewelry and art from Mexico and Central America to the US. Sadly, her husband had died a few years earlier. Instead of returning to the US, she felt happier living in Mexico and only returned to the US to visit her adult children and grandchildren twice a year.

As we tried on and admired each other's shoes and chatted, I finally settled on a pair and paid for my new sneakers—one for each foot this time—and said goodbye. When I exited the store, I found Henry lingering outside, enjoying the beautiful weather. I clutched my shoebox as we made our way back to the car. On our way, we saw the dock for the ferry that shuttles tourists and locals between San Miguel and Playa del Carmen. Ferry tickets were cheap, and we decided to go back to the hotel, get changed and go get dinner in Playa del Carmen that night.

I had no expectations of what the ferry would be like. I'd learned from interrogating better-traveled friends and family about their experiences overseas that what Americans often assume about other countries— and how they're portrayed in shows and movies—is often very wrong. So I can't say I was surprised to board the ferry that looked like any ferry in the San Francisco Bay, taking tourists to Angel Island or Sausalito. When we docked, I was delighted to find a vibrant street, full of art galleries, silversmiths, live music, and packed restaurants.

We settled on an airy corner restaurant with billowy white curtains in the wide-open glass walls. We enjoyed local seafood and tequila. I did all the ordering for us. I was so proud of myself that I could speak well enough to get what we needed. People were so generous, they would repeat my sentence back to me with the necessary corrections and then breeze right along, never embarrassing me or making a big deal out of my elementary language skills. I was sure to use 'please' and 'thank you' more than anything else, hoping that being polite and respectful would make up for any gaffes or inconvenience.

After dinner, we walked up and down Calle Cinqo, a playful nod to New York City's Fifth Avenue. We browsed galleries and jewelry stores. I even picked up a couple of pairs of earrings I liked. Having cash was a bonus allowing me the novelty of negotiation and getting a better price. Since it was getting late, and we didn't know when the last ferry was leaving, we decided to head back to Cozumel. The ferry was loaded with sunburned tourists and locals, tired from a day of work.

The next morning we woke up before dawn and grabbed a quick breakfast before setting out to San Miguel to catch the ferry again. I went out on the deck as we were crossing the strait that separates the island from mainland Mexico. The sun was rising, shocking pinks and oranges, while flying fish zoomed past. After docking, we quickly made our way to the rendezvous point to meet the tour van to head to Chichen Itza.

We boarded a large white van with another 20 or so tourists and set out northwest to the pyramid complex. The drive wasn't boring; it was fascinating to see how people lived—concrete houses with dirt floors and hammocks for beds; chickens and dogs playing with toddlers and young children; women hanging the wash to dry on clotheslines. The land was flat, dusty and hot, but not unlike parts of northern California.

Three hours later, we were entering the very busy and crowded parking lot for Chichen Itza. Our guide was a university professor of archaeology, so he was a wonderful resource, explaining the purpose of the buildings and the lives of the ancients. Many of the buildings had been cleared and cleaned up, but were closed to tourists. The complex is huge—so many buildings: an observatory, an infirmary, a sports field, cenotes for fresh water. Our guide explained that divers had found so many bones in the bottom of the cenotes. Men, women, children, and animals were sacrificed to encourage rainfall; their bodies flung into the wells.

Eventually we made our way to the main pyramid. The steps were steep and a rope was installed to help tourists climb the pyramid. Once I was at the top, I realized how flat the valley was and marveled at how magnificent the pyramid must have appeared to people coming to Chichen Itza. I enjoyed the view for as long as I could before I grabbed the rope and began my descent.

I continued to wander around the complex, mesmerized by the ornate details of the buildings, bas-relief, and walls. There was an eeriness to the place I had never before experienced. The stories of all the bloodshed, the sacrifices, enemies taken as slaves: I wasn't exactly uncomfortable, but there was a definite strangeness to the place that was distinctly 'other.' It was eerily quiet, lacking birds or other animals.

I decided to go find Henry and walked to the museum and gift shop at the entrance to the site. I found him browsing the Mesoamerican history books, trying to decide on a gift for the love interest back home. He looked up and smiled at me, holding up two volumes. I pointed to the one devoted to Central American art history and he assented and went to go check out. I wandered back out to the hallway to peer at the displays while I waited for him.

Soon, everyone was back at the van and we were on our way to another venue for some entertainment and food. As expected, we were taken to more gift shops, many offering to write your name in ancient Mayan hieroglyphics on a gold pendant, or a ceramic reproduction of the Mayan calendar for your wall. By late afternoon, we were back on the road towards Playa del Carmen.

I felt unsettled and irritable. At first I thought it was just because I was fatigued and weary of sitting in a van with strangers. My thoughts kept returning to the stories of savaged captured enemies and sacrificed children, whose bodies were thrown into those deep cenotes to encourage rain and continued successful crops.

Was human life so expendable? Did the conquering Aztecs survive to adulthood more easily than their European counterparts? I knew that elsewhere in the world, it was an accomplishment to grow old. Were children so easily born that they could be so handily sacrificed? Or was this perhaps a sign of their great devotion, to make so large a sacrifice? Was their need so great? Was this dusty land always this dry? Perhaps the archaeologists had it wrong. Maybe those were children of their enemies? Vanquished competitors whose women and offspring would be flung into these deep freshwater wells to nourish the gods?

I grew snappish with Henry and knew I wouldn't be good company. When we returned to our room, I excused myself, showered and went down to the bar. I didn't understand my own thoughts. Why would human sacrifice that happened long ago bother me so much? What was it about that strangely quiet place that haunted me? I walked past a table full of drunken hotel guests towards the bartender. There was another guest placing his order and I waited patiently. Once they were done, one of the men from the noisy table stumbled in front of me and started barking an order at the bartender. The bartender very firmly told him that I was next, then turned to me and asked me what I would like.

Speaking in my imperfect Spanish, I thanked him for his hospitality and asked for a margarita. He took his time, probably as a jab to the rude man, and I slipped him a tip. I followed the signs through the small grotto and out to the resort's private beach. I was surprised to find myself alone. I walked to a lounge chair at the far edge of the beach and drank my cocktail. I looked out across the ocean at a few boats and one cruise liner. As my eyes drifted heavenward, I gasped. There were so many stars. I could see all the familiar constellations: the big dipper, Orion, the little dipper. I lay back, still sipping my drink when the tears began to fall on my cheeks.

How did I end up here? I was in a foreign country with a man who was not my husband, not my boyfriend, by the grace of his generosity. I had just visited a place that left me unsettled and upset, though I had experienced no personal sleight or unpleasantness. I was actually communicating successfully in a language I had just begun to study less than a year prior. Back home, I had an ugly divorce to conclude. Yet, here I was surrounded by unimaginable beauty. The twinkling stars and quarter moon above, the soft splash of the waves on the beach, and the solitude of this lovely beach. And I was crying from the overwhelming absurdity of the whole thing. But now, I also knew this experience was repeatable. While my fears of traveling alone were reasonable, I knew that I could confidently add more stamps to my passport.

IN SEARCH OF SORROW
G. Clark Hellery

The Traveller entered the dim tavern. She didn't bother to make eye contact with the smattering of locals who made it financially prudent for the tavern owner to stay open long past the time other folk were in bed. Her boots stuck to the film of damp sawdust: the assorted smells of the night before, cheap alcohol, vomit, even more than a little blood clung to her as she walked towards the bar. The Traveller crinkled her nose slightly as she eased herself onto a creaky stool at the bar. She gently placed her ukulele on the stained wood, nudging some dirty glasses out of the way as she did so.

The tavern owner approached, giving the Traveller an appraising once over. Her calfskin trousers were slightly baggy, as if made for a bigger person, and tucked firmly into well-travelled boots. Her top half was shrouded in a colourful poncho featuring stylised birds, animals and geometric patterns. Not the work of the local tribes, he mused. Her wide-brimmed, sun-bleached leather hat was pulled low over her face so only flashes of a tight mouth could be seen. He saw no holster at her waist, a mistake in this town. She carried no backpack or other belongings aside from the ukulele.

She didn't look up as the tavern owner made a show of cleaning the glasses and moving the dirt around the bar with a stained rag.

'What'll it be?' he asked, one hand already floating by the bottles of alcohol.

'Whiskey,' the reply just audible over the noise of the drunks, having the same arguments they'd had the night before, and the night before that, and the night before that. The Traveller laid a protective hand on her ukulele as the tavern owner poured her drink into the smudged glass placed in front of her. She waited a moment, then in one swift move the glass was scooped under her hat, and returned to the bar empty. She gestured for the tavern owner to refill the glass. He did so and hovered to see if she would knock it back like before. When the Traveller started to swirl the amber liquid around in her glass, he put the bottle back on the shelf.

'You ain't from round here,' he said, more a statement than a question.

'Nope,' replied the Traveller, her hat not moving while the liquid in her glass continued to dance around.

'Don't get many travellers in these parts, neither,' pressed the tavern owner.

'Don't imagine you do.'

The tavern owner frowned. 'You looking for something? Passing through? Ain't much round here, 'cept some farms. No work goin' neither. Mine closed some years ago, after the accident what killed all them folk.' He paused, but there was no reaction from the Traveller. 'Farmlands only good if you work it hard and this time of year no one needs workers. Ain't no gold in the river and no one dare go up in those hills, no wi' them,' he paused, searching for the right word, 'things up there. Name's Jacob. I own this place. Been here a long time, helped 'em build the town. I know all what goes on around here. Seen a lot o' people come and go. Mostly go recently.'

The glass momentarily stopped swirling, then a slight

nod from the Traveller and the liquid in the glass disappeared under her hat. 'Kinda talkative, ain't ya,' she murmured.

Jacob's glare was wasted on the hat, but he was not going to be easily dismissed. He'd heard the gripes and arguments of the bums he served too many times to be deterred from hearing a new story, and he had a feeling the oddly dressed traveller had an interesting story to tell. He took a deep breath.

'S'what does bring you to these parts?' An edge entering Jacob's voice, as he looked once more at the patterns on her poncho.

The Traveller shrugged. 'Gotta keep moving. Looking for someone. A girl.' The dregs of the whiskey puddled in the bottom of her glass. Jacob topped up her glass, hoping the liquid would loosen her tongue. It seemed to be working so he hovered, holding the bottle in readiness to refill her glass. 'I'm guessing t'ain't much to do round these parts.' The Traveller gestured with her glass. 'I visited a lot of these small towns. All the same. Only entertainment is drinking, whoring.' She paused. 'Fighting. Fighting be big business, especially in small towns like this.'

The change in her tone caused Jacob to swallow hard. He carefully put the whiskey bottle back behind the bar and wiped the counter, pressing the cloth hard into the wood to stop his hands from shaking. 'Don't hold with fighting m'self. So, who's the girl you looking for? Sister? Daughter? Doubt you'll find her here, ain't no young 'uns and ain't no unaccounted girls around here.'

In reply the Traveller reached out. Jacob took an involuntary step backwards. Under her hat he caught the flash of a smile, then the Traveller gently picked up her ukulele. She lovingly stroked its wooden curves, running her fingers along the strings, producing a small whine then placed it just under her breast, as a mother would her nursing child before beginning to play. Her voice wasn't particularly melodic, more than a little raspy from lack of use, but her words were clear. The drunks stopped their arguments and looked over with renewed interest at the Traveller, as her voice drifted with the dust to reach the darkest corners of the tavern.

I'm searching for a girl-child,
Don't know her real name,
Lives down in the south,
With a growing kind of fame.

Living in the darkness till the sound of the bell,
Knowing she'll be forced to fight again,
Fighting through a special kind of hell.

In the ring she survives,
Using her hands, her teeth & her wiles,
Forced to fight beast and fight man,
While people come to watch her from miles.

Stolen from her family,
She don't know her kin,
All alone in the darkness,
Don't know if she'll see the light again.

The last note gently floated away through the tavern. All eyes were on the Traveller as she lay the ukulele on her lap, her head remaining bowed.

The silence was broken by someone scraping their chair against the sawdust floor. The Traveller cocked her head towards the sound as one of the men rose unsteadily to his feet, the assorted glasses on table clattering their annoyance at being disturbed.

'Mighty pretty singing, there, but we ain't got your girl, an' I think it's time you be on your way,' he said.

The Traveller spun around on her stool, her back to the man and gestured to Jacob for another drink. The ukulele reminded in her lap, her hand lightly over the strings.

The drunk staggered around the table, knocked it with his hip and sending glasses, liquids and playing cards tumbling. One of his companions threw up his hands in annoyance at the end of their card game while the other swatted stale alcohol from his lap, then they watched as their friend approached the woman at the bar.

The drunk pointed at the Traveller. 'You hear me lady? I said it's time for you to leave.'

Jacob waved his dirty cloth at the drunk, 'Now sit down, John. Let the lady finish her drink. She'll be on her way soon enough. Won't you, miss?'

The hat bobbed slightly before the whiskey disappeared under it. The empty glass was placed upturned on the counter. 'S'right. Don't want no trouble here boys. I'll be on my way,' said the Traveller, slightly slurring her words. The growing tension in the tavern eased as the Traveller began to stand. Then, as if the alcohol had suddenly hit, she slumped back onto the stool.

A few of the men closest stood to help, but the Traveller raised a hand to stop them while a few, including John, leered and sniggered. The tension eased, replaced by a lusty expectation.

'You need to take it easy,' jeered John. 'Looks like the lady can't hold her drink. Perhaps we need to show her some small town hospitality.' John moved closer to the bar, his hand on his belt.

Jacob looked around nervously, unsure of what he should do. 'Pr'raps you should be going, miss,' he said.

'I ain't going nowhere, not till I find what I'm looking for.' The Traveller's tone, clear and strong made the more sober men pause. John, however, too bull-headed or too drunk to notice the change in the Traveller's tone, continued forward. Her hand tightened on the neck of the ukulele and just as John reached for her, she struck, jabbing the head of the instrument into his neck. He staggered back, struggling to breath. Two of his drinking buddies sprang up and caught him under his arms to stop him from falling. He gagged a few more times before pushing his friends away roughly.

'You dare touch me, you bitch!' He roared, launching across the bar once more, this time with some of the more drunk locals at his back. They pulled up short of the Traveller as she sprang to her feet and raised her ukulele, the head pointing at each of the men in turn.

The hat gently swayed, as a cobra assessing its prey, her earlier act of inebriation replaced with deadly focus. 'Don't have to be this way boys. I know what you got going on here, your fight club, betting, whatever you call it. Folks and animals been going missing from about here. Word's getting round it ain't safe in these parts.'

There was a derisive snort from one of the men.

'You should'a listened to them words,' growled John. 'It ain't safe. But don't you worry none, you won't live long enough to tell no one.'

'Thing is,' continued the Traveller as if she hadn't heard John, 'Word also says you took what you shouldn't ha'. A girl. Her family travelling through these parts looking for work. You killed them and took her.' The Traveller's voice broke a little at the end but her stance did not falter.

A low chuckle rolled across the tavern. 'We only kept her to feed to the dogs. Little scrap of a girl. Turned out, she was our best fighter. Earned some o' us a lot of money. You ain't taking her nowhere.' The Traveller turned toward Jacob. He had a shotgun raised, and was pointing it at her head. 'I told you it was time to leave, miss. I had a feelin' you was going to be trouble. That little girl you was talking 'bout? She bigger now and what skills God gave her, been trained into something that's more deadly than any coyote or rattlesnake I ever seen. But why am I bothering to tell you, when I can show you?'

Jacob gestured with the shotgun. The Traveller

slowly raised her hands. As they drew level with her shoulder, her right hand lashed out, the ukulele spinning in her fingers. The body of the ukulele hit the end of the shotgun and there was an explosion as it fired. The Traveller spun around, into a crouch behind the bar as the shot struck John and the other drunks in the bar. They screamed as the buckshot entered heads, shoulders, arms and stomachs. Some fell, dead before they landed, while others staggered back, checking themselves for injuries. The Traveller somersaulted over the bar. She struck Jacob in the throat with the head of the ukulele. As he staggered backwards holding his neck, she pulled one of the strings from one end of the ukulele. It came away easily, unwinding in her hand. Forcing Jacob into the bar, she pushed her knee against his back to stop him turning around while she slipped the string around his neck. With practiced speed she twisted the wire string, ignoring Jacob's screams and flailing hands. Once tight, she used the tuning pin to hold the wire in place.

The Traveller stepped over Jacob as he dropped to the floor, thrashing around while clawing at his throat, his face slowly turning the same red as the drops falling from the garrotte at his throat. It wasn't long before he was still. The shotgun he had dropped was kicked under the bar. The Traveller swung the ukulele, now missing one string, slowly in her right hand. Climbing slowly onto the bar, she surveyed the remaining men.

Some of the men lay on the floor, screaming in pain from their gunshot wounds, but others had only received minor injuries from the buckshot and were picking themselves up, suddenly sober and looking to fight. John and his drinking buddies wiped blood from their faces and spread it on their chests, like streaks of war paint, or flicked it onto the floor where it mixed with the blood and piss of the fallen. John flexed his shoulders, causing more droplets of blood to seep from the wounds to his face and arms but he made no further move to stop the flow as he growled, 'Gonna teach you a lesson.'

The Traveller jumped down from the bar, landing sure footed. She planted her feet, digging her heels into the floorboards and flicking the arms of her poncho onto her shoulders, revealing a spiral of tattoos rising from her wrists and coiling around her arms.

John and three other men moved to surround the Traveller taking points of the compass in front, behind and on either side, with John facing her. Weapons appeared - knives, chair legs and even a whip but she did not move. They jostled between themselves, murmured bets as to who would break her first, then louder taunts and threats, specifics as to how they would tear or rip, gouge or smash the Traveller. She did not move. Following the preening and the jostling the men grew uncomfortable. With no reaction to their bravado or answers to their threats they were unsure of what to do next. The man on John's left feigned a lurch at the Traveller. She did not move. The man to her right snapped his whip against the floor. She did not move. Moments passed.

Without warning the man behind the Traveller launched himself at her, swinging a chair leg wildly. She deftly stepped out of the swing and brought up the ukulele, causing a crunch as it broke his nose. As he staggered around and raised his arm to swing again, the Traveller stepped closer, forcing the shards of broken bone into his brain with an upward jut of her wrist. He fell backwards like a felled tree, the chair leg falling from his arms as a broken branch.

The other men stood shocked until the crack of the whip broke the silence. The Traveller cocked her head to one side, as if curious to find the strip of leather around her waist but she didn't stay still for more than a moment. Spinning, she danced towards the man, the whip wrapping around her. Bringing her elbows up, she struck the man in the face, sending him reeling. He still held on to the whip and for a moment the Traveller started to lose her balance as he toppled backwards. However, grabbing his hand which held onto the whip, she pulled him upright. She grabbed the bottle of whiskey from the bar and smashed it against the man's head before jabbing the jagged bottle into his neck. A front kick sent the man tumbling over tables, as blood pumped from his neck, a red rainbow arc. A shimmy of her hips loosened the whip and it puddled at her feet.

Turning, the Traveller pulled a tuning pin from her ukulele, holding it between the fingers of her clenched left fist, with the sharpened end facing out whilst the ukulele remained in her right, the body held high like a bat.

John and the remaining man looked at each other. A tiny nod from John and both men launched at the Traveller, knives and teeth flashing. With unnatural speed she dodged aside as the man swung his knife upwards, barely missing her kidneys. She stepped in close and rammed the tuning pin into his eye before kicking him away. He screamed as his hands flew to his face and the damaged socket. The Traveller flicked her wrist, shooting the eyeball off of her tuning pin and hitting the man on the chest. The eyeball fell to the floor and was crushed under the man's boot as he bashed into tables trying to escape.

The Traveller ducked as John swung his knife at her head. Powering from her legs, she caught him around his middle and drove him backwards. They crashed into one of the tables and amazingly it didn't collapse under their combined weight. John pummelled the Traveller's back. Jumping, she flipped over and forced John onto the table, landing on his stomach, her knees pinning his arms to the table. With a loud groan the table gave way and they crashed to the floor. The Traveller was thrown off John. With a roar, he climbed to his feet and turned towards her. The Traveller spun, her leg raised in a roundhouse kick and kicked him in the face. However, he remained standing, and spat teeth at her as blood dripped from his mouth. Tightening her grip on the tuning pin, the Traveller launched at John, wrapping her legs around his torso. Faster than a quick-draw she shot the sharpened tuning pin into his chest, punching multiple holes. She landed heavily on top of him, amid the debris of the tavern.

'What the hell are you?' John asked, putting the last of his energy into asking one final question.

The Traveller lifted her head for John to see her face. He died screaming. Her eyeless sockets were crudely sewn shut with coarse thread, tiny droplets of dried blood still clinging to the fibres. Her cheeks a criss-cross of purple scars and her mouth pulled into a tight, one-sided grin.

The Traveller took a few deep breaths. Gently picking up her ukulele, she plucked the tuning pin from John's chest with a loud squelch. Limping slightly around the bar she cleaned the blood from her ukulele using the tavern owners dirty apron. She poured whiskey into a glass and dropped the tuning pin in. Small tendrils of blood and gore drifted through the amber liquid like clouds at sunset. Pouring herself another generous dose of whiskey into what passed for a clean glass, the Traveller knocked back the shot and wiped her mouth. Picking up her instrument and replacing the pin, she eased her way past the bodies on the floor, ignoring groans and occasionally kicking anyone who appeared to be on the verge of getting up. Around the back of the tavern was the outhouse, an overly generous a word to describe the shallow trough dug in front of the back wall that was filled with piss and faeces, dead rats and insects. The Traveller swallowed the bile in her throat with difficulty as she walked around to the tiny shed which backed onto the 'outhouse'.

The door caved after the fourth kick and she pushed aside the splintered wood. The inside of the shed smelled even worse than the outhouse but the Traveller forced herself not to flinch. She didn't move into the shed, instead waiting to try and sense any movement from the darkness.

'Hello?' The Traveller called tentatively. A quiet rustle, and a low growl was her reply. 'Hello? I'm here to help. I'm going to get you out of here.'

Movement in the dark. The Traveller turned her head. 'You're safe now. Come on. Those men ain't coming back. You don't have nothing to fear from me.'

A small girl, not much into her teens appeared from behind the door. She was covered in a dense mix of dirt, excrement, sweat and blood. Her hair hung in matted clumps. A cord hung loose at her neck and wrapped around her wrists, pinning her to the wall of the shed. Only her eyes were clear, shining as bright a blue as on a cloudless day. She peered nervously around the door, her small hands clenched tightly and her stance ready to fight should any threat appear.

'That true? Those men ain't coming for me?' She croaked with a voice which hadn't been used in a long time. She swallowed hard and tried again. 'Where's my family?'

'What's your name?' asked the Traveller, ignoring the girl's question. There would be plenty of time for explanations later, about how the girls parents had been killed but came to the Traveller, begging her to help their daughter. The Traveller had listened impassively as the ghosts had shimmered in front of her, only leaving when she promised to do as they bid. She slowly pulled one of the tuning pins from her ukulele and using the sharpened tool, gently cut the cords around the girls wrists and neck. The girl flinched at her touch but obediently stayed still. The Traveller returned the tuning pin to her instrument. 'What's your name?' She asked again.

The girl looked confused for a moment. 'Don't remember. The men called me The Beast.'

The Traveller nodded sadly. 'Well, you ain't no Beast. Time for a new name. I think 'Hope' will do. Yup, Hope sounds just perfect.'

Hope stepped towards the Traveller. The Traveller reached out her hand towards the girl, but Hope flinched backwards. A sad smile could be seen under the Traveller's hat. 'You ain't got nothing to fear from me, Hope. I been searching for you a long while. There's others like us, Hope, other women and girls I'm searching for that need to be free like you. I'd be glad of your help, if you'll give it.'

Hope tentatively reached out to the Traveller. The Traveller raised her head and looked at the small girl with sightless eyes, twin fires burning behind her closed lids. Hope barely quenched a scream as she looked into the Traveller's face. She paused for a moment, took a deep breath, then gently grasped the Traveller's hand.

They smiled at each other, the warmth of a shared bond flowing between them. Dawn was inching over the mountains, its blush light sending shards of warmth onto Hope's upturned face. She smiled a happy, relaxed grin as she looked up at the Traveller.

'What's your name?' asked Hope as they began walking out of town.

The Traveller spun her ukulele as she squeezed Hope's hand. 'M'name's Sorrowful Jones. People call me Sorrow.'

FREEDOM OF VOICE
Jessica Marie Baumgartner

I've always been one to let the wind blow me in the right direction. By my senior year of high school, I was working a full-time job and had my own apartment with my sister and a friend of ours. If it had not been for music classes and my love of English I might have given up on education altogether. During my studies I found that the greatest lessons come from one-on-one moments with others.

Wandering through life has led me down a path of independence, but with love for the human connection. I need to be my own leader and always chart my courses based on intuition and signs from the gods (the creator(s), the universe, God; whomever or whatever you give your faith to – it's all the same to me). After battling to be noticed in the music industry, I found myself gifted with the opportunity to put stock in something way more creative: Motherhood.

It is not for every woman, but I come from a long line of ladies with a maternal touch. My mother did her best to instill a strong sense of family in my upbringing. Despite her efforts, I found her financial difficulties, lack of education, and difficult marriage to my father, akin to elective prison. It made me resist the urge to settle down and allow my nurturing nature to flourish for years.

Although I attempted to sabotage every relationship I entered, I found myself cared for by a calm reasonable man who offered me the kind of security I needed at the time. We got married, bought a house, and then had our first child. There is nothing more healing than being afforded the opportunity to right past wrongs by providing for the ones you love.

My husband worked full-time and I stayed home to care for my daughter. She brought out the best in me, making me examine my own childhood to do better. I had been raised on mac-n-cheese and Little Debby snacks. For years I had tried crash diets and exercised until my fingers and toes went numb, but once I desired to be a mother I had to lead by example. The 'do as I say, not as I do' approach never seemed to work with me. Improving my own habits gave me more insight. Suddenly the bitter taste of green beans led to sweetness—and a healthier figure. My daughter loved peas and carrots, and I enjoyed sharing her enthusiasm to take care of myself.

Exercise was not a chore; I loved dancing her around to my eclectic musical tastes and found that she was a born dancer. Watching her wiggle her little baby arms to the cheesy synthesizer in the 80's song "Oh Sheila" cracked me up so much I would laugh until my mouth felt too tight for my cheeks. It inspired me to pull out my guitar and play her some of the songs I had written years before.

Dust flew off my guitar case. I brushed it away, half ashamed that I could neglect what had once been such an important aspect of my life. Setting my baby girl in her bouncer, I pulled the Dean out and strummed my finger down the strings. The most hideous noise erupted from it and I cringed. "She needs a tuning real bad," I apologized to my daughter who eyed me with a glowing face.

I pulled out my tuner and adjusted the pegs. I took up my natural sitting position and began playing an old country song my aunt had taught me. I'd never been very fond of country music, but certain songs break all genre barriers. My daughter cooed and kicked in her seat with a grin.

Audience reaction had always been a big part of my performancing days. I love drawing from the energy of others to pour everything I had into my songs. Her enthusiasm encouraged me to try and play one of my originals. "It's been a while, sweetie. But mommy wrote this one."

From the moment I found out I was pregnant I talked to my daughter. There are always new ideas and thoughts attacking my mind. I'm not good at holding much in. She seemed to love it and really listened. It made me wish to do more for her.

I played one of my favorite Lauryn Hill songs next. Stroking the first chord I cocked my head at her. "You know, everyone has a chord. One that fits them perfectly. If I was a chord I would be this one," I played the bar cord and let the flowery notes echo loud.

I leaned forward and rested my chin on the glossy wood of my guitar. "I'm going to try and find your chord."

My rusty fingers failed me and I was unable to get back into practice so soon. But I started playing more. Each day we danced a lot, and I found myself telling her stories. One of the main reasons I always loved music is that it allows people to tell a simple story in a short time. I made a couple of stories up off the top of my head and kept at it, telling my daughter tales of my childhood and from my musician days.

After while she began staying up later at night. By the time she reached her first birthday she required longer stories, or little mini-concerts before bed. It was during those nights that I wrote her theme song: The

Annabella song. Upbeat and simple, the words were shaped from her very being. It didn't take long for me to pull out the guitar and find her chord after finishing the lyrics.

Bright and bluesy, my daughter's song became a regular performance. She danced to it, sang with me, cuddled up with me after hearing it, and asked me to tell more stories. I had some friends who were interested in my take on parenting. "You make it look so easy," my sister-in-law said to me at a family gathering.

I just did what felt right. I loved my daughter not only as my kid, but as a person. I wanted to let her be whoever she wanted to be and give her the necessary guidance along the way. This led me to take her to the annual Pagan Picnic. I'm more of a spiritualist but Wiccan in more ways than one.

The sun shined on the booths as we took the walking path through the side shops. Anna was a sturdy walker at a year and a half and she charmed everyone we walked past, as most toddlers do. When we stopped to make a crafted crown at kiddie corner, the woman running the booth talked to me about how nice it was to see someone sharing their family with the community. There were not many families at the event, but we had a great time. I said as much and she looked deep into my eyes, "You seem to have a knack for this. You should write about it."

I'd never given it a thought. Writing was a fun pastime for me, something to do to get my feelings out and have a bit of fun with make-believe. I looked over to my daughter as she rolled oversized beads on the table, wearing her new crown like a proud princess. "I might," I laughed.

The lady at the booth told me about a few Pagan publications and I shrugged it off. From sun up to sun down I was Mom. I cleaned house every day, made every meal from scratch, played learning games with my daughter. But that night, after another "go to sleep" concert for my daughter, I wrote a simple piece and submitted it to The Witches' Voice. Not only did it get published, but I got emails from readers asking for more, so I kept writing.

Writing was fun, but not as enjoyable as making up silly stories for my daughter. She laughed so hard at one of them I wrote it out and very terribly self-illustrated it. The big sketch-pad drawings were less than amateur, but she kept grabbing her father's Kindle and saying, "Your story."

"Sorry baby, my story isn't on there." I tried to explain to her that my book wasn't really a book, but she refused to stop asking. I researched Kindle self-publishing and decided to put it on Kindle for her for fun. It had no place competing with the world of children's books, but I sold a few copies.

Nothing much came of it and I began to wonder what my writing meant. The warmth I received from the few readers who continued to praise my work kept me thinking about going further. Maybe I could write something of note. Maybe.

My mother, who had an off-again-on-again relationship with college, had finally achieved her Associates Degree the summer before and sparked constant thoughts of my going back to school. Ready to try it, I enrolled and got into classes with ease. While studying and taking care of my daughter, I found that I could do more. I longed to write more, teach more; learn more.

A friend of mind told me about a paid writing opportunity with the St. Louis Examiner. With no experience it seemed like a long shot, but I sent in my information. They hired me as the Pagan Events columnist and I now had a writing career (not a world renown one, but a start). Once accepted I sat on my couch and stared down the hall to my bedroom where my daughter was sleeping. This new job required at least one article a week. A tight fear gripped me. Could I keep up with my work, school, and continue to be a good mother?

The fear of failure at any or all of these aspects of my life left me questioning myself. I decided that if my work interfered with school, I would resign. If my work and or school interfered with my parenting, I could always push one off or quit. Challenges make me enjoy life more, and I was damn sure going to try and take on the ones presented to me.

My schedule became tighter than a corset on a Victorian prostitute. I woke up and took care of my daughter, studied during her naps, and worked on writing at night. My English Comp 101 teacher taught me to "never get married to my work." She had the opportunity to publish with one of the big 5 and refused to compromise which led her to be turned away with nothing. She funneled that experience into her teaching and also drilled me in editing.

As a dyslexic with rapid thought, my hands often fly over the page way too fast, and my typing isn't much better. After many revisions, my assignments were all turned in early. One of my articles was published on the front page of the St. Louis Examiner as the editor's pick. Anna's vocabulary flourished, her motor skills were right on, and I continuously worked to keep balance. However, I slept very little.

Then I got pregnant with my second child and spent my pregnancy keeping active. Pregnancy always makes me sleepy, but I battled through nausea and swollen joints to keep up with everything. Most of my remaining classes were available online. It made it easier for me to schedule everything around my daughter and my pregnancy.

Despite my love of writing and learning, the main concern was making sure that my firstborn knew that the baby was hers too. My older sister and I fought a lot growing up, but we also helped raise each other and I wanted that for my children. We sang to my bump, read to it, told as many stories as we could.

When my second little girl came into my life, she multiplied my creativity. Growing up as a tomboy, I never dreamed that I would end up with two girly-girls who changed my entire perspective, but the adventure of discovering all the things I never did helped me to find a hidden aspect of myself: femininity.

The past always has a way of repeating itself, but thankfully it's never exactly the same. My eldest was very much like my sister, and the little one was a tiny version of me. She came out fighting and hasn't stopped since. Her tenacity helped push me farther.

I gained my degree just 3 months after giving birth again. I had no interest in the self-congratulatory pomp and splendor of a graduation ceremony. That drove me nuts when finishing high school, so I chose not to walk. My classes were done. I had made it!

The swell of pride that rushed through me as I buckled myself in the car to go pick up my diploma remained wrapped around me the entire drive to campus. I parked the car with shaky hands on the wheel. Getting out, I stepped onto the pavement with my shoulders back and went in to beam on the administration.

It didn't seem like much to the lady who gave me my diploma, but I ran my hands over the leather cover. I skipped back to the car like a child. A few heads turned but I didn't mind.

On the way home, I was struck with a very vivid story idea. It was a children's book with a very clear theme. I'd never seen a children's book that presented all religions together and pointed out the similarities in a simple way that would appeal to children and give parents a teaching tool so they could help their kids understand that we all have different customs and beliefs but most of us want the same thing: freedom and respect.

I did my best to breath deep and control my racing

heart, but I had to get home and write everything out. My foot wanted to push the pedal all the way to the floor of the car. I tapped my toes just above to try and be patient, something I had taught myself in my teen years after getting a few too many speeding tickets.

When I finally got home, I rushed around to find some paper. I always have notebooks lying around the house. They seem to turn up whenever I'm looking for something important—diapers, shoes, my big cooking spoon—but when I need one, there is no paper to be found. I grabbed a little pad hiding under the phone and wrote out my first children's book.

The paper was so small, only one line would fit on each page, but it did the trick. Once everything was out, I sat on the couch and flipped through the worlds. *This is really something*, I said to myself.

I had no idea where to start. The rush of exhilaration pumped through me. I jumped up, grabbed the laptop and started researching the world of book publishing. Children's book publishing looked to be a world of rejection. I needed an illustrator and to somehow get a publisher. The more research I'd done, the more I found publishers and agents who would not work with religious material, but this story wasn't pushing any one religion; I even put a page about Atheism in it.

All of that was put on hold when Anna woke up from her nap and ran for me. I picked her up and hugged her close. Turning around, I grabbed my diploma from the table and let her hold it. She opened it and stared at the paper inside. "You really finished?" she asked me.

I gazed over her hopeful features. "You never really stop learning, honey. And it's only my two year degree."

She wrinkled her chubby little face and pressed her forehead to mine. "Good job mommy."

Those words. That did it.

"Thanks sweetie!" I squeezed her tight.

She handed my diploma back and watched me with a

careful gaze. My husband walked into the room and smiled through his bushy black hair.

"You wanna see?" I raised my eyebrows at him.

"Sure." He looked at my diploma and nodded. "Nice!"

"Thanks." I laughed and he hugged me. "You're next," I nudged him.

He had gone back to school as well and was on his way to earning the same degree. While we balanced his work and schooling, and the girls, I determined to get my book out. Since I wasn't much of an artist, I posted on Facebook: Hey if any of you artist friends and family are out there. I'm looking for an illustrator for my new children's book. Message me.

The first person to respond was Laura Winship-Fanaei. She was my husband's friend's sister and we'd gotten along well at the few gatherings we'd been to together. Her super-friendly nature didn't deter me from staring at the screen, curser blinking. My mouth went dry as I forced myself to describe the premise to Laura.

Most people are cool, but there had been enough people who had verbally attacked me or even once pushed me out of an event for being a Pagan that I did my best to be cautious. I don't know why. It's right there on my Facebook profile. Religion: Wiccan. Right under Political Party: Libertarian. (Yes I am a Wiccan libertarian, quite a conundrum, but I don't care what everyone else is as long as they don't try to tell me what to believe or how to vote).

Her response: "That's perfect! I'm an Atheist."

Goosebumps rippled my arms and I nearly felt like crying. When you create something that comes straight from the heart, it means the world to you, and you take a huge risk of heartache. "Heartache is a part of being a writer. Get used to rejection," My English Comp 101 professor's words came back to me.

"I cannot pay you up front, but we can split the royalties 50/50," I told her.

She was on board and got to work. Every image she sent me was as if she could see the inside of my thoughts. I didn't have a clear idea of exactly how the illustrations should be done, but she made them a reality. The vivid colors and childish nature of the pictures were perfect for what I wanted to do.

I showed my daughters as the images came in. My eldest loved them. The baby blinked her little eyes and rolled into me for more cuddles. Sleep deprivation from having another baby began to set in, but the extra time to stay awake helped me to look into publishing options.

I didn't have a lot of money to throw down on agent books, and everything I read said it would take years to get published. I perused lists of children's book publishers that accepted unsolicited material. Many specifically stated that: We do not accept religious material.

It put a weight on me, but I continued looking. I submitted to a couple of publishers, but got nothing back from one and an immediate rejection from the other. My stomach tightened whenever I thought of it. My work for the Examiner suffered and I eventually resigned. It was becoming too much.

After a nice day out at the park with the girls, I sat down and wrote a new piece for The Witches' Voice. It had been a while, and the welcoming response from that site is where I got my start. Then it hit me, I haven't looked for PAGAN publishers!

I went through their book listings and found as many Pagan publishers as I could. Narrowing everything down, I ended up with a small list and got to submitting. Within a few weeks the book was signed and we were on our way. In the fall of 2014 my first book was published and from there I was able to hold a book signing at the Pagan Picnic.

Being on the other end of the booth gave me more insight than any fan mail I had ever received. Getting out face-to-face to speak with individual readers recharged my creative energies and helped me to know who I am writing for. The simple act of shaking hands with book lovers, or offering a hug to a mother who thanked me for writing something she needed told me I was doing something right.

I continued to get better deals with bigger publishers and hungered for more events. My husband did not fully understand my need to keep going. He grew frustrated at his job and I threw myself into my work and taking care of my children. We realized that we are better parents than lovers and had a very amicable split. Our friendship is important to us and our children, and I find that no matter how my romantic life goes, I cannot ignore my creative life.

Getting married and trying to conform to societies standards did not work. No one can cut a part of who they are out completely and expect to be successful. It is when I found my creative voice refusing to be silenced anymore that things started moving forward again.

In 2016 I decided to really get out there and self-funded a mini book tour to "take the show on the road." The people in Kansas City and Chicago were as caring and interesting as everyone I met in my hometown of St. Louis. I started trading my books with other authors and gaining a wealth of material, from non-fiction memoirs to King Arthur fantasy, and beyond.

Sharing my love of stories has led me to find more acceptance and insight than any classroom learning I ever received, but without those technical skills, I would not have been able to do it all. Expanding to Wisconsin and Kentucky and more, I find freedom. Packing as much as I can into my tiny hatchback Yaris (or the pregnant roller skate as I call it), I relax into my seat and absorb the meditative stretch of road that leads me to more people, more connections, more perspective.

My children are now old enough to make the trips with me. It's only fitting, being that they are my inspiration. They helped me start it all and they continue to teach me while I try to aid them in understanding the world around them. Connecting with others through the written word has afforded me many opportunities. It is not a solitary life. The wind has blown me around like pages on a wayward book, and I am happy to read others as they read me.

HOW COULD I DISAPPEAR?
Sandi Hoover

I'll run away!

That was my frequent threat, or promise, to myself. So I said it again—out loud. "I'll run away!" I thought about running away from home much more as an adult than I ever did as a child.

Daydreams maintained my sanity and became my escape during weeks that sometimes became months when my husband was working overseas. I mused on the law discussed by women whose husbands were out of town—Murphy's Fourth or something. It stated the difficulty of a situation at home would be directly proportional to the distance and problems involved in contacting a husband. This didn't even encompass the day-to-day challenges of raising children, and the logistics needed to keep a family with only a single adult functioning—barely stably.

Considering throwing it all to the wind and abandoning home and children for freedom occurred on an irregular basis, frequently stimulated by a combination of small events—the papercuts of the daily responsibilities—children's behavior, hormonal fluctuations, and parental and managerial demands, adding up to an overwhelming need to flee.

I was already mentally gone from the lineup of cars dropping children off at school when brake lights on another mother's car just ahead startled me. The squabbling kids, both mine and others' bouncing in the back seat, reached a fever pitch, but I was past reprimanding them.

My turn at the drop off point came. The children were led away to classrooms by adult overseers, and I was freed. Cranking up an oldies station on the radio, and rolling the windows down to pretend my tired sedan was a convertible, I didn't fight the steering wheel when the car turned unbidden in a direction unrelated to anything on my day's list. What would happen if the car just kept on going? Somewhat dreamily, I watched city blocks slide past with no sense of almost there, and the impending need to be galvanized into action. My 'to be done today' and shopping lists sat unread and ignored on the passenger seat as I started conjuring places where no one would think to look for me if the car went on and on.

How far could I get? Where would I go? What could I do? Like persons in the Federal Witness Protection Program, or author Erma Bombeck, who said move and leave no forwarding address for children, I plotted places to live where no one would expect to see me. Various locales demanded my attention. I have always loved travel, so liberating my imagination with a mental road trip to free myself was exciting.

Was the other side of town and a room in a cheap motel, or living in a trailer park, far enough away to be lost for as long as I wanted? Probably not, and I started mentally examining the United States map for alternative places to live.

Even though they were as perfect as a non-English speaking foreign country for someone living in southeast Texas, I immediately eliminated the top tier of states in the U.S. They were just too cold to endure, even for escape. It meant I'd have to live there, looking and feeling like the Pillsbury doughgirl or the Michelin woman, in layer upon layer of clothes to fend off frostbite. Nope, none of those states was a possible haven.

Moving along, my next area of contemplation and elimination was the southeast. My progressive views would be expressed too soon and were certain to get me killed, or at the very least—noticed. That outcome would not fulfill my goal of hiding and being innocuous.

The northeast was out mostly because of crowded conditions—easy to hide in the throngs, but uncomfortable to live there. And yet once again, it was cold in the winter with snowstorms and shoveling snow making it miserable for a wimpy person who was chilled when you said 'fifty degrees,' much less said 'freezing sleet tonight and blizzard conditions tomorrow.' Although New York City was without question huge and one could get lost there, I didn't own a wardrobe of black clothes for more than a week, so I would stand out in their monochromatic crowds. Besides, I don't look good in black. Vanity strikes again; another thing moms don't have a chance to develop.

Now where in the rest of the country, and there was still a large portion of the United States to choose from, was I going to vanish? I wanted somewhere large enough the neighbors didn't care who you were or where you went to church or preferably even if you went to church.

It couldn't be too near my current home. It needed to be inexpensive because I wasn't going to have a high-paid corporate position to fund my life. Plus, I didn't want to accidentally run into an acquaintance, or catastrophe—family—while grocery shopping.

While worrying over where to go, I thought perhaps the first thing to do was change my appearance. I'd cut my hair really short and dye it purple, get tattoos and work at some big box store. No, it was just too public, and while purple hair was a dramatic difference for me, it wasn't inconspicuous.

Even though my friends were environmentally and socially correct—they said they recycled before it was popular, and avoided corporations whose payment policies treated their employees like slaves—I'd bet money they occasionally backslid and shopped in a forbidden store.

Paying everything in cash was going to make it difficult as well. While daydreaming, I tried to avoid thinking about practical things such as new identification and other actual details, but some inserted themselves unasked.

Enough sunshine was a must. My hiding spot needed to be somewhere with a nice climate and interesting scenery. How about a city with a large park or botanic garden? I would hide in plaid flannel and work planting annuals for every change of season. Under a big hat, long sleeves, with gardening gloves, and looking at the ground, I'd never be discovered. I got an instant backache thinking about that vocation, not to mention sore knees and behind.

Perhaps I could assume a sort of 1940s Veronica Lake look with blonde hair draped over half my face. Hair in my eyes, something I normally hated, and wouldn't wear, would bar recognition from a casual glance. Veronica in her mid-thirties wore slinky attire not currently chic. So I'd opt to wear demure pastel sweater sets with pearls. If I sold perfumes in an upscale boutique in Dallas, I'd never be found.

Never mind, I forgot about my allergies to strong aromas and whatever many colognes were made of. Since I also didn't own the required sweaters, I'd better think of something else to do. Well, I had scratched that occupation, but I thought I would like to keep the hair. Maybe I'd find out if blondes really had more fun.

As a teen, I had helped my dad work on our cars. He wanted a boy first, but there I was. Perhaps that was an answer. I'd work in the parts department of a large car dealership in another state. Even though I already spent my days in the car with children, hanging out in a car parts sales area was so far from my current life, it was an unthinkable place for anyone to find me. Not a plant in sight, no greenery or a breath of fresh air. Arrgh. Just the thought made me slightly stir crazy. I wanted escape, not purgatory.

New Orleans' charm had always intrigued me. I'd become a redhead to match my Irish temper. Then I'd sit in a garret, a phrase sounding artistically reclusive and poetic, and write florid bodice-ripper novels or dramatic plays where the heroine loves unwisely. Did garrets even exist anymore? How would I find one? More importantly in New Orleans, were they air-conditioned? Most importantly, what if a hurricane came by? And the odds were good that one would in the foreseeable future. That lovely city is below sea level! Not to mention the pressure of writing.

My mind idling with the engine, I considered and discarded Oklahoma, another state easily reachable from my location. It would be only a day's drive to disappear in rural country there. The tanned hiker-chick look with sun-streaked blonde hair, rough and ready khaki shorts and boots had great appeal. Hmm, not exactly city attire, but my attitude changed just thinking about the freedom of being out in the open. Could I learn to be useful on a farm? I was quite accustomed to cleaning up after small animals (after all I had two children), but the possibility of having to slaughter my own dinner, made me consider being a vegetarian without even leaving the city.

Eek! No more tornadoes, thank you. I saw one up close. It was extremely impressive, and I never wanted to live in tornado alley after watching transformers on power poles flash with brilliant blue and shocking red before going dark inside the oncoming funnel. Hiding in a bathtub with a mattress over me held no appeal.

Especially if all I could live in was a trailer. I'm convinced they are tornado magnets.

Clearly, northern Texas, Oklahoma, and those flat rectangular states were out of the question. Calm weather was high on the list of my necessities after growing up with earthquakes in California as a child, and living with hurricanes in Houston as an adult.

So, the possibilities were getting slimmer. No snow, no tornadoes, no hurricanes, I was getting pretty picky about the location. I needed a place large enough to not become the object of interest as the new person in town, but still I wanted to find a niche.

If I hid in a big city like Los Angeles, where any extreme was standard, a severe black hairdo, with fishnet stockings, plus a rerun on platform shoes with a short skirt could work and had a retro appeal. On second thought, it had been too long since I wore those clothes with the English mod look of the time. Although retrieving both youth and the freedom of childlessness were attractive, the desperate appearance of someone hoping to recapture a lost era was not who I wanted to be.

Time for an assessment of what I thought might work. Okay wearing casual clothes, having blonde hair, and some way to make a living out in the open was settled. Lots of negatives in location, not many positives yet. Where was I to go?

How about some territory where I could leave my hair straight, grow it long, and wear it in braids like Willie Nelson. I'd add denim, put on a bandana and hair net and work in a school cafeteria in a large town.

Great heavens no, what an awful idea! Was that prompted by some country and western song I just subconsciously heard on the radio? The object was to avoid children, not be subjected to even more of them. Of course being completely opposite of any expectation of something I would do, it might work. But emphatically no! It was painful to even think about standing surrounded by noisy children with low blood sugar or alternatively, a sugar high.

That outfit, without the hairnet, and with a blouse showing my décolletage could possibly work elsewhere. What about a rural biker bar? Those were prevalent in east Texas piney woods where no one would expect me, but the aroma of stale beer, loud music, and burly ruffians covered in tattoos, didn't appeal for even one second. That idea was conceived, envisioned, and discarded in a shudder of relief. Sigh, I wasn't getting very far in making an escape decision.

Driving through the green tunnels of Houston's streets stimulated pictures of northern California and the immense trees living there. The image following those trees was of the cold fog, rain, and gloom essential to grow something gigantic. As the sun-loving woman I am, no way could I be happy living in that environment. Those hiking shorts and boots I was imagining left lots of space in between for goosebumps. Another large sigh of regret. As much as I loved visiting there, as a permanent location for me, a dreary climate wasn't going to happen. Trading one form of depression for another was no answer.

While coastal Oregon is the same as northern California, only more so, inland it is quite desert-like since the coast range blocks rain. Aha, that meant a bearable number of cloudy days. Interior Oregon seemed like a possibility, and it was a progressive state with laws to protect human rights. Okay, what about a frizzy 'fro, to go with long skirts and loose gauze blouses with lots of beads? A bit of an unrepentant hippie, this was so similar to my standard self it wasn't camouflage. And too, there was still the colder winter and hotter summer climate by virtue of location to contend with. Heavens, it was difficult to find the ideal place, and persona to disappear into.

I looked south. Perhaps Arizona. It has always been a state with lots of sun, and warm, no, make that searingly hot, days. The compensation were the charming, almost human, Saguaros, and the mountains were elegantly exposed—a delight for a person with geological training.

Parts of the state held appeal, my favorite town being Sedona. However, the cost of living there was too high, and not only was it small enough to have to tell one's story and keep track of what had been said, it also had a significant snow season. I still was spoiled, thinking I wouldn't live where I had to shovel the white stuff.

So going further south, Tucson was entrancing with its Spanish and Mexican flair. Best, it had no snow, but at the other end of seasons, the number of days over one hundred degrees was frightening. Bad idea after all, and Phoenix was turning into a hotter Los Angeles, without the ocean at hand. Scratch Arizona.

I even considered Mexico, but the complications of language and nationality overwhelmed my imagination as I considered a quick getaway. If only I had taken Spanish instead of German in high school!

I got this far in my thinking more than once, but never could decide on the perfect international or U.S. location. This inability to settle on a hideout saved me from making a column headline—Unfit Mother Abandons Children. Or across the entire page—Mother Disappears, Father and Children Distraught—with a heartrending photo of sobbing children clinging to their father.

Usually I had driven to the Houston City Limit sign by then, and was startled to see open rice fields looming ahead and buildings diminishing in the rear view mirror. And at that point I wondered what the kids were doing in school? Were they behaving? Wasn't it almost time for recess…were they having a good time with friends? I could imagine laughter and smiling faces. No way could I miss the next installment in their young lives.

I pulled into a gas station parking lot, with Brubeck's Take Five on the radio—absolutely right on target. I snapped back to the present and realized with just a few more deep breaths, I could cope with a day's normal duties. My imagined freedom—sanity saving. Being a grownup isn't always easy.

I filled up the car for the week ahead, and thought about the chauffeur license I didn't have, although it was an important job I fulfilled. One of my responsibilities was getting dancers to class, and soccer players to games. Those weekly routes had become so routine I was a moving map of the city.

The adult benefit of handling car pool was open time after children were busy with their games and classes. Then there was the opportunity to talk with other mothers who faced the same things. Comparing notes made us laugh and kept us sane. We were a sisterhood of women coping with life and creating bright, curious children.

The trip back toward town flashed by as I reviewed my various selves. Oh well, they would probably be boring in short order. I discarded them one by one. First to go was Ms. Goth. I wasn't very fond of her, and black hair wasn't flattering to me anyway. Next on my list of abandoned personas was Miss Prim, the fragrance saleswoman. I would have had a hard time maintaining that level of decorum. It wasn't difficult to leave her behind.

My gardener in the big hat and the hiker chick were really variations on a theme. Off they went together. Hopefully to some bright green space where they could lie on their backs in warm sunshine and discuss merits of native plant species.

Ahh, lastly, the redhead in the garret. No need to be a non-operatic version of Mimi and die in my impoverished hovel, but writing still had appeal. It offered an adult outlet I could indulge in after all were asleep, but a garret sounded claustrophobic and confining. Keeping a journal and throwing away the fear of hurricanes, I could salvage some of her.

Time to face life. Picking up my list at my first stop, I added a lined notebook to it and headed for the grocery store, but veered off when I saw a beauty salon sign saying, Walk-ins Welcome. How much, I wondered, would it cost to become a blonde?

Forget concern when children threaten to leave home. It's more serious, yet both funny and pathetic, when moms do it. Or just think it. I know wasn't the first, nor will I be the last mother to contemplate running away from home.

Daydreaming about freedom from responsibility was a way to maintain a certain stability of behavior. Those urges to drop out of sight occurred as I was caring for children as a temporarily single parent, and gave me much more empathy for women who managed it years on end.

This was all long ago, and the youngsters who precipitated thoughts of running away are now busy parents with children of their own.

I have never asked if they ever thought about leaving home with no forwarding address.

THE WEEK I WAS JODIE FOSTER
Leanne Breiholz

"Are you alone?"

"Uh, yes." I was clearly alone.

The customs agent looked at my passport and then at me again. "You are traveling by yourself?"

"Well yes, I flew by myself but I'm meeting a friend here in Japan." This was getting old fast.

"Are you certain your friend is here?"

"Yes, he works for [giant Japanese corporation] and has been here for several weeks. I'm meeting him at the hotel."

The customs agent made a face, "You are sure? You will not be here alone?" Was I in the wrong country? This was Japan not the Middle East. I have always looked young for my age but I was a pretty well traveled 27-year-old. I had never had this problem before.

"He is here, I'm sure."

"Okay then. Enjoy your stay."

What would he have done had I not been meeting someone? I flew 10 hours to get here and had all my required travel documents. Could they actually send me home?

Before traveling to Japan I had joked around with

my fiancé, Brian, that when we got married I would start following ten paces behind him with my head bowed. I would occasionally hand him something and back away, shuffling my feet, hands pressed together, not making eye contact. It was our little joke, me becoming a proper Japanese wife so he would not be shamed. I knew that in the year 2000, women in Japan nonetheless mostly adhered to traditional gender roles. At [giant Japanese corporation] there were female employees, secretaries and engineers, but not managers and executives. Infidelity was widely accepted among men in Japan and often looked at as nothing more than blowing off steam—completely unrelated to the state of their marriage. There is a Japanese saying "It is a shame for a man not to eat a feast placed before him." When managers came to the US to work for a time, they often hooked up with the Japanese translators that worked in the office, sometimes even paying their rent during their stay in the US. These same employees also had to be warned, when working at the US headquarters, pornography was not to be seen on their computers between the hours of 8 a.m. and 5 p.m. but a blind eye would be turned the rest of the time. This was the climate I had just entered and I was not sure how I would be treated during my stay.

I exited the airport and followed picture signs to the taxi line. I did not speak Japanese and had a slip of paper written by my fiancé's co-worker with the hotel address. Luckily my driver spoke no English so he did not interrogate me about traveling alone. It does however, take some extra trust to hand someone a paper you cannot read and sit in silence for 45 minutes hoping you end up in the right place.

My driver found the hotel with a little help from dispatch—I assume, because I did not understand the conversation. The hotel staff was waiting for me and called me by name when I walked in. I was easy to recognize as the only American woman staying at the hotel. Tourists visit places like Tokyo, Osaka and Kyoto, not smaller industrial towns with little to see.

The room was small, as are most things in Japan. There was a bed jammed into an alcove so that one had to crawl into it from the foot of the bed. A strip of carpet between the bed and a low dresser was the only floor space in the room. The bathroom had a shower with the nozzle at eye level to my 5'5" frame, a sink and luckily, a completely normal toilet. At the airport I had encountered a control panel to the right of the commode with numerous buttons, pictures and symbols that I could only begin to decipher. I was pretty sure one button activated a bidet feature, and another appeared to provide a heated toilet seat, but there were so many more. I was not feeling adventurous enough to actually push any of these buttons and was satisfied to just find the flusher.

I was too excited to rest even though I had been awake for about 20 hours. I waited for my fiancé to get off work so we could attend a welcome dinner at a nearby restaurant. I flipped through a few channels on the TV but none were in English. Instead, I pulled out my novel and read.

. . .

We arrived at the restaurant after 9 pm as the Japanese work day is rarely 9 to 5. The décor was exactly as one might imagine, almost like walking onto a movie set. I removed my shoes as the paper screen slid open to reveal a long table on top of which sat four giant tuna heads, each pointing nose up to the ceiling. Twenty or so Japanese men and women sat cross-legged around the low table, pulling bits of meat with chopsticks, directly from the fish heads into their mouths. Various bowls of unfamiliar looking vegetables also adorned the table. Although my surroundings were what I had anticipated, the banquet before me was not the sushi rolls and miso soup I expected. "The adventure continues," I thought entering the private dining room. Brian introduced me to the assembled crowd and in a haze of jetlag and culture shock I nodded politely, quickly forgetting each name. I sat across from a group of "office girls" as they call them, the secretarial pool, who giggled and pointed at me saying "Ah, Jodie Foster." I was familiar with this tendency of the Japanese to assign nicknames based on their knowledge of "western culture." Brian's broad shoulders and pale blue eyes had earned him the moniker "Mel Gibson." My long blond hair and high forehead made "Jodie Foster" a fair comparison.

I was confused about what exactly to eat. The helpful gentleman next to me said, "Eat stuff behind eyeball, very good for brain!" I had no idea if he was joking or not. Instead I spooned some green pods, what I now know as edamame, onto my plate along with a generous helping of rice. Carefully using my chopsticks, I put the pod into my mouth and bit. "No! Like this." a hand grabbed the pod and showed me how to pull it open to eat only the insides. I was going to starve. However, first I had to use the restroom.

Brian instructed me to put on the bathroom slippers. Sure enough outside our private dining area were several sets of slide on slippers. I chose a lovely blue pair and found my way to the restroom. There was a step up into the restroom and as I opened the door what awaited me was a porcelain trough in the floor, maybe a foot or so long and half a foot wide. I had heard about Japanese style "squat toilets" but this was the first one I had actually seen. So here I am in borrowed slippers, exhausted after 22 hours of no sleep and I need to squat over this glorified hole and pee. I assumed the position. Nothing happened. I was tense and wobbly, afraid to fall over backwards out the bathroom door with my pants down, flashing half the restaurant. I breathed deep, "You can do this." I needed a pep talk to pee. "Don't pee on the slippers, breathe, aim, don't pee on the slippers." Finally, success.

...

The next day I was on my own as Brian was here to work, learning how to install manufacturing equipment he would then assemble in the US. I was in Japan to see the sights and learn about Japanese life, as we could someday have to relocate for a 2- to 3-year assignment. Armed with my guidebook and a plan I boarded the train for Nagoya, and found myself surrounded by business men and uniformed school children. I was the only *gaijin*, foreigner, on the train. I knew from my subway map how many stops the train would make before I got off. The subway lines were well organized and color coded, but if you were not in downtown Nagoya, you were completely at a loss. Nothing was labeled in English outside the city.

I had chosen to start my day with one of the best known landmarks in the area, Nagoya Castle, figuring it would be easy to spot once I got off the train. What I hadn't counted on was the confusion I had on the platform after I disembarked. I had the right subway stop, but there were 5 different exits to street level, all emerging in mystery locations labeled only with a number. I chose the "2" and climbed the stairs. A quick spin around revealed I could not see my destination. The streets were practically empty with everyone starting their work day and I could not read any street signs. I had decided before my trip my "Plan B" would always be to find a man in a business suit, figuring that was my best chance at finding an English speaker. I saw one and quickly trotted up to him. I said "Nagoya Castle?."

He looked at me for a moment then extended his arm out to the side and said "This way, then this way." Indicating a left hand turn. I thanked him and walked that way. A moment later quick feet approached me from behind and I turned to see my business man. He swept a hand toward the sky and said "Trees, trees." With a polite Japanese nod, he turned away and headed to work. After I walked a few blocks I saw trees and turning left a large street sign with an outline of a pagoda type building with an arrow.

The castle, now a museum, had many English signs and the restroom even had "western toilets" at the end of the row of stalls. I was sad to read that the castle and many building on its grounds were destroyed by US air raids in 1945. Apparently the castle was being used for military purposes during the war. I successfully ordered tea in the restored tea house, adding five years to my life, my guidebook claimed. Outside the castle walls I found a beautiful opera house with a display of costumes and set pieces to view.

I was doing great on my own, right up until lunch. Many restaurants in Japan have either picture menus or a large glass display case with plastic food models of the dishes they offer. This was the day I learned to doubt the accuracy of plastic food models. I pointed at what looked like a chicken and rice dish in some mystery sauce and hoped for the best. I reviewed brochures and maps while I waited for my meal. When it arrived, it was covered in onions and looked quite different from the plastic model in the case. I am severely allergic to onions. Having assumed pictures and food models would be an accurate representation, I had not properly prepared for this contingency. There was nothing I could do but attempt to eat around the onions. It's hard to explain food allergies and return a meal when you don't speak Japanese.

The food adventures continued through my travels. I ate cow tongue cooked before me on a hibachi grill and it was surprisingly good. I ate chicken feet, which had more meat then you would expect but were disturbingly crunchy. I learned I am not a fan of raw fish and that alligator tastes like chicken that's been hanging out in an aquarium. Green tea flavored ice cream left a lot to be desired as did most desserts I encountered. Gelatinous masses of various colors derived from red bean paste and algae were often set before me at the end of a meal. Some resembled translucent hard boiled eggs while others were fancy layered concoctions, but they were invariably tasteless blobs.

...

An American wife was due to arrive during my stay, and I made arrangements for some activities for us. Actually, I chose the activities and Brian had his Japanese coworkers make the reservations due to that pesky language barrier. My guide book said there was an English speaking tour of the Noritake factory where you could see dinnerware being made. Shawn, the American wife, and I traveled to an industrialized area of the city that appeared deserted. A few factories billowed smoke into the sky but most of the surrounding businesses were closed, their windows covered in paper and magazine pages, many with pornographic images on them. It was the only time I felt a little unsafe in what is a very clean and friendly city.

We entered a show room and glanced around at the assembled crowd. There were about two dozen Japanese tourists awaiting the tour, the English tour. We checked in with a young woman behind a desk who assured us we did have a reservation for the English tour which would begin shortly.

Two gentlemen entered the show room, one spoke to the Japanese and they followed him into a small theater with a movie screen. Shawn and I were approached by the other man who said "English tour?" and prompted us to follow him to a 19- inch television with a VCR. Our guide inserted the VHS tape which gave an introduction to Noritake and the china making process. Apparently the English version of the movie was shorter than the Japanese version and when we finished we headed out to the production floor with our guide. Our private English tour got us up close to the action, while those behind us in the Japanese tour stood on tip-toe to see over each others' heads at each station along the tour. The best part was product testing. Each plate, bowl and cup was individually checked for quality. First there was a visual inspection and then each piece was struck with a black Sharpie marker to make sure it would not chip or crack. Any piece that did not pass inspection was immediately smashed and thrown into a bin so it would not accidentally be sold to the public.

As we progressed, our guide continually looked ahead in a large blue manual referring to notes on what was coming up and what to tell us on the tour. I assumed that he was either new to the job or needed some help with his English. However, we later discovered our tour guide was an executive from the corporate office. He had received a call early that morning that they needed someone who spoke English to give a tour because some Americans had actually signed up for it.

...

I constantly turned to my Fromer's Japan guidebook during my adventures. For seven days it was my bible. Fromer was my trusted and only source for the correct subway stop for each sight I wanted to visit, insight into specific points of interest, tips on dealing with money and ordering food and led me to believe that the recommended places to visit were actually frequented by Americans. I was constantly the only English speaker at any given tourist location, like at the Noritaki factory, so I saved one especially out of the way trip for a group outing. Fromer had told me all about Inuyama, a town of about 72,000 people at the time, that had some great places to visit. The Museum Meji Mura is a huge architecture museum with over 60 buildings that have been transported to a scenic 250-acre lake side property.

The buildings were all originally constructed from 1868-1912 and include things like a sake brewery, Kabuki theater, bath house and prison.

Inuyama is also one place to see cormorant fishing. Nightly, men dressed in grass skirts and pointy hats, like big garden gnomes, head out in boats with fires suspended in cages over the water. Trained seabirds dive into the water to catch the fish attracted to the lights on the boats. Special collars on the birds prevent them from swallowing their catch and the fishermen pull the birds in on a leash to retrieve the fish from their mouths. It's an inventive and interesting 300-year-old tradition, that no Americans ever go see. The people at the ticket office were shocked when we actually arrived for our reservation.

No one in the town spoke English, even at the McDonald's. We were stared at on the train into town. We confused the bus driver when we told him we wanted to go to the Museum Meji Mura. The boat captains that took us on the water to watch the fishing were at a loss for what to say to us and fretted we might wear our shoes on the *tatami* mats that lined the boat floor. We had an interesting experience, but we made those around us nervous.

...

Brian was often required to entertain visiting Japanese business men when they came to the United States. This usually meant taking them golfing and feeding them steak, two things that are very expensive to do in Japan due to limited land for golf courses and cattle raising. This fact I was reminded of constantly as almost any spare space was converted to a mini rice field, whether nestled among buildings or on rooftops. Brian's friend from [giant Japanese corporation] wanted to return the favor and offered to take us to Kyoto for the day.

Kyoto is home to many Shinto and Buddhist Temples and Shrines. The *Kiyomizu-dera* Temple encompasses several shrines that were of particular interest to me. One area was dedicated to mothers who had lost young children. A statue stands adorned with bibs left by mothers to help ensure their child will be carried safely to the next world. There is also a love shrine. Two boulders standing 18 meters apart, are set up as a test to see if you will find true love. An individual must walk from one to the other with closed eyes, a successful journey means true love is to come. My fiancé tried it, veering drastically off course about 14 meters in. He wandered blindly with outstretched hands, searching for the stone, sending Japanese tourists screaming and running from his grasp.

We visited other famous temples: *Ryoan-ji* known for its Zen rock garden and *Rokuon-ji*, home of the Golden Temple or *Kinkaku-ji*. We were taken from beautiful location to beautiful location for the entire day and treated to a fantastic tempura and sushi lunch by our hosts.

Kyoto is perhaps most famous for its Geisha district though there are not many who choose to train and preserve the traditions of the various Geisha art forms. We saw several walking to their evening's engagements as night approached. It costs several hundred to several thousand dollars, as well as some social connections, to reserve a Geisha to entertain a group for several hours.

...

My final morning in Japan I decided to look for some souvenirs at the mall call *t-FACE*, about a mile from my hotel. I arrived a few minutes before the doors opened and waited with the gathering crowd. Just before 10 a.m. music began to play and the staff came to push open the doors and welcome us inside. I entered a fancy department store where uniformed employees stood at their stations waiting to help customers. As I walked past, each one bowed low to me as if I was their queen. Bowing in Japan is an old tradition and common custom but has become more casual over the years. Often a polite nod with maybe a slight bend of the shoulders is sufficient for most social and business interactions. This was something quite different. I felt both undeserving and special at the same time. As much as I enjoyed the experience, the department store was too pricey for me to purchase anything for friends and family. Near the end of my mall wanderings I discovered the 100 Yen Store, Japan's version of a dollar store. Along with some snacks and small hygiene items, Japanese fans, chopsticks, tea cups and origami paper filled the store. Perfect.

...

Sad to leave after only one week, I boarded a bus back to the airport. I didn't get a chance to visit the hot springs or hike around on Mt. Fuji. I missed out on the zoo and botanical gardens. I did not get to see the inside of a traditional Japanese home. I felt open to returning to Japan for another visit or even for an extended stay. However, my husband eventually left the company as he was constantly required to travel away from our growing family.

The flight home was long and crowded and I made the mistake of not moving around enough. I developed a giant bruise under my big toenail that took weeks to disappear. Once home I made another mistake. Too hyped up from the trip to sleep, I stayed up until midnight and did not set my alarm, figuring I would wake up about 9 or 10 the next day. I slept until 3 pm, my body clock so confused by the 13-hour time difference. It took days to readjust to US time.

Eleven years after leaving our Japanese experience behind, our home still reflects the culture's influence on our lives. We do not wear shoes in our home and expect others to remove theirs as well. Bonus, this custom really reduces the need to dust and vacuum. Art work with Japanese symbols and orchids adorn my living room walls and a Shinto good luck charm hangs in my car. I use my Japanese rice cooker on a weekly basis even though I can't read the instruction manual.

I'm not entirely sure what I expected from my trip to Japan other than weird food and communication problems. Whether it was my private tour of the Noritake factory, our day trip to Kyoto or the stranger on the street who gave me directions, hospitality was the recurring theme. I'll never know how I, as an American woman, was really viewed by the Japanese. What I do know is that Japan is a beautiful place full of proud people who love their country and they will go out of their way to make sure you love it too.

THE TIME I WENT TO MALTA
Holli Shan

I hadn't planned on going anywhere that year. But sometimes you receive a flyer along with a music order that stops you and makes you say "I need to do this." The year was 2014 and Jennifer Berezan had just come out with a new CD. My thought was I needed to see what else she had done (in addition to *The Returning*) so I ordered a couple of her other CDs. In that package was a newsletter that offered a "Women's Pilgrimage to Malta" that Jennifer leads every couple of years. The Pilgrimage talked of learning about the neolithic cultures, visiting the stone temples and watching the sun illuminate the back altar at one of the temples during the Autumn Equinox. The moment I read all that and saw the imagery something inside me stirred and I said "I have to go." As I did more research on what this trip was about, the more I said to myself "I need to go where the Goddess walked when she was a little girl." So began a year of planning to travel by myself internationally. To this day I can still hear my mother's voice when she said "What's this I hear you're going to a place I never heard of?" I told her where Malta was and she said "Oh, that's nice. Have a good time!"

I have traveled by myself domestically before and countless times for business or other retreats. But nothing this large, this long or this foreign. I tend to develop a fear of going somewhere I haven't been. I studied the map of Frankfurt airport I don't know how many times to make sure I could have a decent idea of where I was headed. Luckily, when I arrived in Frankfurt to make my connection, it was easy to find the gate. Their lines of security, were much like ours: a lot of hurry up and wait. But I still made it to my gate on time and everyone was very personable and welcoming. When I arrived in Malta, I made it a point to get this new money (Euros) and to figure out its system. Luckily, there was a driver waiting to take us to our hotel, and just like we had been told in our preparation e-mails ahead of time, we could expect to wait since nothing was ever really **on time**. It was more, *we'll get there eventually, so just relax about it.*

We thirty-nine women (from the U.S., Germany, Canada and Australia) were in Malta for about two weeks. As you can imagine, 39 women and 39 distinct personality types. It was a great lesson for me, facing my own insecurities and my own preconceived notions/prejudices about other people and their personalities. Some personalities just clash and some you're not sure what to do with them. There were only a few people I didn't completely gel with, but we still managed to keep things professional (as it were). We stayed on the main island of Malta for most of the time, and we spent a few days on the smaller island of Gozo. Each day began with singing or chanting led by Jennifer. We visited a church while on Gozo, and were welcomed by their clergy. We stood before the Black Madonna and chanted "Om Tare Tuttare." The harmonizing we did filled the church with an amazing beautiful sound. I'm not sure how long we chanted, but it was powerful.

While we were on Gozo we visited the Gigantia Temple during the day to learn more about it, its rooms and to get the layout since we were going to have our full moon circle there. The legend of the Gigantia Temple is that it was built by the Goddess with a baby suckling at her breast. She was the origin of it all. And she did it one-handed.

That day we were divided into four teams and we all collaborated on what we wanted to do for our full moon circle. One group was responsible for the beginning, the second the opening, the third a meditation and the fourth for the closing. Our humble ritual began as soon as we left the hotel for our shuttle that night. Everyone brought a glass enclosed candle. When we arrived as twilight fell, the first group was already there, welcoming us under a spring of flower-scented water as the ladies whispered, "Remember." We filed in a large circle in front of the large stone temple and again it was repeated: *remember*. Our full moon ritual had begun. The second group did their opening and the third group led us in meditation.

During the meditation, we were instructed to select a place to sit or lay down in the temple and have a quiet meditation. I picked one spot, but a flying insect would not leave me alone. So I took the hint and moved to the other side of the temple near one of the other altars. At that point I could feel and see things propelling forward at a rapid pace for me and my growth. It felt right to be there and it felt like home. When we were called back to the circle my group was responsible for closing our circle. While my group chanted we asked everyone to say what they were going to give out to the world via a singing bowl. We whipped everything up into a crescendo and released all of these blessings to the world, as we danced and sang and remembered. All the while, the great temple seemed to come alive, like a grandparent who is so delighted to see her grandchildren after a very long time. I felt love, empowerment and kinship with so many diverse ladies under that full moon. I wondered just how long it had been since anyone had done a purposeful ritual at the feet of Gigantia? How long had she waited for us to be there to play and commune with her and to leave her offerings?

That night was capped off by Jennifer's singing. I forget what chant she started with, but she had tuned her guitar down and went into "A Song for All Beings." Between the wonderful, energetic high of the ritual and the community of women and my fanship of Jennifer's music, I felt myself lose it just a little and I sang so deeply with her and with everyone. The chorus being added to the memory of these blessed stones: "May all Beings, Be Happy. May All Beings Be Safe. May All Beings, Everywhere – Be Free." We retrieved our now charged candles and headed back to the hotel.

We had a couple of days on Gozo where we could relax and do whatever. For one of our dinners, I guess the chefs weren't prepared to cater to a group as large as ours. So some of the entrées came out very late. One lady who was sitting next to me did the most incredible thing. She told the wait staff, "Take this back to the chef. I don't want it anymore; he took too long." I had asked her about that later on and she said that she felt that some chefs feel they can get away with bringing out your entrée much later than is acceptable. So she decided she was not going to tolerate it. I didn't even realize that something like that was even possible. But as she showed me and everyone—it most certainly is.

That night we stayed up late because there was a little four piece band that kept playing music and we kept handing them Euros. We stayed up singing, laughing and just enjoying ourselves. The next morning, one of my fellow Malta Sisters (that's what we call each other now) wanted to get up at 6:00AM and walk by the cliffs of Gozo that are right outside the hotel. After about 5 hours of sleep I did manage to haul my butt and the rest of me out to meet her and another Malta sister as we walked out back and along the cliffs. The sight was breathtaking and all of Malta is a welcoming land.

As we walked, I saw a group of people off in the distance. It looked like they were doing some form of "vocal yoga." It looked like it was being led by one of the ladies in our group. I asked my walking partners if that was she, and they thought it could be. In my gut I felt this *hurt*. This "why wouldn't she ask us to join her in this thing that looked like fun?" We walked back to the hotel and got ready to assemble in the lobby to get our stuff and go back to the main island. I saw the one who I thought was leading the vocal yoga group earlier in the morning. I asked her about it and she said no, that wasn't her. Immediately, I felt terrible. I had made this assumption about her that wasn't true. I told her about it and I apologized. She gave me a warm smile and a hug and accepted my apology.

Back on the main island of Malta, we visited Valetta, its capital city. The majority of the streets are made of limestone and hills. I was glad that no one really set a vigorous pace for walking from place to place. While limestone is beautiful, it is also slippery. We got to visit the National Museum of Archaeology, where the majority of the excavated finds of Malta's temples are stored. In some outdoor temples, replicas have replaced the real thing so it doesn't erode due to weather. While I was wandering around an outdoor market, I heard my name being called. It took me a little while—but I realized it was Jennifer calling me over to where she was sitting. So I joined her and another Malta sister for a light lunch. She asked me how I came to know her music and how I came to know about this trip. I told her I was introduced to her music when I was initiated into my coven and I fell in love with this *sound* that was emanating from the speakers at the time. I told her about how I ordered more music and saw the newsletter. We had this wonderful discussion about her music and being in Malta. I will always treasure that time in the marketplace with her.

Another one of our stops was at the Hypogeum (where Jennifer recorded *The Returning*). When the Hypogeum was excavated, they discovered a small figurine called "The Sleeping Lady." The original figure now sits in Malta's Museum of Archaeology (I had no idea who or what this figure was until I visited). A few of my fellow Pilgrims already knew about the Sleeping Lady, but I had no clue. What I came to learn from my own feeling is that she was the representative of eternal blissful sleep, since she was found in this great underground burial chamber. While we were at the Hypogeum we had to go down in small groups due to the small passageways. Jennifer gifted us with going to the one "oracle hole" (which is a hole in the middle of one of the supporting rocks) placing her head inside the hole and toning all of our names, which reverberated all throughout this underground temple. When I heard mine, it was as if my name was being called to my ancient ancestors. We stayed in this beautiful ancient burial chamber that was decorated in spirals that spiraled out and back inward, that energetically pulled you apart to rebuild you and give you new life. We got to sing here, if only for a moment. And for that moment, our voices reverberated within those walls with respect, honor, love and joy. When I walked out into the Mediterranean sun I felt changed. No, I *was* changed.

The next day was more free time and visiting another city that had a restaurant whose cakes were legendary. I'm not one to turn down a legendary slice of cake so I went with my fellow Malta sister and had cake and a frozen latté. Everything was delicious, except by the end of the day, I wasn't feeling very well. I thought I had too much caffeine and not enough water. I bought a bottle of Gatorade and hoped that would help. I was wrong. I was very, very wrong. That night we were supposed to have a little fun show and I wanted to sing a new chant that I had recently learned from an artist who was new to me. My entrails had other plans. I spent the night in my hotel room, between the bathroom and under the covers of the bed, with the heat turned up. My thought was that the cake did it, since I've been growing more sensitive to sugar. But then it was brought to my attention that it most likely was from the ice of the frozen latté. Malta desalinates its water with a very concentrated chemical process. No one drinks the water out of the taps. The water is fine to brush your teeth with, but crushed up in a beverage that's about as large as your average daiquiri? Not so much.

The next day, I was fine enough for the boat ride to go swim in the Mediterranean. A few ladies asked me how I was and what had happened and I told them. We were all glad things worked out. We took a boat ride out to one area, and this was my first time swimming in the Mediterranean. I knew the salt concentration was high, but I didn't realize it was so high that even a person with negative bouncy could float. It also provided a great resistance exercise to swim back to the boat! That day, I watched as my cliff walking Malta sister, faced her fear of water and got in with a life preserver and all of us around her telling her she was alright and we had her. We all had her. Watching her turn her fear into complete joy was a blessed moment to witness.

The final temple in our visit was Hagar Qim. This was the one where on the Autumn Equinox we would watch the sun rise and illuminate the back altar of the temple. We gathered in the dark, walked down the narrow path to the temple, walked around, communed with this sacred place and began to take our places along the sides to allow the sunlight to come through. There was a small glitch: it was cloudy and overcast. We could see the sun a little bit and even began to sing "Here Comes the Sun" by George Harrison. Jennifer had her guitar and began playing a song about a sun dancer, dancing through the night. She repeated the song over and over again, as we spiraled out from the temple into a circle right in front of it (this area we came to know as "the fore court"). I guess that day we weren't meant to watch the sun rise since we had other things we needed to do.

In our circle, and one at a time, we walked to the center and gave a voice to what we would take with us. Then the circle would echo back your name and "You are (whatever you said)." I waited until the last moment to hop in the center. I wasn't sure what I wanted to say or how I wanted to say it. I knew I would take with me the gratitude and kinship that I found and that I learned here with these extraordinary ladies.

On our last meeting together, we all got to say what was the most important thing that we experienced on this journey. Mine was that somehow, I worked through my fear and my insecurity to embark on a 15 hour, international flight by myself that I never thought was possible. I'm not bi-lingual (but I would like to be) and I walked through that fear and met my other fears and prejudices. Malta and the Mediterranean held us all and cleansed us all in some form or another (one lady was very sick with a raging ear infection the whole time, and other women had some form of an illness or a night of being sick). At the end of two weeks I had fallen in love with this archipelago that is located between Italy and Tunisia. On my last day, I was glad to be going home, yet I wept bitter tears into my coffee because I would miss Malta, her people and her spirit.

While at the ticketing counter at Malta's airport, I struck up a conversation with the lovely agent who was checking my now overweight suitcase. We chatted about the Maltese language and how it was this amazing combination of Italian and Arabic. I told him I would be glad to pay for any overage for the weight of the suitcase and his response was "Hey, it's no problem, you're in Malta!" and he didn't charge me at all. We waited a while for our flight to depart from Malta to Frankfurt. I was freaking out a little on the inside because I didn't want to miss my connecting flight! Our flight eventually did get off the ground and we did make it to Frankfurt. Of course, my connecting gate was on the opposite side of all of the retail stores you have to walk through to get to the passport juncture. Once my passport was stamped, I power-walked to my gate and they stopped me, since I hadn't been through security. So they have me go the side and they ask me a few questions including if I was carrying any electronics. I told them I had a laptop and I asked "Would you like to see it?" in a very calm, customer service manner. The gate agent told me no, that was fine. I also let them know that there was a lady with four children traveling with a stroller who was on her way as well. They made sure to look out for her.

I finally arrived home, 15 hours later. I gave the gentleman at customs my form and he simply looked at me, smiled and said "Welcome home." There wasn't anything on my form I could claim, like various souvenirs, books, treats etc. So there was nothing to technically claim. I waited in baggage claim while a security lady and her contraband sniffing pup came up to my carry on pile of bags. She asked me if I had an animal in the one bag that I had been using as a purse. I looked at her and simply said no. Then I told her that my dog had recently decided he wanted to mark that bag, so her dog might pick that up. Her dog sniffed around and found nothing in my bags. Then I gazed down the line and the little dog sniffed at the traveler's bags at the end of the row, and sat down. Inside I became a 10 year-old that wanted to exclaim "OO! YOU'RE IN TROUBLE!!!" But I took a deep breath instead and waited for my big bag to come around the carousel.

I talked about how being in Malta changed me. Do I still have some issues to deal with? Sure I do. But they are not as severe as they once were and I have a greater understanding of dealing with other people and their own way without me getting into a twist about something. Would I go back for another Pilgrimage? Yes, I absolutely would when the resources allow.

SALLY LUNN
H. Byron Ballard

My colleague Ann is in London for the summer, working and playing. Her photos on social media remind me how much I used to love that town. I first saw it as a wide-eyed seventeen year old on a six-week study tour of Europe. London opened the world to me in ways that have stuck with me down all the years since our first encounter.

They say that at seventeen, we are likely to do many of the things that will stay with us throughout the rest of our lives and that has been true for me. We had seen Amsterdam and West Berlin (which tells you how long ago this was). I had waltzed in Vienna, eaten pounds of chocolate in Switzerland and drunk bier at the Hofbrau Haus in Munich, where you could never get away with stealing the earthenware steins. To this day, I remember learning to count 'one' with my thumb and to recite giddily, "Ein, zwei, drei, vier bier!"

In July, we woke in Paris to tanks rolling through the streets and to the sound of distant cannons. For children who had grown up on our fathers' repetitious tales of World War II and weekly episodes of Rat Patrol on television, it took us a moment to remember what day it was. We dressed quickly then, scrambling down the stairs and into the streets, shouting and laughing. Bastille Day was perfectly perfect with sour wine from vending machines and French kisses from French boys. I'm not sure where our chaperones were but we danced far into the night, roaming the streets of Paris, following the call of the music.

The tunes of Strauss were everywhere in Vienna and we waltzed with Austrian boys and with each other. We went to the famous Hotel Sacher and ate sachertorte and washed its cloying sweetness down with strong coffee. The street vendors there had such beautiful fruit: I recall walking through the park that holds the statue of Johann Strauss, eating cherries from a cone of paper, spitting the pips into the bottom of the cone.

There were delicious museums in every place we stayed and we soon learned that when you entered a mediaeval cathedral, you paused inside to let your eyes adjust and then turned to look for the loft above the doorway, ornamented with its piercing rose window.

The basement of Chartres held a secret that could only be seen by dragging all the rickety folding chairs to one side, which the energetic students were requested to do—a labyrinth that could be walked with our clumsy American feet. We could stay in the cool darkness a little longer, waiting for our orders to replace the terrible chairs and watching the old women plodding their way into the Mystery.

But it was London that consumed me. The London of Shakespeare, of Boudicca, of the Queens Elizabeth, both One and Two. We saw a blue-jeaned production of the musical Grease and were treated to Angela Lansbury in Gypsy. Afterwards, we swarmed back to her dressing room only to find there was a problem with the spring on the door. Mark and I and another boy whose name I no longer remember chatted with the actual real star Angela Lansbury while we fixed the door of her actual real dressing room. She was charming as well as grateful, declaring us to be both helpful and entertaining. We were so delirious we didn't even get her autograph. But we did repair her door.

Years later, my business partners, my daughter and I flew into London to begin the planning trip for a pilgrimage we were to lead the following season. London was grimy and noisy and brilliant, as she always is. Our route would take us, clutching our BritRail passes, west into Somerset, Devon and Cornwall and we would pick up the pre-arranged rental car for local excursions.

We were planning a pilgrimage that would take our guests to ancient monuments, walled cities, flower-clad meadows. As it turned out, we never did do the tour. In fact the business partnership didn't survive the organizing trip. As it happened, we were fine as long as we sat around a planning table in western North Carolina but found ourselves at odds once the road starting taking its toll.

But we were still innocent when we checked into our guesthouse in Glastonbury, a charming place where one could sit in the front room in the evening and watch badgers in the yard. Glastonbury is very like our home village and we found ourselves immersed almost at once in the local politics. There was the inevitable tour up the Tor but my sacred Glasto was the tithe barn at the Somerset Rural Life Museum and the cool chapel at the old almshouse hospital. There was also a nice incense shop, tucked away in an alley off the High Street. I had had enough of witch wars at home and wanted only a decent cuppa and a sausage roll.

A couple of days after our check-in, we rose before dawn and filled the rented car with our ritual gear and ourselves. Our destination was a re-dawn rendezvous inside the ropes at Stonehenge. Our destiny took us at the end of that fatal day to Bath and that famous House. The House of Sally Lunn.

It smelled like every decent tea shop in England and

contained the cool damp that is April in that moist land, but we were grateful to be sitting in the warmth. We had arrived in town hungry enough to eat spotted dick and had gone through the museum at the Roman baths again. Aquae Sulis, we intoned solemnly, while discreetly pouring vials of water as offerings to the sacred baths. The overwhelming ennui of the place combined with our very long day to give me a kind of Regency malaise.

Yes, I am a Jane Austen fan but not a fan of Bath and for the life of me I don't know why. It is a pleasant enough town, well-sited, loaded with the usual burden of English history. But I never feel right there, not even in the museum. My Austen-fiend associates assure me it is the most perfect of towns, but it leaves me cold. The spotted dick was good though.

So, I was sitting with my business partners and my kid in this decent tea shop and we were drinking strong tea and trying to recover from the morning. Our early rising did get us to what is arguably the most famous ancient monument in Britain before dawn where we met a woman named Peacock, a researcher of crop circles. She asked if she could make some photos of our shenanigans inside the henge and I wonder if she ever did any of the things she talked about that morning. We had gotten lost, then found and we were glad to discuss crop circles as we stood shivering in the rising sun of that famous place. Ms. Peacock finally wandered off and the kid fell asleep. The partners argued about something irrelevant except that one of them liked to argue and talked as though she knew everything, which she didn't. I wandered around, getting the lay of the land, plus a little frostbite. Our ritual gear was puny against the power of the stones so we did a bit of chanting and called it a morning.

But, friends, the day had but barely begun for this intrepid witch and folklorist. Our next stop was Avebury. Yes, we were young then and the idea of doing this enormous undertaking was not daunting in the least.

We had a rental car and strong tea and a lust for life and an insatiable curiosity about the inscrutable Ways of the Ancients.

We were on a deadline. Obviously. We were considering this pilgrimage and wanted to spend a little time at all the places we'd haul our eager American seekers. Most of us had already been to all the places on that day's itinerary so we figured we could knock them out in a short while and spend more time at places like Boscastle and Tintagel, where we were pilgrims ourselves.

Ah, to be in England now that April is here! Avebury was colder than Stonehenge and windy and, as I recall, there was a little snow. We trotted down the Avenue, dashing from stone to stone, using them as windbreaks whenever possible. Silbury Hill stood squat on the horizon, inscrutable as ever. Yes, we murmured. Lovely. Our pilgrims can spend the better part of the day here and finish up with a ritual and a pint at that nice pub. Having noticed the nice pub, we had to inspect it and test the quality of their best ale. So we did, claiming we were having lunch, which we also did.

We were so proud of ourselves at that point. The ale was good, the pub was warm and uncrowded. We pulled out an Ordinance Survey Map of the area and circled other delicious Tidbits of the Ancients, that we had no intention of seeing. The ill-fated Cadbury Castle was another day, and another story entirely.

One of the partners was both a Regency fan and a practitioner of a pre-Catholic Roman religion. She gazed around the pub, eating whatever morsels were left on everyone's plates, murmured, "Bath" and gave a little sniff.

She pronounced it *baaahhth* with her mouth turned down at the corners in what she may have thought was a jaded little moue. So we ended that cold day with a disastrous trip to the dreaded Bath. Only moderately disastrous—we did get that spotted dick, after all. But we overstayed our welcome in the car park and it cost us a dashing lieutenant's ransom, to tell you the truth. I was especially whiny and not at all winsome. So when the same moue-wearing partner suggested a 'jolly' visit to Sally Lunn's to partake of the Bath Bun, I dug in my slippered heels and balked at it. "Never!" Said partner turned on me like a vicious dowager aunt and suggested, with an accompanying sniff, that I might prefer to spend my time taking the waters. I shook my head mournfully, followed at a respectful distance and found myself seated in a decent tea shop, with cakes.

Now cakes—all kinds of cakes—always cheer me up and give me the necessary courage to continue living. These did the same. I avoided the famous bun in favor of scones and fairy cakes. I became positively effulgent. Our uncomfortable morning was fast becoming a tale worth telling. My voice rose a bit and I was recounting the cold mess of the Great Henge with enthusiasm.

Across from where I was seated was an open doorway and the wait staff passed back and forth, removing tiny plates and empty cups and returning with huge trays of sandwiches and steaming pots of tea. They were doing their jobs and we were doing ours. But, as sometimes happens, I was gesturing with one hand and relating, in a companionable way, the Story of Stonehenge when the shop went almost silent. A Chekhovian moment in which the shop was treated to the delectable phrase "…asleep so sweetly under the Heel Stone." The staff member who was, at that moment, crossing the open doorway, stopped and turned to face the room. His eyes met mine, as they say.

I knew him. In the biblical sense of the word. Country matters. The beast with two backs. You get my drift.

But it had been years, gentle reader. Decades actually.

Cue misty fog to suggest memory and there I am in my 80s hair. I have taken my BA in theatre and my broken heart to London where my plan was to become an undocumented resident alien and leave my miserable American life behind. I have hennaed and permed hair to the waist in a time and place where sleek and elegant is the prevailing style. Like some pudgy Boudicca, I strode the streets of Victoria in flip flops and angst, mane of hair flowing behind me.

It was a hard time and hard times require madness on a Byronic level. I took some acting classes, saw lots of great theatre, and slowly my broken heart healed. And one of the things that helped heal it was a Scotsman named Terry. I can't tell you his last name because I never knew it. He caught up with me one mid-morning as I was headed up Victoria toward Westminster Cathedral.

Hiya.

Um, hello.

You're American, aren't you?

Yes. You're Scottish, aren't you?

Aye.

We both stopped and turned.

Cuppa?

Yes.

I followed him to a little café where he worked. We did indeed have a cuppa and we talked. And talked. He had me repeat words and phrases because he liked my accent. I did the same to him. He was a few years older than I, had left Scotland in his early 20s for the glamor of London. He was some sort of artist. Sculptor, maybe. I don't honestly remember.

What I do remember was the feel of his hands on my body and the way he said my name. He had a terrible little flat on the edges of Camden Town and we spent much of the next few weeks there, cooking beans on toast and having the sort of ferocious and extraordinary sex that only two broken young people can have. We exhausted each other. Sleep came in intervals and between those intervals was Anais Ninlevel exultation.

I had a part-time job at a tailor shop with the requisite under-the-table wage, but ready cash began to be an issue so I called home. This was a calculated risk because in those days a phone call between the old country and the new one was an expensive proposition and a collect call was certain to raise hackles at home. My mother did accept the charges but refused to send money. I'd gotten myself into this mess, she reasoned, and could get myself out of it.

But she did tell me a letter had arrived for me from the graduate program I'd been wait-listed for. She asked if I wanted her to open it. I didn't but I also needed to hear the contents so I agreed. She read it to me and it contained the joyful words: We are happy to inform you...

Grad school. Dallas. The possibility of a life in the theatre doing what I loved, what I had trained for, my heart's desire. A master of fine arts. A conservatory program that included costuming and acting and directing. My London life was exciting, but temporary, ephemeral in spite of the earthiness of every day's encounter with my manic Scottish lover. As I hung up the phone, I knew then I'd have to come home. And I did. I gathered my bits and bobs, checked my return ticket. I took Terry out for a drink at the pub that had become our local and told him I was leaving London. He was chuffed to hear the news and raised his glass to my success and happiness. We parted with a sweet kiss and no regrets at all. His last words to me? "Yer a fine lass," which sentiment was accompanied by a tender squeeze of my left buttock.

Fast forward now to tea and the Chekhovian moment with that black-haired server. The reverie had been instantaneous, fading as my hand dropped back to the teacup in front of me. We were frozen in that moment, he and I. I smiled slowly as the shop spun around me. Terry dipped his chin and placed his free hand over his heart. I nodded, too. And he slipped back down the hallway and to his job.

My partners, my kid and I paid our bill and returned to the car, ready to make the run back to Glasto, where we were based. I told them, in an uncharacteristically subdued way, that I had known the man in the shop years ago when I lived in London. I did not make it a tale nor elaborate further.

Until today.

The memories of both those distant times rise before me, sweeter than they were then. My life is every bit as exciting now and I still carry the wanderlust that began all those years ago in that adventuresome seventeen year old. I have never returned to Paris or Berlin or Vienna but London is usually my first stop when I return to the United Kingdom, which I do every few years. I still wander down Victoria Road to the statue of Boudicca and to Westminster Abbey. The shops are all changed, of course, but the feeling of London is always and forever the same. I no longer stride about in flip-flops and my hair is shorter, thinner, no longer red. But London is the same.

Thinking now of Terry, I reach for my ear lobe. The left one holds a dent that used to be a piercing, healed now to a small scar. Terry and I and a couple of his theatre friends got roaring drunk one night and we had an argument about who Shakespeare really was. It ended with drunken hugs and the unquenchable desire to have our ears pierced with a tiny gold ring, like our hero in the Chandos portrait. We found an all-night piercing parlor and emptied out our pockets, howling with laughter at each moan of pain. Somewhere there may yet be a faded picture of four bleary-eyed young Londoners. Their heads are turned in exactly the same way, mimicking a painting of the Bard of Avon, now found in the National Portrait Gallery in jolly old London.

My colleague is in London this summer and she has

visited the Tate and seen a new show in the West End. There are photos of Victoria Road in my news feed and I recall those days when an American woman and a Scotsman found each other and healed themselves.

GOOD FORTUNE
Ellen J. Perry

Dear Mr. John P. "Jack" Winters, CEO of the Winters-McKenna Distillery:

My name is Heather Hunter, I'm twelve years old, and I live off Sam's Branch in the Red Bird Trailer Park a little ways outside of Paw Paw, Kentucky. This is a real place even though it don't sound real. (In case you wondered, the paw paw is a fruit that tastes kind of like a banana. There's even a song about it: *Where o where is pretty little Susie? Way down yonder in the paw paw patch.*) I usually say I'm from Pikeville since it's a bigger town in our same county, but I want to tell you the truth about everything Mr. Winters so you'll see I'm a honest girl with smarts, good sense, and a big favor to ask. Maybe you can help me out.

Other day me and my big sister Holly-Beth were sitting around at home watching a repeat of one of her soaps on TV but all I could think about was how the Kentucky Derby was coming on later, the big horse race in Louisville where you live. Holly-Beth calls it "LOOvl." She laughs when reporters on the national news say "LOO-ee-ville." She says to nobody, "Where do these news people come from, the moon?" and lights a cigarette. Do you all in the big city laugh about this too?

Anyway, I got tired of watching Marlena on *Days of our Lives* and the Derby wasn't going to start for another couple hours so I went outside for a little bit, thought my brother Harlan might need some help. Him and our dad sell parts from old cars in the junkyard right by the Red Bird trailers. Well, Harlan and Daddy call it the Hunter Auto-Body Shop but really it's a junkyard with a run down old office, and I help sometimes with sweeping or whatever needs done. I took off, riding the best Christmas present I ever got: Holly-Beth's old pink bike. It has white tassels on the silver handlebars and when I pedal fast, those tassels fly.

"What are y'all doing?" I asked Harlan, putting my bike up carefully against the wall (I take good care of things) and peeking in the back room of the office. Harlan and his friends were working on something but it wasn't a car engine. "Dadburn, Heather, go on home," Harlan said, mad, standing up fast and walking to block the door.

Mr. Winters, I'm a good girl that won't ever get into bad stuff. My teacher Mrs. Banks made us all go to a program on drugs to see what can happen if we try them. METH KILLS, the poster board said. There were these pictures of ghost-looking people with awful scabs, and teeth half gone. It scared me to death.

I said, "I'm gon' tell Daddy," but those boys just laughed at me. "Yeah, run tell Daddy," Harlan said. "He's 'bout ready to start selling. Now get out of here, go on."

It still wasn't time for the Derby so I rode away from the junkyard to see what Miss Alma was doing over at the church. Bike tassels blowing in the wind, I daydreamed I was the great horse American Pharoah, coming in first place with those extra-long strides he has. I knew he'd win that day and I couldn't wait to sing "My Old Kentucky Home" right along with those pretty women on TV – Mama might even be in there with them – wearing big feathery hats and dresses that cost more money than Daddy makes in six months selling door handles and steering wheels. That's why Mama left, least that's what Holly-Beth thinks. She got tired of being poor. "Mama probably drinks mint juleps every day of the week, not just Derby Day," Holly-Beth says.

Mama left two years ago with her boyfriend, a man from Lexington who talked big on a dating site about his family's coal money and got her excited about sparkly things, I guess. She calls home every now and then, says she's done with the paw paw patch for good, but her little baby paw paws can come out and visit with her anytime in the condo, haha. Holly-Beth and Harlan don't want nothing to do with her so they won't take me. Now, Mr. Winters, how can a girl ride all the way to Lexington on a pink bike with tassels?

"Hey, Heather," Miss Alma, the preacher's wife, called when I rode up. She was sorting clothes outside the parsonage near the old graves. I grabbed up a basket to help when Miss Alma went over toward the road to run off a old stray dog. "Git!" she hollered and then one of the Frisbie twins who mows around the cemetery distracted her, got her talking about what a hero the county clerk was for saying he'd quit before the state ever told him what to do about the gay marriage business. "God bless Brother Bill for not giving in to the evils of the world," Mr. Frisbie said. "Amen," Miss Alma said, "This country is headed toward damnation unless people like Brother Bill stand up. Best clerk we ever had." Mr. Frisbie nodded real slow and looked down, chewing on his toothpick.

All of a sudden while I was fooling with what turned out to be the dirty clothes basket, something fell out of a pocket in Preacher Bob's dress slacks. (Lord, there I was holding the preacher's pants! That hadn't been washed yet!) And the something that fell out was a folded up business card that read, "Mr. John P. 'Jack'

171

Winters, CEO of the Winters-McKenna Distillery." There was something on the card, written by hand, a phone number and a message: "Bob, call or write if you ever get in a tight spot."

You know what, Mr. Winters? Or could I even call you "Jack" like your card says? I'm not sure about Preacher Bob but if there was ever a tight spot to be in, I've found it. See, those cars in Daddy's junkyard just sit there, sit and rust like the people here do. Some days it makes me crazy that I won't ever be able to get in one of them broke down cars and drive off fast away from Paw Paw toward Louisville, way faster than I could on my bike, wear a mint-green hat on Derby Day, and watch the horses fly. To make things worse, on the other side of the Red Bird Trailer Park is the church graveyard where Miss Alma hangs out clothes and sings hymns and sometimes lifts up her hands and cries, the sad kind.

My teacher Mrs. Banks tells me I read and write way better than a lot of the other kids in my class but I dance around stuff too much, I need to get to the point. Well, Jack, here's the point.

I live right smack in between dead people in the cemetery that don't go nowhere and a bunch of junk cars that don't go nowhere.

That's where you come in. You must have a lot of money being in charge of a place that makes bourbon, and you probably need a handy girl with smarts and good sense to sweep up or make deliveries or something, anything. If you can just get me to Louisville some way, and give me a job, I won't be no trouble. Please write me back because I am stuck and I can feel the rust on me starting to itch, it scratches my skin. Please write me back so maybe I can find Mama and we'll buy matching dresses for the Derby and I won't never have to wonder what it's like to run free and wild like American Pharaoh, the horse that wound up winning the Triple Crown and stood tall wearing those roses on his back, he was so tall and proud and strong.

Sincerely,
Heather

Dear Heather,

I found your letter in my father's study a week ago, just before he moved out to live with his boyfriend Tim (I still can't believe it), and I've been thinking about you ever since. I don't know whether or not he wrote you back since it has been a month or so since you sent the letter, but I wanted to say hello and tell you that you are a brave girl. I also wanted to say that I know how you feel even though our lives may seem as different as the Wild West and the Deep South. Here's what I mean by that.

I am twenty years old and going into my sophomore year at SCAD in Georgia. That stands for Savannah College of Art and Design. Growing up in Louisville I always wanted to be an artist; my father told me I needed to do something more practical, maybe study marketing and advertising at a state university, but luckily Mom talked him into letting me go to SCAD. She told him I'd probably meet a reliable, grounded boy at SCAD (translation: Clark, my boyfriend from high school, was neither reliable nor grounded), someone who would go on to design corporate websites or something like that, and we'd head back to Louisville with fresh college degrees, a wedding date set, and maybe a few baby names picked out for the future. Mom says she wants her grandchildren to call her "Nana."

So I moved to Savannah last August, and my favorite classes so far are introductory Photography and Art History. You would think the Equestrian Studies program they have here is neat since you love horses so much. For a class project last semester I went several times to Bonaventure Cemetery with my roommate to take pictures. Bonaventure means "good fortune." It's so spooky and beautiful there! I wish you could touch the Spanish moss hanging from the trees, see the CSA (Confederate States of America) markers showing where Civil War soldiers are buried, stare into the blank hollow eyes in statues of women and angels, feel the humid air beating you down but also lifting you up to some other plane – a plane where ghosts walk beside the tombs and watch us. They walk some but most of all, they watch. I feel them every time I go to Bonaventure and I wonder: do they know they're dead? Then one day I thought, maybe I'm dead and they're alive! Because when I think of what happened a few weeks ago during my trip out west to visit Clark, I feel like a lonely ghost.

I met Clark, the only guy I've ever dated, when we were in the 10th grade. He was really different from most of the others in our private prep school because he refused to abide by his parents' rules, said forget college, and decided to forge his own path like in the pioneer days. I admired this about him. He's really outdoorsy so after graduation he moved to Colorado to work as a raft guide and ski instructor. We talked every day either through text or FaceTime. He'd say, "Lisa, I can't wait for you to come out here and see this amazing place! You won't believe it. The air is so clean, and you can see mountains for miles." I was excited about visiting him, too, and made a plan to go out there for the first time during my spring break.

It was mid-March and already getting warm in Savannah, so I packed mostly t-shirts, shorts, and sandals. When I got to Denver, Clark met me at the airport with a quick kiss and a long list of things he wanted to do, places he JUST HAD to show me. All of these activities involved the outdoors and I hadn't brought the right clothes or shoes. "We'll get you some other stuff, no problem," he said. His parents had cut him off financially by this time but he had enough money saved to buy me some hiking and camping gear.

Heather, I learned something about myself on this trip: I don't like camping at all, and a little hiking (especially without my art supplies) goes a long way. I learned something about Clark, too: he loves singing John Denver's "Rocky Mountain High" as loudly as possible around a campfire. This would be okay except for the fact that Clark can't sing, which I already knew from our time together in the youth choir at Trinity Episcopal Church back home.

Clark shares a little apartment near Vail with three guys who are just like him. They work for the same rafting company and talk a lot about local beer. They are avid mountain bikers and trail runners; they shop at REI on a regular basis. Somehow all this wilderness fixation hadn't bothered me when we lived in Louisville. Clark was different from everyone there, and I liked being just a little bit rebellious by dating him. In Vail, though, most people were Clark-ish. I felt like the oddball for once and I didn't like it.

When he took his friends and me out to Eagle's Nest for a day trip to hike one of the trails, we drove eight miles off the main road to get there. I felt jangled and jostled and carsick while everybody else was having a big time on the bumpy, dusty dirt road. Clark drove and called out every so often, "We're just about there!" I'd never seen him so happy.

Finally we made it and got parked. Stepping out of the jeep I looked out on the lake and the rugged mountain peaks still lined with snow. "Isn't it breathtaking?" the girlfriend of one of Clark's roommates – her name, of course, was Meadow – said to me. Meadow was right: I was literally out of breath from the high altitude, and I didn't know if I could even keep up with Clark on the trail much less enjoy what was supposed to be our shared adventure in the wild west.

I made it as far as a bench-like rock formation before I had to sit down. I collapsed on the hard edge and fumbled for my water bottle in what Clark called the "day pack." It was a big black bag that held everything in the world these folks needed: energy bars, water, toilet paper, a first-aid kit, and God knows what else.

"Y'all go on ahead," I said to Clark, my head throbbing. "I'll catch up."

"You sure, Lisa?" he asked. I nodded and watched him march forward with long strides, whistling and laughing with the others.

I looked at his back for the longest time. It just moved farther and farther away from me. Heather, somehow him walking ahead made me mad even though I had said it was okay. Weird, isn't it? But I watched him go and knew he was gone for good. Things would never be the same between us because we had both grown up and away from each other.

When I caught my breath I managed to wander up a little further to the aspen trees. This forest turned out to be the prettiest part of the trail, and I really wished I'd brought my good camera. The sound those leaves make when the wind blows! It's like a sigh, something sad but hopeful at the same time. Sunlight poured through the branches and lit up the ground with dancing specks. A little bit of moon rose overhead. I listened to the cold water running fast over smooth stones in a brook.

On the aspen tree bark I touched the initials and names of those who had been there before me: *DFL luvs CEP. JW was here. Izzy. TK + RY.* These people had all carved out a little bit of tree for themselves, just enough to make their mark. Clark was doing that, too, by starting fresh in Colorado. I needed to do the same in my own way, and all of a sudden I missed Savannah so bad I couldn't stand it. The south, not the west, was where I belonged; I wanted to go home and hide in the nooks and shadows of Bonaventure Cemetery among the ghosts. I wanted to lie beneath the oaks and look out through murky, secret-filled swampland. I needed to be a part of that darkness, our haunted landscape. Clark will never join me there again, and it took a lot of courage to tell him I was leaving Colorado four days early.

To wrap things up (it takes me a long time to get to the point, too, ha), this is why I think YOU are also brave: you're only twelve years old but you know who you are, and you're willing to *work* to make your way in the world. It's scary to get started, though, especially when you feel alone like I did when Clark and I broke up. Luckily Mom and my sisters are supportive of me, and about the stuff with my father I'm sure I'll come around. I might not even mind Tim so much.

Thanks to my own "good fortune" (remember, *bonaventure*) that I did nothing to deserve, I want to help you shake off that rust you wrote about. I'm sending you some money to set aside for when you are old enough to go wherever you want to go. Can you ask your teacher to help you get a savings account started at the bank? If not I can set one up here. You are also welcome to visit me in Savannah any time. Taking the bus might be good. I can show you around the Equestrian Center at SCAD and let you talk to some of the people there about riding and taking care of horses, and we can go walk with the dead in Bonaventure Cemetery to find new life.

Love,
    Lisa Winters

FIVE POEMS
Miriam Sagan

Cross Country

you are driving all night

but have not yet

arrived

in Oklahoma

in every body

of water

anywhere in the world

the moon

reflects back to us

the loneliness

of beauty

(untitled)

pass the checkpoint
in the dark
driving south
towards the border, no need
to explain
why you are heading away
from the country of your birth.
Venus as
evening star
on the right hand
shining over the neighborhoods
of Las Cruces
lit for X-mas
houses outlined
in lights
forming
the luminous shapes
of houses
Orion's belt
hangs vertical
before us while overhead
dim Pleiades.
in our conversation
you driving
me with my old feet
still up on the dashboard.
the checkpoint is
down, no need
to stop
it's possible
to tell the truth
without recrimination
as the past
continues on its own
story, with or without us,
darkness

like braille
surrounds us
with a tale
we can understand
just by
touching it.

We're in the story

on the little barge of just
the two of us
afloat on an ocean
of upside-down stars
we hung out
our white laundry to dry
on a line
beneath the moon
while an aerialist
sound from the crescent hook
and a girl
with a parasol
and red dress
ran by,
and even though
we could dance without music
the love we saw in the mirror
was no longer young
and even though we were barefoot
and had crossed
both the tropic
of cancer and
the tropic of capricorn
we grew old
and even though the rocking boat
held our white bed

and I held you
in my arms

Fortune

born in the indivisible
divided
canyons of Manhattan
W. 81st Street
beneath the Bull
city sustained
by the flow
of fresh water
from upstate
dammed reservoirs
abandoned villages
flooded out
drowned houses
at the bottom
of the lake
inhabited
by amphibious ghosts.
what floats
to the surface—
blue willow teacup
a kodak print
of a small
distracted dog
raised in our own
submerged house
despite a persian rug, a fireplace,
recurring nightmare
that the basement
is the tomb

of an Egyptian pharaoh,
what's hidden,
how our gene pool
came out of
central siberia
bear shaman, tent pole, hallucinogenic
speckled mushroom
and men on horses
in felt boots
out of the north
and not just
for good

(untitled)

to see the lit house
from outside—
that moment
turning back
from the faded blue mailbox
when I might be
two places
at once...

FROM WARRIOR TO CHAPLAIN: GIVING THE MIDDLE FINGER TO THE PATRIARCHY
Tiffany Andes

Full-on career changes are nothing new; and seem to have become much more in vogue over the last decade as more and more people follow their "heart" rather than the all-mighty dollar. My story has some elements of that, but is nothing so romantic as a career lawyer suddenly choosing to leave the world of corporate drive to open a bakery or become a life coach and yoga instructor. This story has a lot more anger, stubbornness, and grit. I am currently the first Pagan chaplain resident to ever work in the Department of Veterans Affairs—an institution that by and large has functioned under the premises of a Judeo-Christian model of spirituality since its inception. My future plan is to become the first Pagan staff chaplain (fully paid and employed) in the VA. This distinction is crucial because Paganism is one of the fastest growing spiritual identities among veterans and members of the Department of Defense, and yet we are grossly under-represented. The DoD has yet to actually install a Pagan chaplain in the uniform. Some of my story includes details on that journey too.

I served seven years in the United States Air Force as a communications officer, and while my heart has never regretted the choice to serve my country, my soul and my body are irreparably changed by my time in service. As a veteran, I am honored to be able to give back to my brothers and sisters in arms, because I came to realize we are all changed by our service. Some carry the scars of it on their bodies. Some of us carry the scars of it inside. Many of us go for years before we can talk about the events that changed us, violated us, or took something from us. Much of my story is also about finding myself after I left the military—the person I am under the uniform.

I commissioned as a second lieutenant in 2007; and made my way to my first duty station at Lackland Air Force Base, San Antonio, Texas. I didn't want to be stationed in Texas; and I didn't want to be a communications officer. In fact, I had studied mandarin Chinese and lived in China for a while in the hopes of becoming an intelligence officer. I had also wanted to be stationed over-seas for my first assignment. But, as I would soon discover, once you sign on the dotted line Uncle Sam owns you. I managed to survive two years in San Antonio, realizing how much I despised my job, and just how misogynistic military culture can be. I had a civilian boss who thought my brown eyes and pretty curves were his for the admiring, and despite my Southern no-nonsense upbringing, I also began to realize the influence of power dynamics and military chains of command on the success of my career. I learned early I could not trust men in power. Instead, I began working on my master's degree in the hopes of furthering my professional career and to give me another outlet for my sanity. I had the sheer luck of running into a local Pagan group that offered open circles and services on the base, and it was through this connection that I learned of the Pagan chaplain "quest" and my life took a new direction.

Chaplains have a unique function in the US military. While they are commissioned officers, they are endorsed by churches and professional organizations of their faith as ministers and clergy. In federal settings, they are required to ecumenically serve everyone regardless of faith orientation, and to refer to other chaplains in very specific cases of need (like Catholic sacraments, etc.) Many service members have reflected they feel chaplains are more inclined to proselytize, judge, or try to convert them rather than support them in their time of need. In the case of Pagans, two organizations had been trying to present a viable candidate for chaplaincy to the Department of Defense for over ten years, but the system continuously found reasons why the candidates were not acceptable. One of the candidates was a very dear friend and mentor of mine, whose career was ruined in attempting the quest.

In 2010, I attended a conference with my coven, where we discussed the chaplain quest extensively. I was feeling an immense amount of inner tension at this point, realizing that I was not living authentically, but not quite sure how to remedy that feeling. The chaplaincy discussion had piqued my interest because it had the right amount of social justice mixed with f*** you to the establishment. I will always remember the moment I made the decision to walk my path. I was in a community ritual where we had drawn down aspects of Brigid, Demeter, and Hekate as Maiden, Mother, and Crone. We had the option of interfacing with any of the aspects and asking a question. I remember approaching Brigid and asking what I should do. She looked at me, and said, "My child, you already know what you need to do." I remember walking away understanding that my life had changed.

Later that year I was attending the retirement ceremony of a friend who had served for thirty-five years as a chaplain. The guest speaker for his ceremony was the Chief of Chaplains for the Air Force, who happens to be the highest-ranking chaplain capping out at two-star general. By this time, I knew I wanted to attempt the Pagan chaplain quest, which meant identifying an appropriately accredited seminary and enrolling, then finding some way to pay for this second graduate degree, plus convincing my husband that I might be crazy but this was something very important I was being called to do.

My commander at the time was a lovely human, and knew of my intentions to pursue chaplaincy. In an effort to do some grooming of his younger officers, he introduced me to the Chief and mentioned that I was interested in becoming a chaplain (this poor man had no idea I was Pagan). The Chief looked at me and said "Oh really? That's great. What denomination are you?"

Only years later would I learn how incredibly rude that question is, but in the moment, I was stunned. Do I tell him the truth? Or do I tell him what I think he wants to hear? I had a small niggle at the back of my brain that prompted me to be honest in that moment, and so I told him I was Pagan.

"That will never happen." He looked at me with severe gravity.

"Excuse me?" I asked.

"It will never happen. There just isn't a need for it. There aren't the numbers to justify a Pagan chaplain." And he continued to mansplain to me why a Pagan chaplain was unnecessary. I had looked up the denominational breakout of numbers less than a week before and Pagan/Other across DoD had outnumbered Mormons, but there were four Mormon chaplains. I politely thanked him for his time, excused myself, and enrolled in seminary two weeks later.

'Moral injury' is a term few people are familiar with unless they are involved in pastoral and spiritual care circles. A term that is much more prevalent, particularly with veteran populations, is post-traumatic stress disorder. *The Diagnostic and Statistical Manual of Mental Disorders (5th Edition)* finally incorporates a very specific set of symptomologies to diagnose PTSD, but does not yet recognize moral injury as a formal diagnosis. Clinicians and researchers in the field of pastoral and spiritual care have determined that moral injury is just as prevalent and damaging as PTSD, and deserves due diligence for treatment purposes. Moral injury is present when there has been (a) a betrayal of "what's right"; (b) either by a person in legitimate authority, or by one's self—"I did it" (Litz, Maguen, Nash, et al.); (c) in a high stakes situation. Both forms of moral injury impair the capacity for trust and elevate despair, suicidality, and interpersonal violence. They deteriorate character. I make this distinction because for me, much of my military career was a dance on the moral injury line. It was violated two distinct times that I will mention here, because these events have shaped my life in irreparable ways.

My second duty assignment after Lackland was at The United States Air Force Honor Guard. This unit is unique in that it is tasked to be a ceremonial unit that performs the funerals in Arlington National Cemetery, as well as Presidential Arrivals, wreath layings, parades, and other showy displays of pomp and circumstance. It is a special duty assignment, and they are selective in who they hire for the job. I was the third female officer to ever do the job I did. The unit's primary source of manning comes straight from basic training, so an overwhelming majority of the members are young, immature, and away from home for the first time. The gender breakdown of the unit is about 5% female to 95% male, though if we are lucky it can be as much as 10 to 15% female.

I was the highest-ranking female the entire time I was in the unit. I cannot begin to explain what it was like living in a fishbowl every single day of my life for three years straight. Because I was leadership I was held to impossibly high standards of performance—and because I was the only female in leadership the standards were higher. This led to a variety of different outcomes; the most prominent being working out far too much and an eating disorder to maintain unrealistic weights standards. I also became a functional alcoholic to cope with the stress of that system. Additionally, there exists this pervasive culture of objectification of women in the uniform that no one talks about, yet it is so ubiquitous it's like the air we breathe. I think this quote from *A Few Good Men* sums up my dilemma perfectly: Col. Jessup: [*during lunch in Cuba with Markinson, Kaffee, Galloway, Weinberg, Kendrick present*] "There is nothing on this earth sexier, believe me, gentlemen, than a woman you have to salute in the morning. Promote 'em all, I say, 'cause this is true: if you haven't gotten a blowjob from a superior officer, well, you're just letting the best in life pass you by." I was a living, breathing, walking sex symbol to the many of the men.

Needless to say, it was a matter of time before my personhood was violated. What I wasn't expecting was the reaction from my leadership. I was given the choice to either rock the boat and blow the whistle on my leadership's gross mishandling of discipline and good order—or I could be promoted. I chose to be promoted, at the cost of my pride and the infliction of a deep and abiding wound. We often don't talk about these injuries, preferring to focus our energies on combat related suffering because it is easier to point a finger at a cause there instead of facing the monsters in our collective mirror. It is hard and uncomfortable to hold our brothers accountable for the atrocities they commit at home to each other and to their sisters.

Fast forward two years: I transferred to a job at the Pentagon, working as an Executive Support Officer to the Secretary of Defense. I was no longer a functional alcoholic, and beginning to have some semblance of a normal life again despite doing shift work. I was solidly half-way through seminary, but because of work I could only attend part time to keep from going insane. I felt the familiar pangs of longing for a more authentic existence, including wrestling with whether or not to stay on active duty. I hadn't met the magic "ten-year mark" which is half way to retirement, so if I separated at this point I wouldn't feel like I was losing out on that benefit (in fact, the thought of working twenty years in a career field I hated was horrifying to me). My leadership at this assignment wasn't anything to write home about, and in fact they repeatedly threw us under the bus in order to make themselves look better. My coworkers were decent for the most part, but once again I was almost the only female working in an entire office of males. There was one exception to the decency: my Navy coworker was the kind of guy that finds anything with two legs and a vulva something worth hitting on— that is until I find out I'm pregnant. Suddenly, because my uterus had an occupant, I became some sort of harbinger of the plague. I found his shift in behavior a little strange, but relieved to be free of his unwanted advances. At some point, my doctor put me strictly on day shifts and swing shifts due to the persistent danger of me falling asleep at the wheel and wrecking my car after working night shifts. This does not bode well with Navy coworker. One morning after shift change, after a very frosty reception and an exchange that bordered on rude, I stopped him in the hallway to inquire if anything was wrong. To my surprise, Navy coworker took that as an opportunity to let me know how selfish I was for making everyone else work my night shifts just because I had gotten knocked up. He also let me know a few other choice phrases and went about his way. I can't say at this point in my life I was surprised. I had internalized the knowledge that women in the military are less-than, and nothing I could say would change that.

I separated from active duty in 2013 and had my son

that same year. In the span of a year my husband and I bought a house, had a child, and I had a career shift. I did all the things you weren't supposed to do at the same time. I also basically had an identity crisis as I worked to figure out who I was without the military, and who I was as a mother whose body was now also affected by an autoimmune disorder and chronic depression. Because of my health concerns I was no longer serviceable for active duty, which meant chaplaincy on the DoD side was no longer an option. I had to completely re-examine my goals and my game plan. There were some amazing positives that came out of the transition off active duty—I could finally be unapologetically Pagan all the time, I could express my sexuality and gender however I wanted, and it gave me the space to find myself without the confines of regulations hanging over me. I went back to seminary full time, and focused on my family and healing myself.

I chose the VA for several reasons. I want to give back to those of us who have served. Because of pain and darkness in my own journey, I can be a companion and a witness for someone on their journey. I also want to be on the forefront of interfaith work. I feel it is important that we make space at the table for all faiths, and that we do the work of true pluralism rather than just tolerance. But really, I just think back to that conversation with the two-star general, when he told me there would never be a Pagan chaplain—and in my mind I say, "watch me."

NOTES FROM BARAKHAMBA
Kate Telma

Alone, it was too easy to retreat into the dark cool of the first floor apartment. The other students I would share the rooms with started working later in the summer. My first few days in Delhi coincided with a heat wave that even people who lived their whole lives in the capital couldn't bear. I went out in the mornings, trying to see my fill of the new city before the temperature crept over 100.

Moments of stooping on the plaza to untie my shoes before entering a mosque, or standing back to take a single picture of Humayun's tomb, the red stone Taj Mahal precursor on the eastern edge of the city, became moments of impossible exertion. The sweat beaded along the roots of my hair, gathering in drops that slid down along my face and spine. The stream rolled over my butt and snaked down my legs, stopping in the backs of my knees before dripping to the ground. Soaked clothes stuck.

I considered it a victory when I had drunk enough water that I looked for a public restroom once during the day; in my first week, I don't think I ever won.

The heat choked, so that stepping out the door I

often couldn't feel it at first. Like shocking pain receptors on a boiling pot, it took several minutes to feel the burn. I lost my appetite walking between my room and the kitchen, a trip that required only a moment in a tiny open courtyard.

I reached my limit in three hours. The car dropped me off at the end of the subdivision, and within minutes I would be back on the bed, the only light fighting through the curtains, drifting back to sleep with heat exhaustion and jetlag. No one was there to remind me that I wasn't eating, that I hadn't eaten more than a couple packaged food bars in the days since I landed.

An afternoon three days in, the stupor broke. Maybe the nausea wasn't from the heat; somewhere I had read that it could also be a symptom of hunger. I wandered out along the subdivision, trying to find a square that I thought I had passed the day before, picking my way through the dust, napping stray dogs and discarded packaging. Shutters covered the main food stalls. A single man dumped scoops of red spice blend into a pot of raw chicken thighs that reached almost to his waist, stirring with his hands and brushing at the flies that settled on his shoulders and neck. The dogs were too sweaty to show much interest.

But two semi-permanent stands along the side road seemed to be serving food, regardless of the weird afternoon time. Men stood eating at the metal counters, dipping flat roti bread into thick sauces. A boy passed out fresh breads, and a man behind the counter used the same ladle to spoon more beans onto the plates as they emptied. Large aluminum pots lined the front of the stand, each with a gas flame underneath. I approached the one that seemed to have menu, lines of Hindi followed by numbers painted onto the blue metal of the shutters.

I watched. The men crowded around, standing close without room between their elbows. New men came as the full ones drifted away, barely exchanging a word with the stand keeper, or the other customers.

Eventually the keeper looked up, and beckoned me forward. "Yes, ma'am?."

"What were the choices?" I asked. He shook his head, and filled a metal plate with lentils and kidney bean stews from three of the pots. He came out from the stand, and set the plate on a particle board desk that served as auxiliary standing room, off to the side. He added a flattish spoon, as an afterthought. The younger boy brought me breads on a plate, too hot to handle with just fingers.

I couldn't remember the last hot food I had eaten—maybe some eggs two mornings before I flew to Delhi. I scooped up the beans, almost frantic, burning my fingers in the sauce and on the bread. As I finished one compartment of my plate, the boy came back with another metal saucer full of that dish, and dumped it in the empty spot. I ate the last bite of my roti, and he was back with more steaming bread.

A plump man with a shock of white hair broke away from the counter, and came and stood next to me, without a word. He poured himself some water from the metal pitcher, and got a glass for me and poured me a drink. Nodding, he returned to his beans.

. . .

I didn't know if it was the relative obscurity of *Nature India*, the online journal I would spend the summer writing for. Maybe it was a clash of our spoken Englishes. Likely, it was because I was a young foreign intern, visibly delighted by opportunities and excited to learn anything new, and these men knew how to handle the media.

When I asked for interviews, the first line of my email was clear. *I am a science writing intern at* Nature India. *I am writing about the legacy of the Open Source Drug Discovery project.*

The OSDD launched several years ago, with the ambitious goal of bringing a new generic tuberculosis drug to market. The traditional Big Pharma timeline for getting a new and frequently inaccessible drug to patients was ten years, and the people couldn't wait that long. By creating an open platform where scientists could share data ahead of publication, the founders argued, it would be possible for a new antibiotic to be discovered quickly and cheaply, something that was needed more and more desperately as the number of new cases—especially multidrug resistant cases—of TB crept up around India each year.

The first few years of the project were a resounding success. Labs from around India and around the world were drawn to the challenge, chipping away at the traditional silos of academia and engaging younger students in ways no one had seen before. But the leader of the effort had several 'misunderstandings' with other scientists, and the media. Then the funding from the five-year plan expired. The government changed. The new five-year plan did include new funding, but the scientific agency managing the project announced bankruptcy. The project stagnated, and scientists began to move away.

It had been ten years since the birth of OSDD, and I wanted to know what they accomplished. No new drugs, yet, but the effort of thousands of scientists surely produced something. At least the start of a new drug? More interdisciplinary lab groups? A culture of open electronic lab notebooks?

I spent the first several days of my internship in my 11th floor office on Barakhamba Road, wading through old websites and abandoned web servers. I scanned papers for traces of data, searching for the names of people who had been involved since the beginning, names of people who had moved on partway through, reading papers about drug targets and novel compounds and chemoinformatic models. I began asking for interviews.

I contacted academic offices at different universities

scattered around Delhi—and made some calls via Skype or the phone—but got variations of the same interview. I started each interview introducing myself, and saying that I was working in Delhi for the summer, and that I was writing for *Nature India*. Older academics recalled their frustration at traditional pharma, or philosophies around data sharing, and realized that they needed to join the platform, and the movement. They disagreed with the direction that the few pharma companies with a TB research program were taking, thought that the software available was inadequate, and retrospectively, that the clinical trials for new tuberculosis treatment regime had design flaws. They had wanted a better way to share work, and they had been trying in their own labs, and the OSDD popularized what they had already been doing. They were working on a new collaboration, details to be announced shortly. They didn't want to go into details, but it was a shame that personalities sometimes got in the way.

The fragments I had been grabbing at for two weeks began snapping together with clarity, like the moment a critical piece is added to a jigsaw puzzle and every subsequent fit is a match.

But the interviews became routine in another way: an hour into speaking freely, explaining truthfully, and maybe venting, they would pause. What exactly is this for? So you are writing about this for your thesis? Publishing? When?

And then: *If you quote me, I need to review all of my quotes. I don't want to ruffle feathers—not that I'm afraid, but I don't want to answer unnecessarily. I need to know how you will quote me, before you publish.*

I blamed myself the first times this happened— likely, I had just not spoken slowly or articulately enough, my American accent was confusing, and my source truly didn't understand my intentions. But by the third or fourth time, emboldened and increasingly more direct, I grew suspicious. None of these men were media-naïve. This project had been written about before. They knew what these interviews were about. And they also knew that I was new, to India and to journalism and to writing about things happening overseas, and that they had a chance to cover up moments where they had spoken too honestly.

...

Every guidebook touts the grandeur, the expanse, and the ease of the government-owned Indian Railways company.

Before I could buy any tickets, I needed to register for an account. My first attempt taught me I could not create an account between the hours of 9:30-11:30. The reasons for this window were not entirely clear, and might have something to do with daily website maintenance. Returning an hour later, I entered a code that was texted to my phone, clicked a link I received by email, and entered a Captcha code, and then I seemed ready to browse for my first tickets.

Friends and tour guides alike had warned that train tickets sold out weeks in advance, and that while tickets will be available for sale, the purchase of these tickets would not necessarily guarantee seats on the train. This paradox was beyond me and my friend, both Indian Railways e-ticket virgins. We decided on a Monday that we would go to the Golden Temple in the northern city of Amritsar that weekend, and looked for trains timed ideally for leaving straight from our offices. Clicking quickly through a screen that asked us to select backup train preferences, which we decided we wouldn't need, we were eventually issued tickets designated 'RLWL' or tickets for a place on the Remote Location Waiting List. This particular waiting list had a separate priority, and confirmations for actual tickets would depend on the cancellation of a Destination Confirmed ticket. Something about a ticket being issued for intermediate stations that were not the main stations at the origin and destination, but actually the most important on the line.

I mostly read the 'for this type of ticket there are less chances of confirmation' line.

The trains connect every part of the country, a limitless combination of paths across. Ideas for side trips and weekend plans months in advance grew. I chatted with women in my office on Barakhamba Road at lunch, explaining my plans for what I wanted to see.

"You must take this train." "No, that one is unreliable." "The highest class on the Chennai Central Garib Rath is third, but you will find that it's much better than first class on the Tamil Nadu Express."

A recent regulation made it so that an individual could only buy six e-tickets a month. "This has been done to prevent any possible misuse of online booking facility as it has been felt that a genuine passenger does not require to book tickets online for more than six times in a month," newspapers quoted a senior Railway Ministry official. Most genuine passengers were probably also able to navigate the in-person booking kiosks downtown and at the stations in Hindi, and could draw on the limitless reserves of friends or travel companions, each of whom had their own Indian mobile verified account. Not *this* genuine passenger.

As we settled into lunch the next day—each woman reaching over and spooning parts of the curries, curd, fried okra "lady fingers," and biryani rice onto the plates of others before addressing her own plate—my train ticket purchasing exploits became the conversation.

I bought the Delhi to Chennai leg after my new friend Madhu decided that I had best leave during the week, and not on Sunday. The Garib Rath was the only reliable option, I knew now. I needed to book Chennai to somewhere on the west coast—maybe Kochi or Thiruvananthapuram—but I would get to Shimla by changing trains at Kalka. The Kalka to Shimla tickets weren't for sale yet, because the popularity of the British narrow gauge rail that led to the summer mountain getaway meant that ticket sales only opened thirty days before the journey.

The review of my purchases was accompanied by suggestions of other places to go, and the best weekends, and whom to ask for friend or family connections while there. One more ticket and I would be over the six ticket limit for the month, though, and having experienced the ferocity of e-ticket purchases and failed last minute attempts that only got me as far as the Remote Location Waiting List, I knew I needed to secure any tickets for the rest of the summer in the next several days. Vidisha, a woman who had approached me one day as I ate alone and introduced herself and her friend, Yashmina, offered me the use of her account, setting off a string of other offers. I thanked Vidisha.

Later that evening, I looked up the routes—it turned out Chennai to Kochi was already sold out, but going to Thiruvananthapuram was still an option—and I texted Vidisha, wondering if she actually wanted me to take her up on her offer.

She responded instantly with her username and password. I finished the purchase from her account in minutes, and texted my thanks. Maybe I was one ticket closer to being a genuine passenger, one who had access to multiple accounts. I thanked her again.

"And next time I am going to charge you 100 bucks for every 'thank you' ☺☺," she answered.

...

An unexpected outcome of the monsoon was a community. I left my office on Barakhamba Road to metro across the city for an interview at IIIT Delhi, a new information technology institute in the southern industrial section of Delhi. To avoid the chaos of Rajiv Chowk, one of the main transfer stations, I decided to walk the 15 minutes to the violet line station where I could catch a direct train. Especially a couple days into a reliable nightly rain, the early afternoons were cool enough to want to get outside during the work day.

I went out the back entrance, and stepped into

Connaught Lane. The lane is a bazaar of sorts. Food stands sell vegetarian and non-vegetarian momos, dumplings fried in shallow skillets of sizzling oil. Women crouch on the ground near heaps of shiny black jamun, pomegranates and mangos, and burn incense to fend off the insects.

About halfway down the block is the 'tea corner.' Here, the chai walla sits inside a little retaining wall built of repurposed cinder blocks, tending a single gas flame that he uses alternately to brew instant noodles and fresh chai. Barefoot but in suit pants, he throws the chai into a pot of roiling milk. He beats green cardamom pods with a rock bigger than his fist, tosses the crushed spice in, and gestures to his assistants to bring more paper cups as he ladles out tea. I justified the beverage as safe to drink because it boils so hard. A milk skin would form as I struggled to hold the paper cup.

Two steps into the lane, it began to rain. Four steps in and I felt my first monsoon.

Men in turbans put plastic bags on their heads, looping the handles over their ears. Fruit sellers whipped out newspapers, moving the piles off the sidewalks and covering up the rest with paper. Others came running with tarps to cover their carts of SIM cards, mobile plans and earbuds for sale. There was something frantic, but with the rain the mood changed. The bustle of the day paused.

Some clustered under the Peelu trees that line the lane, others in the bus stop, or under the eaves of a building. Many were smiling, maybe at seeing me completely unprepared for the weather, but mostly at the absurdity of everyone else. No amount of shelter would keep us dry.

I collected myself under an enormous tree. A young man already waiting there smirked and shook his head. We were only getting wetter waiting. He dashed into the intersection suddenly devoid of cars, because somehow the rain was stopping them, too. I ran after him, because other pedestrians I could use for help crossing the street were disappearing.

At the next intersection I waited inside the covered walkway of a stone building, now packed with other people wondering if they should cross the street. The crowd of strangers seemed chattier than usual. No one was going anywhere so it paid to be friendly. People broke off in twos and threes to run towards the Janpath metro, soaked even before they reached the curb.

Under the roof of the station, I unwrapped my cotton scarf and wrung out as much water as I could. I grabbed at the tails of my blouse and the bottom of my cardigan, and squeezed out another cup.

As I stepped through the metal detector for the necessary metro wanding and frisking, the guard was smiling and had only one question: "Too much rain?"

PILGRIMAGES
Ginger Strivelli

As a devout polytheist Pagan Witch, I follow many Gods and Goddesses from ancient cultures all over the Mother Earth. One of the best ways to follow Them, is to make pilgrimages to Their ancient temples and holy grounds to pray and do rituals with Them at those magical sacred sites. There are ways to do so from your home, thousands of miles away from where They were worshipped thousands of years ago. However, if you can travel, it is even better to invoke a God or Goddess on the land where Their Priests and Priestesses were invoking them millennia ago.

Traveling to such magical destinations is not just a magical working, it is also an adventure. No book can tell you how watching the Sun set over the Sphinx in Giza, Egypt makes your spirit grow and glow. No photograph can make you understand the vibration you feel in the air as you sit on the grass at the foot of Pyramid of Kukulcan in Chichen Itza, Mexico. No video can affect you like riding a boat down the River of Many Faces, on your way to Lamania, Belize to do a bloodletting ritual at the Temple of the Balam Jaguar

Gods. No story I can tell you here about my finding a prayer cloth at the eighth century Hindu Temple of Lord Vishnu near Osian, India, can make you feel the touch of one of Vishnu's many blue hands, like I did when I picked the cloth up from the foot of the temple wall.

Nonetheless, I'm going to tell you about those pilgrimages and many others I have been blessed to perform on my travels. I do so with hopes of inspiring y'all to make some pilgrimages of your own.

Travel alas, can be costly, and time consuming. Many can not ever afford to travel far. I never did much until I was in mid thirties. In 2005 when I decided, that I would find a will and a way to get to Egypt, where I'd always dreamed of going. I found once I put my mind to it, saving up a couple thousand dollars to take that long dreamed of pilgrimage to Egypt was not as impossible as it sounded. Many people spend four or five dollars a day on cigarettes, or fancy coffees. I decided I was going to pretend to smoke a couple packs a day, but instead of buying those eight dollars worth of cigarettes a day, I started a travel savings account, and deposited that money into it. I found a few extra dollars here and there, selling online tarot readings and taking some from my tax refund, outside of my 'smoking habit' to also deposit, and within just a few months I had enough to book my tickets to Cairo!

Now, part of the hindrance to travel on pilgrimages is the cost of the flights, hotels, taxis, meals, and shopping. Mostly the flights as many places, including Egypt are very cheap to stay and eat in. Hypothetically, one could even not spend any on shopping, though I've never been able to manage that magic trick. Once you have addressed the saving and spending hindrances though the main obstacle seems to be courage.

On every pilgrimage I've made over the years since I started traveling 12 years ago, I've been told umpteen times that, "You can't just go there alone" or "You need a tour guide or a group to travel with", "Aren't you afraid to just wander around a foreign country by yourself?" "It is dangerous in such places, you won't be safe." 'How did you plan and book your flights and hotels by yourself; you need a travel agent." "You can't just traipse off to exotic locations on your own."

Well, traipse I did, nonetheless. Often all alone, though sometimes I could talk my best friend or one or two, three or all six of my children into going with me. I booked my flights myself, I booked my hotels myself. I called taxis and wandered around sites without a tour group or tour guide to force me into their schedules and ideas. I loved every minute of it. Even the planning, perhaps especially the planning and the planning took months. I savoured making packing lists and itineraries and notes on my phone of places to go to, things to do and what to eat while I was there. I shopped for the perfect outfits to wear to the sites, and enjoyed all the preparation. The internet is a great resource in researching those things to plan out yourself. Travel guide books are also helpful. You can also ask others about their travels to help with your planning.

I am not saying you can't just, if you can afford it, spend twice or thrice as much to sign onto some organized tour of some place you want to go....then show up and be led around by someone carrying a clipboard and a little flag so you don't lose sight of them. If you are able to do that money-wise, and it is easier for you courage-wise, it is a way to travel and even 'pilgrimage.' I'd not do it, I've never done it....but I usually lack money, and never lack courage.

Once you have decided how to save and how to plan, and you finally arrive at your destination, then there are a few carved-in-stone type rules to pilgrimaging. First rule; there are no rules, there are just some suggestions. Second rule: Suggestions sometimes don't work for you as well as the one who suggested it. Third rule: Don't be afraid to ask for different suggestions from others as you go along. Fourth rule; Making up your own suggestions is also doable. That being said, I have some suggestions:

  ---Always take your camera. Not just your cell phone camera but a second camera, perhaps a third. One might break right when you get to the monument you've been dreaming of going to since you were a kid, and one might just not take good pictures in the conditions you find when you get there. Maybe it is dark inside the tombs, maybe it's hazy in the jungle, maybe you keep putting your pinky in front of the lens of that one camera. I gave each daughter a disposable camera when we were exploring Chichen itza together several years ago. That way we all managed to have photos of each of us, as no one was always the photographer. We had photos from different viewpoints and in both definitions of the word, viewpoint, as the photos my then, ten-year-old daughter, Harmony took, were quite different from the ones her sixteen- and eighteen-year-old sisters Amethyst and Sybilsue took. You want to make scrapbooks of your trips to remember them by, if you are like me, and you want to share way too many photos of your adventures on facebook, and twitter, and everywhere else you can post them, like I do. You need photos—lots of photos.

  ---Wear comfortable shoes. It's hard climbing up rocks. I climbed up the Red Pyramid in Dashur, Egypt on that first pilgrimage to Egypt I made in 2005. It is not something I had planned, as I have a fear of heights, and you have to climb a third of the way up the pyramid to the entrance. I also have a fear of enclosed places and there at the entrance one has to then back down a narrow low-ceilinged shaft on something that is a cross between a ladder and stairs into a dark chamber deep inside the pyramid. I am afraid of the dark. Nevertheless, I went climbing up it. Luckily my sandals were comfortable. They weren't strappy, rhinestone decked, expensive, fashionable shoes that I might wear on the red carpet. They were comfortable and I wore them on the Red Pyramid, for my last minute change of plans to climb up that pyramid.

--- Write your itinerary in pencil. Yes, write one. Research, study, plan and replan it for months before you go, but write it in pencil. When you wake up at the hotel on one of the precious few days of your trip, and it has rained all night, and none of the drivers want to take you far on the wet roads, like happened to me on my first trip to Egypt in 2005. Then instead of going to Saqqara an hour or so away, that day, I stayed around Giza, near my hotel, on foot mostly exploring shops and cafes. I went to Saqqara the next day, and loved it. It was such a beautiful day with a clear lapis blue sky and snow white sand. Had I found a driver brave enough to drive me the day before like my itinerary had said, the sky was grey and the sand was wet and tan. One day in 2010 while going to the Huge Statue of Hanuman, Temple of Hanuman in Delhi, India, my three younger daughters and I were watching some monks chant. Harmony, my youngest knew the chant as we often listen to them at home, and joined in. This impressed the monks so much, they asked us to follow them, and led us to another temple under the statute that isn't in the guide books. As we followed the monks we found ourselves being led down a steep dark staircase into the ground. After a few steps I noted I was ankle deep in water. Before we reached the bottom of the stairs we were half submerged. This underground cave temple was dark, and flooded, with candles and flowers floating by as we were led through the water filled cave to an altar with a statue of Mother Kali. Now, Kali is a rather intimidating Goddess that I'd never really warmed up to, until then. Being allowed to Visit Her private temple was a special rare treat, that we had not planned on, and I wouldn't have pencilled into our itinerary even if I had heard of that Kali Temple beforehand. Sometimes the Gods want you to go somewhere else on the day you had planned to go to another place. Be flexible, move things around on that itinerary you wrote out in pencil. You have an eraser there on the end of that pencil.

---When in Rome, do as the Romans do. You didn't save up, plan, and prepare ten months to be in India, on the other side of the planet, to eat at the McDonald's near the Holiday Inn Hotel where you are staying. Book yourself into a little inn that is run by locals, that is decorated like the homes of locals, or like an old fashioned colonial Indian mansion. In your room there, you will feel like you are in India, not Indiana. When in some far off jungle, and you find yourself hungry like the wolf, eat the fried brains, like my teenage son Balthazar did at the 'You like Restaurant' in Delhi, India. Or if you are a bit less adventurous than my teenage son, eat the kheer (rose water rice pudding) and naan (traditional Indian bread) like I ate there. Do not order the burger and french fries, even if you are in France.

---When packing for a trip, I follow a quote (I do not know by whom) that goes; 'Lay out all the clothes and money you plan to pack....then pack half the clothes and twice the money.' It's clever and cute, but oh so true. Don't over pack clothes. You need a sweater, shawl, or coat, a good dressy going-out-to-dinner outfit, two or three outfits for tromping around in the desert/jungle/woods/rocks/whatever outfits, a bathing suit, pyjamas, three or four pairs of underwear, extra shoes and as we call it, a BUB (back up bra.) Don't just take the one bra you are wearing on the plane, or the shoes you are wearing on the plane. Ya may break a pair and need a second pair. All hotels have sinks to wash things out in and chairs or balconies or towel racks to hang them to dry on, so you can rewear outfits. You don't need a separate outfit for each day. Also, pack things that mix and match to make several different looks. Lastly wear on the plane/boat/car/train your heaviest items to keep your suitcase light. I almost always travel with only my carry-on rolling bag and purse, with no checked bags. Checked bags are a pain in the back, the wallet, and the timetable. Avoid the hassle if you can. Then the 'twice the money' punchline: yes, it is funny, but it is also good advice. You don't wanna run out of spending money before you run out of vacation days. There are some mildly entertaining things you can do for free in any place, but you didn't save and plan and pack and fly, to some exotic location to sit by the hotel pool or window shop on foot around the hotel. Take all the cash you can, you won't regret it. You might even bring some back with you, that you didn't need to spend. It did happen to me once.

Now, that you have decided to and found a way to save up the money, and the gathered the courage and knowledge to savor the planning, and you know all the rules, I mean suggestions, for how to travel. Let's go!

Where are we going? Where have you always been drawn to go? What ancient Gods do you hear call your name? What world heritage sites do you want to see before you die? What is the closest therefore cheapest place you can make a religious pilgrimage? What language do you want to try to learn some of? Where did your ancestors come from? Any of those are great ways to pick a destination or you could toss a dart at a map on the wall.

When I chose to go to Greece with my best friend, Beth in 2011, it was because I loved the Greek Myths, and felt a bond with the Greek Gods; Ares, Hera, Poseidon, and Apollo. I'd been drawn to Delphi, so much, I'd named one of my daughters Sybilsue Gaia after the Sybil of Delphi, the oracle Priestess of Apollo and Gaia, (and my grandmother Sue.) So in Greece, Beth and I splurged on a professional private driver on this trip for the first time. Cost a fortune, but we had a chauffeur pretty much, who waited on us and took us everywhere, answered every question and was at our whims and calls all week. We didn't have to deal with finding, negotiating prices for, and keeping a taxi from other tourists. Of course, one of our days we had him drive us to Delphi, which was several hours away from our Hotel. On our way from Athens to Delphi, we stopped at the site of a battle and a memorial to the battle, called The Chaironeia Lion statue. Lord Byron had visited The Chaironeia Lion Statue in 1809, and I wanted to stand in front of it, as Lord Byron had two hundred and two years earlier. That was the second 'Lord Byron' pilgrimage site we visited on that Greece trip, as we also went to the Monastiraki flea market in the Plaka in Athens where Lord Byron had stayed in the home of 'the maid of Athens,' Teresa Makri during his own 1809 and 1810 Greek Pilgrimages. So, one can make pilgrimages to sites that are historically important to you, not just religiously, as proved my visits to sites for my favourite Poet. Also this story shows one can make a 'pilgrimage' to a famous shopping site like the Monastiraki flea market there in Athens, Greece, which is quite famous. On another trip two of my daughters and I shopped at the Khan el-Khalili, the oldest bazaar in Cairo and one of the oldest in the Middle East, dating from the 1300s, as another 'shopping pilgrimage.'

Of course most pilgrimages are religious in nature, and one can actually perform works of prayer, magic, or ritual while on these magical trips. Here in Egypt, where I live now, after visiting it eight times, we often see tourists praying or meditating at the temples and pyramids. There is sometimes a bit of controversy about that from the more rigid right-wing Muslims in charge of things, but most Egyptians at the sites are quite accommodating to those of us wishing to worship, work magic, or pray to the ancient Egyptian Gods at Their holy sites.

After being forced into a divorce proved hard for me to recover from emotionally, I decided to do a Mayan bloodletting ritual on my trip to Belize with my best friend, Beth in 2016. I hoped it might help me banish that grief and attachment. As I mentioned previously, we had to sail up the River of Many Faces out in the jungle to the lost Mayan city of Lamania. Once there, we climbed up a couple of large hills to the Temple of the Balam. Balam means Jaguar Gods. The Temple is a breath-taking sight of a small pyramid temple, flanked by two large Jaguar faces on the front wall of the temple. Amazingly the altar stone still sits in the grass just a few meters in front of the temple. We sat upon that stone, and Beth, (she's a trained Priestess and a Nurse, don't try this at home,) sliced the heel of my left hand, at the base of my thumb open with a knife. We wiped my blood upon the carved jade Jaguar handled ceremonial blade and then plunged that into the earth in front of the altar stone by the temple base. To say this was a powerful working of magic, an awesome ritual, would be a monstrous understatement. That blade, still stained with bits of my blood, and the Mayan earth, lays on my altar in my cabin back in North Carolina where I visit for the winter holidays with family and friends yearly.

I often hear, or see, or sense the ancient Gods on my pilgrimages. I mentioned before how I found a discarded prayer cloth at the base of a hundreds of years old temple of Lord Vishnu outside Osian, India. When I caught sight of its gold fringe winking at me in the sunlight, I instantly knew it was a message, a gift from Lord Vishnu, Himself. When I walked over and bent to untangle it from some thorns that had held it there waiting for me, for who knows how long, I truly felt Vishnu hand it to me. It brought tears to my eyes then, and again as I type this. In 2009 in Rome, as I stood outside The Colosseum, I clearly heard Juno tell me to not go inside. The past life memories it might have triggered were not something I could handle at that time. I hope to return one day to Rome and go inside The Colosseum as the issues I was working through then have been settled. While there in Rome, I did go in and enjoy the Pantheon. Fittingly, as Pantheon means temple of all the Gods, I heard many Gods and Goddesses welcome me into that ancient magical temple, as I entered. I also felt the touch the Mother Mary's hand and saw the serene smile She wears inside the Saint Maria Sopa Minerva Church behind the Pantheon in Rome. The Church's name means Mary on top of Minerva because the church was built on top of the older Temple of Minerva, the Roman Goddess of wisdom. I sought out Minerva there, and found I heard some words of wisdom from Her as well.

Sometimes on pilgrimages, things don't go as planned or there seems to be some horrible mishap that 'ruins' a day. Try to not let anything ruin a precious day of your limited time at these holy sites. Once in 2010 in Mexico, my daughter Destiny and I were staying near the lost city of Teotihuacan, and were told at the front desk when we asked for a taxi, that we could just walk to one of the entrances. So we took off on foot walking and indeed after not too long a hike on a nice flat paved road came upon one of the sites' entrances. We went in, got our tickets and proceeded to head towards the Pyramid of the Moon and the Pyramid of the Sun. We could see them, from where we entered, but found ourselves on the opposite side of the city on the 'Avenue of the Dead.' We were a bit unsure of our ability to make it all the way across the city to the pyramids as we'd already walked a mile or two to the site, and the 'Avenue of the Dead' looked like it's name was a warning, but we had no choice. We found that on this road we had to cross several smaller temple courtyards which had steps so steep we had to climb down them on our backsides like crabs to get down to the courtyards, then climb back up another steep staircase on the other side on all fours. Alas, the road had several of these obstacles. Along about the fourth or fifth of these temple courtyards in the middle of the road we finally saw another tourist. A young guy with a huge backpack hiking along at a much faster pace than we were. He looked at us rather worriedly, I am sure thinking that I was too old, and both of us were too fat to be on this 'Avenue of the Dead' hike. He was right, but we had no choice, we were halfway there by that time. It was over three hours after we entered the site, that we finally, huffing and puffing, scraped up and soaking wet with sweat, reached the Pyramid of the Moon's courtyard. We sat and recovered for quite a while before exiting at the entrance that was right there beside the main two pyramid temples. The day had not felt 'ruined. However, we'd have never marched all the way across the vast ancient city had we not been given no choice, so it was an unexpected experience, and we enjoyed it (some) and we were proud we made it through it. The following day Destiny, who speaks rather good Spanish, made it overly clear to the taxi driver that we called to take us back to the ruins, repeatedly that we wanted to go in the good entrance not the bad one at the other end of the Avenue of the Dead.

Another nearly ruined pilgrimage day happened in 2014 in Athens, Greece with my two younger daughters. Sybilsue, who was eighteen at the time was the victim of a pickpocket while we were shopping in the Monastiraki flea market. In our defence we were being very careful, as the guidebooks and the taxi driver had warned us that pickpockets were common there. Nonetheless, her wallet disappeared out of her hand as she paid for a purchase. Naturally we all fell apart, and got upset and were crying by the time our taxi driver picked up back up. My daughter's social security card, driver's license and over one hundred euros had been in the wallet. Luckily, we had also followed the guidebooks advice to not carry our passports with us, and hers was safely back at the hotel. After a pep talk to each other, we pulled it together, and did not let it ruin our day, as we only had a couple days left in Greece that trip.

Festivals are wonderful events to attend when making a pilgrimage. Both the trips I made to India—in 2010 with my younger three daughters, and in 2016 with my younger son—were timed for us to be there for the Holi festival. Holi is the spring festival were Hindus celebrate the colours of the blooming spring flowers by throwing coloured powder on each other all day. It is magical and spiritual, but also lots of fun. You start the day in clean clothes looking normal and return to the hotel covered head to toe, clothing and skin decorated in multicoloured powder. Sometimes parties are thrown on any and no date at all in places where people often travel. My daughter, Destiny, my mother, several friends, and I have taken cruises to the Bahamas, where the local bars at port are throwing a party every single day, and you might find yourself conga lining around the bar, getting shots at every corner squirted down your throat by waiters dancing on the bar. This might not seem like much of a pilgrimage, but I always research the ancient original Gods and Goddesses of such places and celebrate Them while we are partying like it's 1999. In the Bahamas for example, the Moon Goddess, Karaya is my favorite of the Caribbean Island Tainos (Gods), and I always pray to Her there before or after the partying.

Lastly, you want to be sure you remember your pilgrimages. I am an artist and writer, so for my trips, I always explore the cultures in my art and writing, for the months leading up to the trip, as well as while I am actually there. I find some of my best paintings or drawings are done overseas on my pilgrimages. They often show the sites themselves, or the local ancient Gods and Goddesses. I write poetry or prose about my experiences daily upon the trips and add that to my trip scrapbook of each pilgrimage, with photos, feathers or such messages from the Gods I find in my exploring, and such. These scrapbooks and artworks are great mementos of my travels, as are the jewelry with images of the Gods, or sacred symbols of each temple, or the statutes or such that I buy when shopping on my pilgrimages.

Now, go forth and explore! Make some pilgrimages of your own! Blessed Be.

CHASING SHADOWS
Tammy Conrad

I sit in my canvas lawn chair under my pop-up tent filled with trinkets, talismans, charms and other unique goodies. Over a weekend or a week, I will move this lawn chair perhaps 20 or 30 times chasing the shadows and hiding from the sun. I think many of us do this both on a physical level and on a spiritual level: chasing shadows, hiding from the sun. I peddle my wares but mostly what I do is participate in, assist, and observe transformations. I am not alone; I am a vendor, author, workshop giver, and a speaker.

For decades I have traveled from place to place forming and forging unbreakable bonds with others just like me. We are! We are cleverly disguised as vendors, speakers, workshop leaders, authors, and singers; we are women. We teach, shape, mold, hold and guide those that follow in our footsteps. And we learn, grow and heal.

In addition to being women, we have other commonalities. We all have movement in our blood. We are compelled to travel and travel we must. Some of us may have permanent homes, and some of us never will, but all of us will continue to seek adventures, travel lands, and lift each other up. And it goes deeper even than that.

The view from a vendor's row is a clear view; we see and know almost everything, whether we share or not. We know things we don't want to know, things we shouldn't know, things we really wish we could not know, but we also see the other side. We watch young girls grow and flourish and transform into beautiful conscientious young women who will be the future leaders of our clans, of our communities and of our Country.

We live in a time where women can appreciate and lift up each other; though it isn't always done, it is getting better. We gather in fields and woods and conference rooms to stand together under the pretence of learning new skills or ideas... but that is only part of it. We are gathered to be among other like-minded women who are standing together against our oppressions. We are healing the wounds of our upbringings, of a patriarchal society that has nearly convinced us that we are not good enough, not worth enough and will never be enough. We burn ourselves out attempting to save the world, living up to the expectations we believe others have of us and we neglect self-care more frequently than not. But in these places, we stand together and KNOW we are enough. We are breaking free from the prisons of our own minds and from our generational beliefs.

I have always traveled, always moved. I either attended festivals or have been stationed or lived in nearly each State of this great America, and have left parts of me, or pieces of my soul in each. Generally the trip is a fast and furious get to the location, do the event, get back home, driving or flying straight through and not really enjoying the journey. Last fall I was invited to be a speaker at a conference in Las Vegas, Nevada at a time that I was beyond burned out; I was burned to a crisp! I was questioning whether I wanted to continue this path or find another. I think we all go through the moments of frustration and confusion, wondering whether we are actually helping anyone or if what we are doing is making a difference in the lives of others.

I made the decision to accept the speaking offer and talked a dear soul-nourishing friend, I will call Lady Di to make the drive from East Tennessee to Las Vegas with me—partly for company, partly to make sure I was brave enough to go, but also to make sure I would come back. We scheduled a few extra days on each side of the conference weekend to be able to drive slowly and enjoy the view. We stopped at every single thing that appeared even remotely interesting. Even though I had passed this route at least a dozen or more times in the past, I was focused on experiencing the journey, not just the destination.

I took time to photograph rocks and flowers and cactus that I have never really taken the time to 'see' before, things that are not common in my current beloved Appalachian mountain home. On the way there we stopped at all types of novelty shops and I posed with a huge stuffed bear in a store and played with maracas. We took back roads to admire rock formations at a closer distance than the interstate allows. We laughed and looked and laughed some more, but every once in a while when crossed a mountain pass or a city, county or state and something inside me would seize. I could 'feel' a terror or tragedy, my head or stomach would ache as though I was going to become ill. And when we passed that particular land, I was well again. Something was stirring within me that I couldn't exactly identify. We traveled on crossing into New Mexico, driving slowly along the interstate taking in the scenery. On the border to Arizona it was there again, that feeling of discord and familiarity and bordering on panic. I couldn't fully understand what I was feeling.

We arrived in Las Vegas after three days on the road overwhelmed and exhausted. There was 'something' else too, more than road trip exhaustion. I have been to conferences in Las Vegas two or three times since… since I was 19… suddenly I felt myself standing on that ground as a 19 year old.

I had just arrived in Las Vegas shortly after my 19th birthday on a greyhound bus and was alone, lost and scared. I saw a security guard standing by the parking lot gate of a casino and was instantly taken in by his easy smile, green eyes, (and broad shoulders) and I walked up to him to ask him for directions. I really didn't know what directions to ask for since I didn't have a plan or know where I was going, but I was grasping for any reason at all to talk to him. It seemed an instant connection that would become a two year whirlwind romance beginning with flowers and dinner and daydreams and ending with a two inch scar over my left eye and a child on the way. But the wound was deeper than the two inch scar; it was a wound deep in my soul. A wound that affected all my relationships after that, that left me less trusting, less compassionate, less loving and it was one that no matter how I tried to resolve it, would fester when least expected.

Snapping back to my current time frame standing in the hotel lobby with Lady Di and checking in to get our room key, I took a few deep breaths and released the memory to my Higher Power and thanked the Universe for the beautiful child I had the honor of calling my son. I thanked the gods and goddesses for the incredible man he has grown into and that—without the unfortunate portion of the experience—I would have never known the years of love for and from him. I felt a piece of my soul return to me as I did this small release and the anxiety I was feeling vanished.

Lady Di and I got checked-in and settled in our room and I slept peaceful and well, something I had been unable to do on previous Las Vegas trips.

Throughout the weekend I continued to think about the releasing experience and how much better I felt in this city than I had previously. Instead of hiding out in my hotel room the entire duration of down time, I went out with friends and saw things. I got to dance with an Elvis troupe and explore and laugh. I was mindful of my distrust…not of other people, but of my own inability to take the time for my own self-care. I let go of 'feeling stupid' by dancing in the middle of the street with whoever happened to be near me. I let go of the irrational, fractured portions of my ego that no longer served me and just had fun. The soul wound from this place had been healed, one I had carried with me for over 25 years. My soul no longer had anything in common with this place and it could no longer hurt me.

I finished the conference but was 'bumped' from my speaking position—in my mind the reason I was there. Even though I was disappointed, the Universe had a different reason for me to be there. Sometimes the Universe has bigger plans for us than we have for ourselves.

I started this piece talking about workshops, festivals and conferences and part of what we do is assist women process and move past the soul wounds of their pasts, or of their past lives, and even their ancestral lines. There is movement in this. There is movement in our blood. What if to fully resolve a soul wound or ancestral trauma we need to physically go to the location of the trauma or event to call our soul parts back; to clear our generational and historical trauma for our own selves and our tribes? With this idea coming forth in my mind more as a statement than a small still whisper, I thought I would test this idea of movement and healing on the return trip.

Leaving Las Vegas, Lady Di and I stopped at 'anything and everything' that appeared interesting. I stopped at a few locations that did not appear to have anything interesting, but I would begin to feel anxious and 'felt' it was a good spot to do a releasing. After the release, it would seem that another part of myself was stronger. We left Nevada and continued this process in Arizona on the way to Sedona. During this next step of the adventure, we gathered stones from each of the lands from each of the tribes in that state, leaving an offering in fair exchange. We hugged the Red Rocks and took paths not recognized by GPS, and each place called another soul part home. We explored caves and dodged cactus, absorbing the beauty of the land and feeling the history, but also of the Sun and of the Shadows, and loved and integrated both.

About 30 miles from Flagstaff as night was falling we saw a location that from the road looked intriguing and called to me. We turned around and went back to the exit and drove into this place, it happened to be Diablo's Canyon, Arizona and a 'ghost town' of sorts now. I walked to edge of the canyon and could hear the drums beating to the rhythm of my heart. It was too dark to see much of anything, but you could 'feel' the trauma and disrespect easing out of the ground and it filled the air. This place was called "Two Guns" and we learned later has a dark history. Over 40 Apache were burned alive in a cave here as a retaliation by the Navajo during the late 1800s and it was also used to as a tourist location in the 1920s complete with a zoo. The cave where the Apache were burned was put on display and people paid money to disrespect the memory of those gone. It was called the Apache Death Cave, later renamed the Mystery Cave and the owner sold 'Apache skulls.' The town has burned down each time efforts were made to rebuild it. It is unknown if I have had family involved in either location or the incidents of them, or even my own past lives but I do know that I was compelled to stop there and after doing the releasing another part of me came home. It would seem I had things in common from many of the physical locations I stopped at.

The next day we drove into New Mexico taking Route 66 and then side roads and back roads to each of the Tribal Nations, gathering stones and leaving offerings, leaving release processes and gathering soul parts and ended up perfectly lost taking pictures and back roads, hiking trails and searching caverns and canyons. We found ourselves at the Continental Divide at New Mexico and Colorado and spent several hours sitting on the peaks in meditation and contemplation. I had previous soul wounds and trauma related to New Mexico from my teenage years, and no matter the inner work or shadow work or releasing I had done, these wounds also seemed to fester when I was unprepared and I never could quite 'fix' it. Now sitting on the Continental Divide, it seemed possible to resolve these wounds for good. And I completed the release process for this space. In my mind I saw the trauma that my mother endured in the lands of New Mexico decades prior to this moment; I saw beyond and before her lifetime to my ancestors and hers, and maybe even our own from a previous life. I stood fast and released each event. I chased the shadows and caught them... and set them free. I looked into the Sun and did not hide.

The next day we crossed Texas and repeated the process. Once into Oklahoma, I could feel my family line and the trauma they endured. My grandfather was born on the Oklahoma Indian Territory now known as Fort Sill. It is interesting to note my son's assignment for Basic Training when he enlisted in the Army was at Fort Sill. It seems however we move or whenever we live, events will take us to the physical place of a soul wound or trauma. We stopped at a beautiful lake and I spent time releasing the historical and current trauma from my family line; from my grandfather for his reservation experiences and from my son for his military trauma. With this it is more clear that there is fluidity with trauma and it travels a time line that crosses generations both backward to past generations and forward to future generations. With each place we stopped it became a firmer thought in my mind, a thought I could feel that sometimes you must physically go to a location or a land to completely resolve the soul wound and collect your missing soul parts. To do the work required, you must have movement in your blood; you must go to those places.

I realized that even though I was 'burned out' at the beginning of the trip that my path was the right one for me, that I would continue the work that I was doing, but become more mindful of the journey and not just the destination. I also learned that I would have to prioritize self-care and not just solitude. I work with and assist women in a different way now and incorporate the releasing process in the work that I do.

Sitting here in this lawn chair under my vendor pop-up tent, I recognize I am 'this' location at 'this' time for a purpose, because whatever land I am on, either me or my ancestral line has a connection to or something in common with it. I know that each event, each location, each land that I step on, these beautiful women are with me for a reason, for a purpose. To learn, to grow, and to heal on their journeys to either continue to teach, shape, mold, hold and guide those that follow in our footsteps or become the conscientious young women that will be the future leaders of our clans, of our communities and of our Country.

I stand to move my lawn chair…chasing the shadows and hiding from the sun and think to a life-altering and beautiful moment when I stood on the peaks of the Continental Divide and place my chair halfway between both, the shadow and sun. I remember standing on the peaks and saying prayers to my ancestors knowing they would flow both directions to farthest reaches. I stood on the Continental Divide and threw my tears to the winds for a history that was never mine.

MOTOSEXUAL
Shannon McRae

Straddling you: leather tugs along my right thigh, your
warm, smooth vinyl yields under me. My fingers curl
resilience, rubber over steel. So cool now, my love, and
quiet: me wrapped around your gleaming silverblack
metal. I want to make you move under me, I want to
make you take me.

My gloved fingers slip over your controls, softly closing
around the slender hard of your clutch, stroking all the
smooth buttons that will make your lights bright for me,
your motor growl for me. Oh ferocity, I know how to
get you started.

Your sounds: so soft and sweet at first.
Solid click—one booted foot moves your sidestand—
back and up.
Thunk: gears falling together as I step on the gearshift.

I open you, so slow, so sweet, control you, throttle and
clutch. My red leather thighs closing around the shiny
smooth black of you. You purr for me, shudder, surge,

voice lowering into a low moan when I shift you. Up,
up and oh now it's you taking me now, fast, easy.

We settle into high gear, slick glide of all your power
roaring under me. My back arched, hips moving with
you, sinuous through twisties, we must be together in
this; I know if I lose you, one of us could break. It's
that delicious ambient terror, knowing how we could so
hurt each other, that keeps me so hard against you,
fingers, wrists, feet moving you and you're so fast, so
fast now, yes faster I can feel you, I can feel all of you,
all along my bones, my skin is hard metal, your tank so
soft, so soft beneath me, shuddering the same,
shattering into speed, into sound and I can hear you
howling now, how fast are we going, the road is hissing,
we're all wind, all sound, we're nowhere at all but this
motion, and it is you riding me now, and then I do not
think at all, and low,
low in my throat, I'm laughing.

And we never have to stop. We could go on like this
all day. And we will, my roaring brightness, my danger,
my delight—you know we will.

TRAINS OF THOUGHT
Shannon McRae

Last time I read Jack Kerouac's *The Dharma Bums*, I was 16. I forgot exactly how I happened onto it then. I think it's because I'd just read Richard Brautigan's *In Watermelon Sugar*, was craving similar, and got a recommendation. I had forgotten all this time, until picking it up again as a woman now over half a century old, the worlds this book opened up for me. Kerouac's version of Zen never really took with my young pagan self—too much attachment, too much aggression in the search for detachment and peace. And I was troubled, even then, by the secondary status of female characters—even as I was wildly identifying with the male protagonists. For weeks afterwards, I kept asking everybody I thought might know how—older college kids and the cooler adults in the vicinity—how to hop freight trains.

It was a physical longing, that wanting to smell the steel, be inside the vanishing point of rails on the horizon, go wherever they took me. And physical anguish when remarkably patient adults explained to me exactly what this kind of life would be, for a girl—what it would mean, what it would cost, and given how very sheltered I was, how unlikely I was to even survive.

It's that bone-deep, heart-deep feeling of possibility lost that came back to me—hard—on rereading. That loss folded into rage long unvoiced, that the careless adventures that seemingly defined the type of mid-century masculinity Kerouac's many fans—those older, cooler kids—taught me to idolize when I was young were not only not an option for most women, but often adventures had at their expense.

I've spent a lifetime traveling anyway, how and when and where I can—hitchhiking across Europe, crisscrossing most of the west coast alone on my motorcycle, solo camping on beaches and parking lots in my van. Nobody has ever walked up to me and called me a *bodhisattva* for it. More than a few strangers have asked me how I dared, but nobody has ever given me a hard time either.

But I still mourn and rage for a whole generation of Beat women who died early and young, who were written out of the stories or got stuck with the bills and the babies, and feel (as I rarely feel) outrage at feminine constraint.

But then, there is my mother. "Hey mom, do you remember when I was a teenager and always wanted to hop trains?" I asked her this morning, frying up the bacon and eggs for breakfast.

"Oh, I used to do that," my mom said, buttering the toast.

RECORD. SCRATCH.

My mother did not have a secret career as Boxcar Bertha. As it turns out though, my very well brought-up young mom and young sister or two used to hang out all the time along the siding near the Oldsmobile plant in Lansing, when they were 10 or 8 or so, in the 1940s. And they'd hop onto the open car-carrier train cars, take a little ride, and hop off. And they'd go home, and their incredibly regal, incredibly proper Irish-Catholic mother, my indomitable grandmother would say, "I hope you girls weren't playing on the train tracks again."

One of my mother's favorite things, to this day, is the echo of the train whistle across the river—the southbound train, heading for Chicago. Every time she hears it, she stops to listen and she smiles and says, "I love that sound."

And like that, my sorrow and rage fades away like the last doppler echo of the train. As it turns out, it is possible to be both nearly as adventurous as one wants to be and as ladylike as one wishes. The best part of all is that negotiating the raging egos and Paleolithic gender attitudes of drunken old-guy Beats is absolutely not required.

Some books, maybe a handful, stay with you your whole life long. I'm so glad that this one stayed with me, even after I thought I'd left it behind. It opened up to me all the roads I've ever traveled, and all the ones still waiting to surprise me. And if I'd never taught it, and remembered, I might never have known that all this time it was my mother I've been following down all these paths that women walk, joyously and in secret.

FIVE DAYS IN SYDNEY: REMEMBERING JUDY GARLAND
Joan Coulson

In February 2012, I had the opportunity to visit my friend Cathy who lives in New Zealand. Many years ago I met Cathy, a New Zealand nurse, in an English Public House in Santa Clara Valley (now known as Silicon Valley) while she was "working her way around the world." Being an anthropologist whose ambition was to wander the world and talk to strange and different people, I was immediately captivated by this young woman who was doing exactly what I had wanted to do many years ago. She was looking for somewhere to live for a few months and as I had a big five-bedroom house, I invited her to join my two teen-aged children and me. She stayed with us for about a year before continuing her wanderings. Her birthday was one day after mine and our Gemini spirits were in tune. She returned to New Zealand, married and had three children, but we kept in touch.

Suddenly here was the opportunity to visit Cathy, renew my friendship with her parents, and meet her children, so I was going. But I asked, can we manage to have a few days in Australia? Cathy thought that was a wonderful idea having been there years before. Her fifteen-year old daughter Chelsea was very excited for this adventure. We plan for five days in Sydney.

Australia is a continent in the southern hemisphere surrounded by the Indian and Pacific oceans. When I was about eight years old and living in England, I spent a year in a geography class studying Australia. I remember at the end of the year I could draw the outline of the coast freehand and could highlight all the different important areas like the Great Barrier Reef, which lies off the northeast coast and extends over 1,240 miles. The whole continent has 21,262 miles of coastline and is the whole size is 3,146,060 square miles. Its size gives it a wide variety of landscapes, some tropical rainforests in the northeast, then mountain ranges in the southeast, southwest, and dry desert in the center. It has the oldest and least fertile soils and semi-arid land known as the Outback—the largest portion of land. This is where the where the earliest settlers lived. These earliest people probably came by way of the sea from southern Asia around 42,000 – 48,000 years ago, and these indigenous people, called Aborigines, lived as 'hunters and gatherers.' This is one of the first terms one learns when beginning to study anthropology: and it is important because 99% of the time that humans as a species, have been on earth, they have been 'hunters and gatherers.' The other 1% is the time of recorded history of man; this is all we are aware of, so to understand the life of a hunter and gatherer is important, because this is our history.

Well, these hunters and gatherers, which divided into approximately 250 groups and spoke different languages, had the entire land mass to themselves for a very long time, but in 1606, a Dutch expeditionary force encountered it. This was a time of great exploration by many of the seafaring countries of Europe: Spain, Great Britain, and Portugal were wandering around the world invading new lands and looking for raw materials for trade to add to the wealth of their countries. In 1770, Great Britain claimed the eastern half of the continent, and starting in January 1788, sent many people in the prison system to form a colony in New South Wales. From then on there was a constant movement of people from and to Australia, and by 1850, most of the country had been invaded and settled, and five self-governing colonies had been established. By 1901, six colonies were federated and formed the Commonwealth of Australia. Now Australia has the world's 13th largest economy, ranks high in the quality of life, health, education, civil liberties and political rights, and has a population of 24 million. In the early 1950s, there was an effort by the government to bring more people into Australia from other parts of Europe and the world and now the population is quite diverse with lots of interesting restaurants with no tipping allowed. Of this population, Australia has the 9th largest number of people born overseas. Most of the population lives in the big cities situated on coastal areas, such as Sydney, Brisbane, Melbourne, Perth and Adelaide, but the capital Canberra is inland.

In the 1970s, my daughter spent her year at an English school on the geography of New Zealand. I wonder if these studies continue at this time. Certainly the young people in England are still fascinated with these countries 'down under' and many of my friends and relatives have young relatives immigrating and starting new lives there. After the end of World War II, many hundreds and thousands of British people immigrated to Australia and New Zealand for a new life. At that time, the journey took six weeks by sea and the great distance meant that often families would never see each other again. Now this has all changed with the convenience of air travel and Australia has become the sixth largest country in the world and has the 13th largest economy in the world.

My secondary reason for wanting to visit Sydney was to be in city where Judy Garland had one of her famous concerts. I was a fan of Judy from childhood and followed her career all over the world. She had a wildly successful concert in Sydney in 1964, so I wanted to visit the city where the audiences had been so appreciative of her talents.

The following is an extract from my book *Always for Judy: Witness to the Joy and Genius of Judy Garland*:

Judy's television series had ended and she planned shows in Australia. On May 11 1964 Judy and Mark Herron, her companion, arrived in Sydney along with conductor, Mort Lindsey and others. There was a large press reception at the airport and Judy seemed relaxed and happy. In the evening, she gave a press reception at the Hilton Hotel for about forty reporters, including interviews for radio and television. On Wednesday, May 13th she gave a successful concert for 10,000 people at the Sydney Stadium and on May 16th she gave an even more successful concert; performing for more than 90 minutes singing about 23-24 songs including 'The Man That Got Away', 'Swanee', 'When You're Smiling' and 'As Long as He Needs Me'. It is reported that the immigration people confiscated Judy's medicine. Medicine stays in the body for a few days and Judy was fine during the Sydney concerts but she had not been able to obtain her regular medicine, probably Ritalin, in Australia. Judy went by train to Melbourne on May 19th which was probably a mistake, and she arrived exhausted. She attempted to give a concert the next day, but it was not a success because she was unwell, although she managed to get through fifteen songs.

The Melbourne Sunday Herald reported on May 20, 1964 how kindly the staff at the hotel thought of her, so the trip to Melbourne was not all bad. They presented her with a toy koala bear and card signed from maids to manager, saying, "A very small Australian mascot, but a lot of good wishes." They found her quiet, polite and agreeable, and when she left she told assistant supervisor, Mr. Clarry Crew, "I really appreciate what everyone has done for me. I think you've all been wonderful. I've never had service like it anywhere in the world." These comments are important because they show how charming Judy was when she was treated with kindness. (197-199)

As I had lived and worked in many of the places where Judy performed, I felt I needed to be in Sydney and understand the city and people who gave her such a great welcome. I know you cannot understand a people until you are actually on the ground in their city. Sydney is the largest Australian city, established in 1788. One can tell a great city by its buildings, museums and infrastructure and Sydney fulfils all these expectations.

When Judy performed in Sydney the majority of the people would have been British. These were the same people who had greeted her in London in 1951, 1957 and 1960, the same people who had loved her in the MGM musicals and listened to her recordings through the years. No wonder her concerts were so successful. Then there is Melbourne. There has always been animosity between the two cities, particularly on the part of Melbourne. I caught an example of this attitude at Sydney airport on my way home. I was waiting with a lady who had flown up from Melbourne, and when I asked about her town, she said, "Oh I love it! Such a beautiful civilized city, so cultured, not like Sydney," which she dismissed as being rough and uncouth. This might help to explain why the people of Melbourne did not welcome Judy with open arms the way Sydney did. If Sydney liked her, they would not. However, the main entry point into Australia was Sydney in 1964, as it is now, and so it was logical for the first concerts to be there.

So finally, I was in Australia with Cathy and her daughter, Chelsea. Immigration officials were smiling and friendly. We must have seemed an unlikely trio.

Cathy and Chelsea have passports from New Zealand, I have a U.S. passport, but I am obviously English. Cathy and I have pale skin and blonde hair and look related, but Chelsea is exotic with dark, dark hair and a very pale complexion. Somehow, we do not have the correct entry forms and rush to try to fill them in while standing in front of the immigration officer. Now, I have gone through many immigration checkpoints and the officials are usually very formal and impersonal. This man was very tolerant of our confusion. It was as much as he could do not to laugh aloud at our antics.

We spent the next few days exploring the exciting city with a bus and ferry pass from our hotel at Potts Point and Kings Cross Station (all stations, trains and buses are clean and well run). My first impression as we leave Kings Cross Station is that it reminded me of New York with beautiful trees everywhere; later I revise this to San Francisco when I see all the many beautiful bays.

We had a nice clean room with two double beds and a small kitchen stocked with tea, coffee and milk. We quickly take off with our bus passes to explore. The 311 bus goes past our hotel and we catch a bus; where to, who knows? Chelsea has eagle eyes and spies the Circular Quay and we get off and catch the first ferry we see, which is going to Darling Harbor.

I am sure that if we had been on an organized tour we would have discovered the highlights of the city quicker, but I wanted to savor the place and try to understand the people. Our bus rides in the next few days took us all over the city, through the beautiful Royal Botanic Gardens once or twice a day. We rode the ferryboats and talked to people; or at least I did. Towards the end of our few days, when I had asked an old lady about the walker she used and tried it out, Chelsea commented, "you really do like to talk to people!" People interest me and so no one is a stranger; one can learn so much from people. One such woman talked to me for half an hour on a bus one day and I learned so much about the city. She came from Chile and was half-Spanish and half Irish; with no Indian blood, she insisted with a smile.

Another day we made our way by bus to Haymarket as Chelsea wanted to shop—well, me too. I can always shop. We planned to meet in 90 minutes. I find a backpack on wheels to replace my old one, determined to travel with only this bag in the future. At the end of 90 minutes, I am completely lost and realize there are several entrances to this market and I have no idea which was our entrance. Luckily, I had taken some photographs on the way down and someone identified our entrance. Chelsea had bought some food. Cathy wanted to find her nursing friend who she had not seen for twenty years, but remembered that she has a dress shop on Williams Street in the Paddington area. This is a very old area of the original city and at one time was depressed, but recently has become very fashionable with haute couture dress shops. I insist that we take a taxi because to navigate the city of Sydney as inexperienced as we are will take too long. I am glad because I always like talking to taxi drivers. Sydney taxi drivers, rather like London taxi drivers, have to be natives to navigate the haphazard streets, which go off at peculiar angles with no rhyme or reason and obviously no overall plan. I commented on this and the taxi driver explained that we were following the paths of the old carriage roads when travel was by horse and buggy (the new immigrants are bus drivers). He tells me that the trees were planted in 2000 for the Olympic Games. The trees are beautiful and line every main street and many side streets; consequently there is shade everywhere and one can walk without sunglasses. The taxi driver found Williams Road and put us down literally outside the shop of Cathy's friend. There was a joyful reunion with Ruth. We arranged to meet the next evening. Ruth had given up nursing a few years ago and took a clothing design course and obtained a four-year degree. She was in the haute couture business, which meant she designed and hand-made clothes for special customers, many of her dresses costing over $3,000 each. I was unfamiliar with this world.

We walked up to the high street and saw a bus to Watson Bay. "Let's go to the beach," I suggested. It was a lovely long ride through so many different neighborhoods. We found ourselves at this pleasant area overlooking a beach and small harbor. We discovered an ice cream shop and talked to a couple from England visiting their children. The place was full of grandparents visiting their children. We find there was a ferryboat going back to the Circular Quay. As always, Chelsea was the leader. At some point I turned to Cathy and said, "When was this child born?" "August," she says. Of course, she is a Leo. I should have known. Leos are born leaders. We ate at the Circular Quay. I get a large sausage roll for $4, which is a complete meal in itself.

There was a Picasso exhibition at the Art Gallery of New South Wales and of course, we go. It takes a big city with forethought to bring such an exhibition from the Musée national Picasso-Paris. The exhibition ran from November to the following March. Chelsea led the way again from the bus, and we walked near the beautiful Cathedral, which we had passed so many times, and up the tree-lined pathway to the Museum. The exhibition was excellent and we had lunch in the museum cafe.

We found our way by bus back to Williams Street in charming Paddington, which so reminded me of New Orleans with its balconies. I met two delightful Greek ladies who had been in Australia for over forty years. One of them has a junk store set amongst the other fancy shops. When Ruth finished with a client, we went down to a local pub and Chelsea and I enjoyed listening to these two nurses reminisce about their training days. They had both worked with elderly patients and very strangely, Ruth turned to me at one point and started telling me this story about a patient on Ritalin. She knew nothing about my interest in Judy and her drug problems. She told me that this poor lady had locked her medicine up for protection. She lost the key and could not get into the box. In her desperation for the drug, she went completely mad and set herself on fire. Ruth said it was ghastly and she considered Ritalin the most addictive and most awful drug on the market. I thought of poor Judy.

On our final day, we took off for Taronga Zoo, situated on 74 acres which one gets to by ferryboat. Most of the animals are in enclosures surrounded by moats with plenty of room to roam about in natural surroundings. We saw marsupials, including the kangaroo, koala, wombat and birds such as emu and kookaburra set in surroundings with many eucalyptus trees. I was particularly impressed with the chimpanzees' enclosure and I am sure Jane Goodall must love it.

The ferryboat landed us back at Circular Quay, and we were loathe to leave. I got a sausage roll to eat again, and we enjoyed the atmosphere. Cathy and Chelsea walked down to The Rocks where they could see the original houses of first settlers. I sat and chatted with a lady who lived inland and was just finishing a cruise, learning much more about life in Sydney and Australia. We wandered over to the other side of the Quay. Chelsea and Cathy talked with a Silver Man while I walked down the shops looking for some Wiggles toys for my grandson. Instead of Wiggles, I found a shop selling opals and of course I am in Australia and I must buy a necklace for myself. I am so charmed by this city that I think I will frame a map so I can plan my next visit.

JOURNAL OF DRIVE THERAPY
Clara Vann-Patterson

I found myself in Seattle, in a ramshackle mother-in-law's cottage called an Airbnb. A few weeks earlier in North Carolina I left a job I hated. At 52 years young I'd decided I would test the Einstein inspired meme "life is like a bicycle, to keep your balance you have to keep moving." A longtime friend invited me to ride along with her on a road trip to her home in Washington state and I packed my dog and my suitcase for a cross country jaunt. I thought I would be staying at her apartment when we arrived, but we were in Kansas when she found out she would have to move from her apartment as soon as she returned.

The 10'x20' Airbnb shed with European bathroom, electricity, a microwave, electric tea pot and a coffee press was cute for about two days. It only had one bed and a tiny old tube TV/VHS player and no Wi-Fi. It was not a pleasing situation for either of us, but we are still friends and we managed to tolerate each other and the situation without it being the end of the road for our relationship. From my perspective, that in itself was miraculous.

After ten days in the Airbnb I helped her move her

belongings to a new apartment. My plan to fly back home changed when Anna told me she would sell me her car for a good price if I wanted to drive back. She knew I had concerns about my dog George if we flew, I pondered that option and after some contemplation I decided to buy the station wagon.

Car camping would help keep the cost down and I began gathering materials to make a bed in the back of the wagon. After all, I needed to maintain the budget that supports my latest pledge of autonomy and freedom. Granted, buying the car was cutting into the budget but it also opened the opportunity to drive cross country and see areas that I had never been. Travel is a bucket list activity that has become more relevant since my mother's passing a decade ago.

Mom never had the opportunity to travel. She worked in a factory to support us and spent her vacation time working at home and in the garden—canning and preserving vegetables and such. She wanted to travel, but my father, who was a trucker in those days, did not agree. She wouldn't venture out on her own with us kids. It was one of her death bed regrets that she did not travel more.

"There's all those places I haven't seen." Her voice faint and cracking, with oxygen tubes in her nose, I listened to the beeping of machines as her eyes drifted across the room to gaze at the wall. Perhaps she imagined the places she'd wanted to go but had never been. It resonated with me and made me more aware of my mortality—the things I want to do and the places I want to see before my life is over.

When we completed moving Anna's things we celebrated at the Airbnb that evening with a fire, marshmallows, beer and cannabis products. Recreational use is legal there and the Airbnb was agreeable. The fire was quite magical and Anna was higher than I'd ever seen her. We were having fun and I commented that it seemed we should be saying hello not goodbye. We both grew quiet for a while and watched the flames consuming the logs. As the fire died down Anna said she had never noticed the little cities inside the embers.

The next day I took I-90 East across the jaw-drop gorgeous Stuart Range, rolling down the progression of the landscape, from mountains, to buttes, to flat lands and into Spokane. In Spokane, I tested my car camping idea. It was about 11:15 pm when I scouted a 24-hour Walmart and discovered that there were 2 RVs parked overnight. I surveyed the parking lot and then went into the store to buy a $2.98 prepackaged salad for dinner. I ate it in the car with George who I gave the bacon pieces from the salad since he refused to eat his own food. I didn't worry since he drank quite a bit of water.

I moved the car and parked in a spot that was well lit. I backed up to the light post so that most of the light would be at the back of the vehicle. The back windows were tinted and would help obscure the view of me sleeping in the back. I also used a seat cushion and small rug sample as block outs for the rear windows – they fit perfectly! My bed was a yoga mat, a cushion from an outdoor chaise I bought for $5 from the Airbnb hostess, and a folded mattress topper all layered to make a bed. I put a fitted sheet around it and then a flat sheet on top, and added pillows. I had managed to make a bed in the back of a station wagon. Now to test it.

I got out and surveyed the surroundings for a moment and decided that I would make the driver's side of the car the entry and exit door, and considered what I would need to do if during the night someone tried to mess with the car (and me). I didn't carry a gun and even if I did it would probably get me into more trouble than it would get me out of. I made sure there was nothing in the driver's seat and that the passenger seat was positioned so I could get into the driver's seat without having to get out of the car. Just in case.

I opened the back door and slid in, stretched my legs out in front of me toward the back of the wagon and wiggled down to get situated. It took several minutes of shifting things around to determine how I was going to sleep. I put up enough baggage/items to block any view of me from the front of the vehicle.

It was about 58 degrees outside and the back windows were down about an inch. The sounds of the parking lot were annoying and eventually I reached for the Benadryl and Melatonin. George was laying to the left of my feet and he made a huffing sigh of disappointment over the accommodations. When I turned over I had to be careful not to kick him. I was grinning as I realized that the bed was more comfortable than the one I had been sleeping in for two weeks. It was snug, but whether it would really serve the purpose for sleep was yet to be determined.

Around 1:30 am a quiet calm settled over the parking lot and I woke the next morning around 7:30 am with the sun streaming in, birds singing, a breeze drifting through, and cottonwood seeds floating about. I survived my first night of sleeping in the car. I felt better upon waking that morning than I did after the last camping trip a few years back. Sleeping on the ground always made my body hurt. This was tolerable. I saved at least $75 and that made it even more tolerable.

After lying there scrolling through Facebook, Google maps, and things to do in Spokane, I rolled out of the wagon through the driver's side back door, instructed my feet to find the ground (they did) and stood and stretched. The parking lot was still relatively quiet as I put a leash on George, staggered a bit as I walked about and he performed his usual morning ritual. I responsibly removed the poo from the ground and walked to a trash can across the parking lot to throw it away, then trotted back to the car then up and down the sidewalk to shake out the stiffness. I opened the driver's side door and George jumped in and took his copilot seat. I went into Walmart to use the facilities, returned to the car, and readied for takeoff.

We went to Manito Park where I found a picnic table and gave George his breakfast and put together a peanut butter and banana sandwich with a zero calorie Lemonade drink from the cooler. We ventured into the grassy area at the front of the greenish body of water and I threw the tennis ball, gradually moving along with him to the other side of the park as we played fetch. I had to leash him as other people with dogs passed by and soon we came to a Japanese garden. It was a little reminder of my son in Japan. I took pictures and sent them to him. He responded promptly and expressed that he was bored. I held him close in my heart and imagined him remedying his boredom by going outside and exploring.

I led George back to the car in a sauntering, zig zag fashion across the rocky hill that was between us and the parking lot, then we were off again. Before leaving the city, I visited a couple of cannabis shops, talked vaporizers with a skateboard fellow (who couldn't be over 21), and with a magnifying glass inspected some flowers, delighting over the colorful strains with little sparkling crystals protruding from the buds. It was time to move on and I turned onto Canyon Street and went into an immediate descent that felt like a freefall into the little canyon and at the bottom was a stop sign. George looked at me with worried eyes and I laughed at how surprised we both were. As I drove out of the city I passed exits for Thor and Freya Streets and just had to smile.

White lines flew by fast as I made a B line for a cheap motel in Missoula MT. I discovered that the bed was less comfortable than the bed I had made in the back of the car, but at least there was a shower and Wi-Fi. I didn't sleep well that night and the next day I was fatigued and depressed. What the hell am I doing? I asked myself. Certainly, it seemed that Kulshan (Mt. Baker), the San Juan Islands, Puget Sound and everything I had experienced during the east to west trip was enough for one ramble.

Why did I want to buy this car and drive back?

I could have flown, still have that money in the bank and be in my own bed resting. I had never traveled outside the southeast and had never really travelled much at all. This was not an ideal trip but I would at least get to lay eyes on some of America, right? My only way home was the road and I would be choosing the roads I took and stopping where I wanted. With the budget that governs my freedom in mind I'd be sleeping in the station wagon again tonight.

Yet I didn't feel pushed to return home. I felt quite removed from the loneliness and exhaustion when I assumed the role of the observer. I suspect it was an accurate view of myself as being alone and isolated, but capable of building bridges to the resources that I needed. Those resources being other people. I typically distance myself from others to protect myself. I'd learned early on in life that it was safer that way, but now it seemed I needed to reconsider my position on that. I observed my uninspired self still moving about from one point on the map to another with no intention other than witnessing Mother Nature's creations and workings. I was in search of inspiration.

When I left Missoula, I texted the Facebook friend I had never met who was also on a cross country trip but going the other direction. We coordinated and met at a Wendy's in Bozeman and I posed with George and her for a picture. Billie asked me where I was off to next and I answered with some tinge of embarrassment that I wasn't sure. I loved the Salt Lake area on the 1st leg of the trip, but was thinking about Yellowstone since I had never been. She encouraged the Yellowstone option and we parted ways. She and her travelling companion went into Wendy's as George and I headed east again.

I took the Livingston exit towards Yellowstone and at 4:30 pm George and I were at the entrance booth and I paid $30 to ride into the park. I stopped at the

Mammoth Hot Springs Visitor Center and I read part of the pamphlet I was given. Dogs are not allowed in the backcountry, on boardwalks or on trails more than a hundred feet from the road. I was not pleased, as what I could do at Yellowstone was just scrapped. I decided that I would go directly to the sites it is known for, the Geysers and Old Faithful. There was no cell signal throughout most of the area. Nevertheless, I felt the connection between my eyes and my soul as I drove south in a state of amazement: neither pictures nor descriptions can do it justice.

I stopped to take some pictures with my cell phone and walked George farther than he was technically allowed to go. We encountered a dying bison at a corner of the geyser field. It was lying on the ground with its head up. Labored breathing, a dull glaze over the surface of its eyes, along with the smell of decay confirmed the animal's state. It held its head up straight and made a snort when it saw George, who did not bark, but perked his ears up and then relaxed them as he seemed to realize that the creature was disabled. Mother nature was at work in myriad ways; I could feel the earth vibrating beneath my feet. The boiling, rumbling, spewing and hissing of the geysers churned on.

It was about 8 pm when I began to look for a parking area near the Old Faithful Inn. It was then that I read that no overnight parking was allowed. I had been driving inside the park for hours and had not considered that I wouldn't have anywhere to sleep. I went into the souvenir store and asked the men at the counter what my options were and they recommended calling the campgrounds to see if they had space.

I went back to the car and called information to get the numbers and learned that the offices for the campgrounds were closed now. The young man on the line suggested I drive about 45 minutes to a town outside the park called West Yellowstone. The only room at a hotel inside the park was still an hour drive away and would cost about $300.

I drove to West Yellowstone and discovered that the rooms were still very expensive and it was already 11 pm and there weren't any places to park overnight either. I felt the budget quiver when I thought about spending $240 for a room at that time of night. I decided that Bozeman from whence I had departed only a few hours earlier would be my next logical stop. It was an hour and forty-five minutes up Hwy 191, a two lane where the bison crossing warnings are posted the entire length of the road and the speed limit is 55 at night. I read a sign as I left West Yellowstone that stated ten bison were hit on the Highway in 2016. Trees lined the road and hovered over the roadway as if to block out any light that might splinter through. I had wanted to spend at least two days at Yellowstone. The tentative plan unraveled again. Damn.

White lines, reflectors and darkness: that was the drive.

When I rolled into the Bozeman 24-hour Walmart at about one am there was a lot of activity. At the furthest point from the front entrance there were at least four RV campers and a couple of cars that appeared to be inhabited. I got out, stretched, staggered and walked George around a grassy area. I put him in the car and went in as if I were performing a routine: facilities, food and stretching. Afterwards I got into the back of the wagon, blocked off the windows and settled in. It was after 2 am when I took Benadryl and chugged a Kulshan Brewery beer.

The next morning, I woke up before 8 am to the sound of car doors slamming and the hum of traffic. The sunlight burned my eyes as they painfully rolled inside their sockets and the assumed culprits - cottonwood seeds, were floating like parachutes everywhere. It was quickly heating up and I debated on whether to go back to Yellowstone. George was the discouraging element of that consideration.

So, the next stop was the Black Hills of South Dakota. On the way out of town I dropped by a McDonald's drive through for a small black coffee and a large sweet tea for the road. Leaving Bozeman, I sipped my coffee and in the rearview mirror the Crazy Mountains cast an irritating, blinding light.

I had to adjust the side and center rearview mirrors repeatedly for several miles so that the light reflecting off the snow draped mountains didn't shine directly into my eyes. I had a strange feeling in the pit of my stomach and my head ached. In my mind, I saw the goddess Kali standing on Shiva's chest with her razing sword of knowledge flashing. I pulled over and staggered out of the car to take a picture of the snow-covered mountain range that was irking me all the way down I 90 East. As I got back into the car I could see glowing imprints of the snow reflections floating in front of my eyes... Crazy Mountains indeed. Crazy me.

Billings was a few miles ahead and as the white lines flew by I began to ponder the symbolism of Kali. It was a bit disconcerting but at the same time there was a feeling of empowerment. Severing the past away, along with the ego, bestowing divine knowledge and acceptance, destruction, creation: It was a compelling vision to have with the sun reflecting from a snowy mountain range into a rearview mirror and into my aching allergy eyes.

I shifted my attention to the communities that I passed. All along the highways of my adventure there were divisions. Communities divided by the type of dwellings that they were composed of: trailer parks, then parks with newer, larger trailers and then modular house communities, gated communities with large homes, real stick-built house neighborhoods and then the isolate ranchers and rural small farms.

Sometimes I would see a lone single-wide trailer with a few healthy-looking horses fenced in around it. I was ushered out of Billings by several miles of little humps on I 90, east of town; they made me feel as if I was hopping like a rabbit down to the prairies and grasslands. It was the first belly laugh I'd had since leaving Seattle. I felt optimistic that the road would lead me to more amazing, memorable places.

I stayed in another cheap motel in Deadwood, South Dakota. It was clean, a place to rest and my emotional state was not good. I was restored somewhat by a walk down the strip with George shortly before dark. I people watched, stopped and read signs, and observed the little town that Wild Bill Hickock had been shot and buried in. The phrase tourist trap came to mind.

George received his usual recognition from the tourists and I slipped off to the side at the end of the leash as he charmed the attentive folks in Deadwood. His tail whipped back and forth at a relaxed tempo and he seemed to smile at people who spoke to him like a baby. I replied to inquiries if needed, usually it was breed information. Walking further I noticed a school house sitting to my right, just a few steps up from the street. The sign said "Lead-Deadwood Elementary School" and I pronounced it as 'Led' rather than 'Leed.' I laughed to myself and took a picture.

We crossed the street to the small park in the center of the town and we encountered two girls about 10 years of age who rode their bikes to the little playground next to the main area we were in. What a cute little dog! One of the girls exclaimed as they zipped past on their bikes. They got off their bikes and walked over to the swings and sat down as they talked. A few minutes later I glanced over at them as I was playing fetch with George and saw them moving about. They appeared to be casting a circle, calling quarters and made animated gestures. I couldn't understand what they were saying, but it was quite theatric.

Wow. Maybe there is hope!

When I got back to the motel I attempted to write a few notes about the day, it was some depression fueled compost that had to be shoveled, I suppose. I enjoyed a long warm bath but found falling asleep difficult no matter how tired I was. The next morning, I managed to get out of the motel no later than 11 am. The sun was shining, it was a beautiful day and I noticed the rear drivers side tire was almost flat. I inquired about tire repair as I left the motel. I followed the verbal directions and went to Central City just a couple of miles up the road to a family-owned tire shop. There were three objects that had punctured the tire. A screw, a nail and a large staple. It was fixed for $22 and I was grateful for the affordable fix and that I had noticed the low tire. It would have been a flat tire on the interstate, miles from anywhere.

I drove north on 85 headed through Spearfish Canyon, a great American biker's route that's near Sturgis. There were evergreens and rock cliffs with Spearfish Creek running through it. We got on I 90 once again and we were on our way to the Badlands National Park, but not before driving by Mount Rushmore and the Crazy Horse Memorial. It was $10 to park at Rushmore and $11 to enter Crazy Horse but I didn't really want to spend much time looking at manmade attractions. Mother Nature was my muse. I took some dashboard photos as I drove by and decided that was sufficient.

I noted that the white man's monument was immaculate while the one for Crazy Horse was incomplete. I read the pamphlet that stated no federal money was used to build the Crazy Horse memorial. Donations were needed to complete the memorial and all was appreciated. I got back on route and soon there were Wall Drug billboards "as seen on CMT." At 5:30 pm, George and I were sitting at the Badlands entrance and I was asking questions.

It will be the best $20 you ever spent. The park is open 24 hours. The attendant said as I debated whether to enter another park after 5 pm. I handed her a twenty and received my pamphlet with the receipt stapled to it. She was right, it was the best $20 I ever spent. I took a lot of pictures and took a good one of a goat that jumped up to the overlook. I sent it via messenger to handful of people I feel some sort of connection to. Why? I am not sure. Perhaps it's validation that this Appalachian mountain goat (me) is still alive and exploring the extraordinary ways life is expressed on this planet. I could not keep it to myself. My reserve escaped me for a moment as I stopped and felt gratitude for the experience I was having. I wished I could share it, so I tried to with a picture.

I left the park earlier than I wanted for fear of not getting back to the campground in Wall before their office closed. I didn't want to repeat the mistakes of the previous national park experience. It was quiet, with Wi-Fi, showers and a laundry room. It cost $15—a fraction of what a motel or Airbnb would and I could play fetch with George only a few steps away from the car. The train tracks were close and I cannot explain how that was not an issue. I was still excited by the experience of bison herds crossing the road, prairie dog towns, and wild goats jumping on rock pyres in front of me. Did I mention the rock formations?

The next morning, I showered, utilized the laundry room and washed and dried everything I could fit in the washer except what I was wearing then after lunch went scouting. The temperature rose to 93 degrees so I drove more than I walked. There were moments I felt sick, it came over me when walking and exploring the Badlands. I was dizzy and near faint at times as George and I ascended the jagged stone formations and mounds. I felt as though I were still riding in the car.

George jumped over the lips of the rock passages without looking where it led and I realized after approaching one ahead of him that the drop from the openings could range from no change in the elevation of the next step to a drop of about a hundred or more feet down into a cavernous floor that looked like a valley of jagged spires. George was trotting along behind me and as we approached another stone opening and I shouted at him to stop. I was so dizzy I was afraid to stand at the threshold to block his path. He slowed and trotted past me but didn't stop, I shouted again, lunged forward, grabbed his collar before he could pass and attached the leash. I stood and peeped over the edge and indeed it was a disaster averted.

At about 9:30 pm I rolled back into the campground and parked in my spot. A man with a wife and two small children were camped right next to my mine where there wasn't anyone the night before. His expression went from smiling and relaxed to horrified when I parked the wagon next to them. His eyes fixed on me even before I got out of the car as if he expected a murderer or a kidnapper. George jumped out after me and I leashed him. I said hello to the man and proceeded to set up my bedroom for the evening. He just looked at me suspiciously and continued what he was doing.

The following morning, I needed to decide where I was headed.

Where am I going now? Do I want to go home yet? The fatigue was making it harder to enjoy the trip and the heat was oppressive. I left the campground still debating on the route I was taking. Minneapolis rolled off my tongue, I liked the sound of it and entered it as destination in Google maps.

White lines were coming up fast as we drove past beautiful prairies and grasslands; cattle sprinkled across the browning pastures and gathered in the green grass around watering holes. Each pond appeared as an oasis, with the wind blowing the surface, making little waves across the entire pool of dark blue water. Sky with perfect clouds casting moving shadows on the slightly rolling hills of the Minnesota grasslands.

I passed a billboard identifying the area as the home

of Laura Ingalls Wilder. My thoughts went to Little House on the Prairie and how my mother loved to read about life growing up on the prairie; I had enjoyed those same books too. I decided it wasn't a stop and went on to Mankato and paused roadside to book an Airbnb in Minneapolis.

Once in Minneapolis I found a parking spot just across the street from my room. I went to the front door and found a week old notice from the Minnesota DOC folded and stuffed into the crack of the door about a level 3 predatory offender living nearby. I checked the directions and the official Airbnb entrance was the side door. I guess no one ever goes through the front door.

The Airbnb was nice enough, but the bathroom was shared, unlike the listing stated. I messaged the owner and asked if it was safe to walk the dog on the Greenway after dark and he promptly answered that it was safe to stay near the hospital. I walked George in midtown Minneapolis that evening and my shirt was soaked in sweat within twenty minutes. On our walk, I noticed plenty of hijabs hiding women's faces, bendy buses, hipsters, and a dark-skinned woman appeared intoxicated seemed to bounce from the window sill she was sitting on and rolled her hips suggestively and said, "Hello sweetheart, you are soooo pretty!"

I don't think prostitutes are allowed at the Airbnb, I remarked silently to myself as George and I ignored her and continued swiftly down the sidewalk. Perhaps she wasn't a sex worker but to a country bumpkin like me it seemed a likely assumption. I thought about what it must be like to pay someone for sexual acts. How the one paying is just as vulnerable as the person performing the acts. Ten seconds later I started to think that the 2-block radius is a little farther from the hospital than I wanted be.

On the way back I noticed there was a tree next to the hospital that had grown between the sidewalk and the street. It had yellow tape tied around it and an orange X spray painted on. The tree looked like it had arms and it sprawled out as if in a (perpetual) dancing pose over the street. I touched the tree and closed my eyes; I felt the undeveloped roots cramped at the base and then a few lifegiving roots shot deep into the crannies far below the sidewalk to pull water and nutrients up to the trunk. The forty-foot-tall tree was robust and thriving despite its limited access to soil and water. Mother Nature often surprises us with such outliers. I felt a moment of sadness about the future of the tree.

The Airbnb was an old 2 story house built in the early 1900's. The place was stuffy and hot, but the box fan was there for that reason. I took the melted freezer packs out of the cooler and put them in the kitchen freezer and put the last two beers I bought in Washington in the fridge for later. After showering I sat cross-legged on the bed and started to scribble in my spiral notebook. I put down the pen and turned on the laptop. Wi-fi had been unavailable most of the time since I left NC in early May.

I kept trying to write but fatigue and loss of sleep was taking its toll. I looked online at what I might do in Minneapolis tomorrow. Prince's city was now a Prince tourist attraction and there was a waitlist for tours of his estate; there was also a downloadable map so you could go see where he did this and did that. Mall of America was apparently a tourist attraction. I didn't figure shopping into the budget but looked to see if dogs were allowed. Of course not.

It was after 2 am before I went to sleep and once again the station wagon bed was more comfy (but much less roomy) than the bed I was sleeping in. George was sprawled out by himself on the futon enjoying his own space. The next morning, I took another shower and determined that Electric Fetus would be the one definite stop I would make. I didn't need records or posters. I just wanted to visit Prince's favorite record store. Vinyl and I go way back.

I fed George, gathered my things together and reviewed the instructions for departing the Airbnb. We were off again and when I walked into the Electric Fetus I felt as though I had stepped into a time warp. The feel of the plastic covers on the records was soft, evoking warmth and the selection was diverse. I came across several records that I would have liked to take home with me, but I have been trying to reduce the number of belongings I have to move about more easily.

I bought a fifty-cent Electric Fetus bumper sticker and went out to my car. I got in and realized I didn't have my cell phone, which meant I didn't have my debit card, credit card or driver's license. I looked in the usual places and then got outside the car and looked underneath and around it. Apparently, I was acting rather panicky as evidenced by the way George jumped completely out of the car and stood there on the sidewalk looking at me as if he didn't know whether to run or listen to me telling him to stay. I walked around and put his leash on him and we walked back into the store.

I looked around for a few moments and decided that if the woman at the cash register would call my number maybe I could find it faster. She began dialing and we didn't hear ringing. I went out to the car and still no ringing. I went back into the store and she suggested that they turn the music down. There it was ringing softly – I went looking for it and several record aisles away on the other end of the store was my wallet/cell phone lying on top of the Tom Petty and the Heartbreakers section with *Southern Accents* in the front. I exhaled deeply in relief and smiled.

The song "Southern Accents" trickled into my stream of consciousness with the ping of piano notes and I felt a new sense of direction. A feeling came over me that although my path and my future are uncertain, I will be the captain of my ship and make the choices that must be made. There's so much yet to be witnessed and so many more miles ahead before my days are done. I got back into the car with my copilot and "with one foot in the grave and one foot on the pedal," I selected home as my destination. It was just after 1 pm in Minneapolis and I vowed I would not sleep until I was in my own bed in North Carolina.

White lines flew by for 1100 more miles. It was almost 5 am the following morning when I took the turn up the little curvy road to home and George remembered where we started almost month ago. He excitedly bounced around in the passenger seat getting a better look at the dark surroundings and poked his nose out the window for a good sniff. I suspected he may have not have been sure where home was anymore. I pulled into the overgrown driveway, stopped, put the station wagon in park and stepped out onto the grass. I stretched and staggered around and breathed in the cool mountain air as I looked up at the stars sparkling overhead. George was trotting around with his nose to the ground and his tail wagging. It was Sunday morning.

It took me several days to recover from what I learned was called reverse motion sickness or land sickness. I guess after so much time in motion it affected my vestibular system. I felt as though I was still moving. George seemed to need some recuperation time too. He wasn't up to more than two or three pitches when playing fetch before he kept the ball and went to the door. I noticed he would go lay on my son's bed to enjoy a good sprawling nap. We'd been inseparable for four solid weeks and the space seemed luxurious.

I am content with the outcome of the spontaneous 8000-mile therapeutic drive I made. It was exhausting but I gained clarity about the direction I need to take at this crossroads of my life. My dreams and the things that aid and sustain me are no longer going to be shelved or put away. While the people I love and need in my life are not always close in proximity, they are close in my heart and I will maintain those connections with tender care.

Living alone is not a terrible thing, traveling alone is not a bad thing either. As long as there are people in my life, whether near or far, I am still part of a human circle. I will tend to those connections I am able to make and must accept the endings, beginnings and possibilities each day that I live. Mother nature sometimes produces what statistics calls an outlier; unexpected results that no one could predict, like those plants, trees and creatures living, growing, and often thriving in unlikely places. They do so seemingly without necessities and the in conditions that do not foster their survival, yet they flourish. Inspiration comes to me through those anomalous discoveries. Acceptance of changes and learning to navigate the choppy waters of transitions are essential for survival.

Thankfully I am not like the dancing tree in Minneapolis; I can move about, set my own course and choose my destinations. The tree is not appreciated in its place of origin and cannot go elsewhere, so it is damned to an ending that is unavoidable. Humans are blessed with feet instead of roots. So perhaps the meme "life is like a bicycle" might bear some truth despite land sickness.

My unexpected, meandering drive to Puget Sound and back revealed to me an expansive and ever-changing land and seascape crafted by the forces of nature. It has prompted many rambling roadside journal entries and reflections. For me, this gift of consciousness is enhanced by the earth's natural beauty and continual transformations. Her cathedrals are all around the globe and I intend to see and experience as many of her breath-taking works as I possibly can before this gift of life expires. I won't be waiting around for a travel companion, but if I happen to meet one, that's fine too. For now it's me, my dog and a station wagon.

GET MILES
Susannah Blanchard

My family didn't travel much; we were homebodies, really, but privileged homebodies. Our vacations were generally close by at one of the two houses my family owned: a lakehouse on my mom's side (20 minutes away) and a beachhouse on my dad's side (an hour's drive to the east). I barely remember a trip across the state to the mountains to ski when I was 6ish. My coat caught on fire. And once, we went to DC. I got dried ice cream from the museum.

As an adolescent, I planned to be a marine biologist when I grew up. My mom went momentarily crazy and let me go to Puerto Rico (chased by iguanas) and then Honduras (harassed by a dolphin) through the marine biology program at a nearby university. In high school, there were field trips (mostly local) and conferences (FBLA, yo) and, most importantly, band: Away games, playoffs, Busch Gardens, Disney World. We were a good, strong band with a way cool band director. I played trumpet, well and loudly, and enjoyed the people and the purpose of each of those band trips

But none of those experiences were as personal as the freedom I found when I got my license. I never doubted that I could drive; just sort of did it. At 16, I was off. My first car (after the obligatory prove-you're-trustworthy Ford Crown Vic) was a Nissan 2000NX, five-speed, and I drove it home from the dealership despite not knowing how to properly drive a manual. The final two years of high school saw me riding backroads, often with my best girl Priscilla, the Queen of the Backroads. We would criss-cross the county from east to west, north to south, and never hit a main road, singing Reba McIntyre and Garth Brooks. Friday nights in the summer often meant a quick hour jaunt to the beach to dance (Salt-N-Pepa, Mary J. Blige) and then back to the aforementioned beach house (different beach than dancing, so that meant another turn down the road).

While these were the days before we carried personal computers in our back pockets, my dad had a Motorola bag phone that he sent with me everywhere. I think that may have been the only way he'd let me out of the driveway. I don't think my parents ever knew quite what to do with me. I know I worried them, especially driving so much. Always on the go, but I reckon all teenagers are.

I often drove to clear my head. When there was too much static from figuring out how to be a teenager, I would close myself into that little Nissan and drive back roads near my house with the windows down and the radio loud. Loops through the same roads, a routine in the shifting of gears.

The physical act of driving (five-speed, remember?) anchored me so I could sort out the source of angst or reflection (a boy; it was usually a boy). I like the control of driving, especially a manual transmission. You can make a car float just before changing gears. Or you can make it grind. The play between the clutch and the gas demanded a good sense of balance and timing. Fluid and just there. Comfortable and easy, never to be second-guessed.

The circles of my travel grew wider when I left for college a little over two hours away. I drove back and forth more times than I should have to see a boyfriend I left behind. He was the first in a string of serial boyfriends from whom I sought, in the worst clichéd ways, validation. For various reasons and like a lot of people, I grew up feeling unwanted and unlovable, so of course I would choose boyfriends who were emotionally unavailable and too wrapped up in their own damage to see my light.

I spent a year and a half driving from my dorm to my hometown then back to my dorm. Those trips were too frequently late-night cigarette-fueled burns up I-95 (around ten years a non-smoker now, thankyouverymuch), often with Alanis Morrissett's ground-breaking album Jagged Little Pill on repeat. Her anger and willingness to communicate that anger— anger toward a man for his lack of recognition of her vital spark—connected with me strongly … and yet I still went back to this guy. After a year and a half of that mess, I finally transferred to the university that sponsored the marine biology trips all those years before … to major in English. It was closer to the guy I still dated, and the trips were shorter, but soon he went off to college in a different city. Before too long, my wheels rolled down different roads to see him. More fool I was.

While I still sought his validation to a fault, I was also beginning to breathe deeply on my own. The move to a new town allowed me to reconnect with friends with shared interests and shared history, and to build a life separate from the boyfriend. The drives up the highway to see him were different than the runs between my hometown and my dorm. Now I drove in daylight and often more leisurely. I looked at the countryside, the differences in land and buildings as I drove north. In the towns I passed through, I noticed people on the sidewalks, sitting in the shade. A dude in a ball cap holding the door for a lady with braids; a group of boys and one girl on skateboards. The need to be with that guy was beginning to wane and I found in the miles between my apartment and his a freedom of the sort I had never really experienced. In between I was free of expectation or obligation or responsibility or, really, identity. Space to think, reflect, ponder, obsess, laugh, and start over again. In those miles, I began rebelling against how he perceived me and shaping who I was independent of his feedback. I left my apartment for his when I felt like it and returned to homebase earlier. The miles between were as constant and dependable as my car.

And this car—a 1992 Nissan 300 Z, manual transmission, long and low, and dusty blue—was a joy to drive. It sat into curves and soared over hills. My car had T-tops (which sadly have been basically replaced by sun- and moonroofs) that connected me to the sun and the sky. And the music: Gomez, the Allman Brothers, Led Zeppelin, Pearl Jam, Janis Joplin, Fiona Apple, Joan Jett and the Blackhearts, Tom Waits, Modest Mouse, Blondie, PJ Harvey, Garbage, Metallica. Loud, independent, brash, rolling stone music filled the miles between.

Sometimes there would be something beyond the road, the sky, the music, and me. Once, I walked into a little convenience store on some back road in the middle of nowhere but close to somewhere, and the smell of it was the same as the smell of my Grandaddy's general store. He used to let me and my cousins fill little paper bags with nickel candy and bubble gum. His store had closed years earlier, Grandaddy had passed on, and the building was being rented for storage. But when I closed my eyes in this little store that sold earthworms and crickets for fishing bait, I was right back in Grandaddy's store. Never since have I smelled that smell. I wish I had bottled it. Or at least noted the name of the store.

I also hit a dog once. It was horrible. Dog liked to run cars. He made a strategic error this one day, and got caught up under my car. I had no clue what to do after delivering death to this poor dog who was bound to get creamed one day because he liked to run cars on a country road in the early days of cell phone coverage. I drove into a nearby town and stopped at a little gas station. Dog had broken a section of the bottom front bumper of my car. As I squatted there looking at it, a cop drove up. No lights flashing or anything. No idea that anything had happened, but he asked if I was ok. I related what happened, and he said he knew the dog and the family it belonged to. Dog was apparently a local nuisance. The officer kindly offered to tell the family what happened. Then he expressed admiration for my Z (ahaaa!); we talked muscle cars for a minute … and then I recalled I had a half-smoked joint in my console. Extrication from that situation without showing him the inside of my car became expedient. And successful. Poor dog, though.

After hours rolling up and down those roads, I knew every nook and cranny (much like the back roads near the house I grew up in). I learned all the best travel spots: where to get Pepsi in a glass bottle or a bag of boiled peanuts; which gas stations had the cleanest bathrooms; short-cuts around the worst traffic (which really wasn't too bad at all); the funniest road signs and billboards; the prettiest views. I began to make the drive less and less as I established more of an identity for myself outside this guy. It wasn't without mistakes, though. I stupidly turned down this lovely man who crushed on me hard in favor of the boyfriend who chose to go to university two hours away rather than be close to me. Saying no to him is one of my only real regrets.

Those solitary but never lonely drives finally ended when my boyfriend transferred to the same university from which I had since graduated and at which I worked on my Master's in English. We moved in together, got engaged, and broke up within two years. I finally realized he was unnecessary. I broke off the engagement and changed my direction. He tried to wrestle the steering wheel away from me for a while, but I ultimately turned onto a side road to lead a different life. It was around that time, too, that my wandering slowed.

I don't have many regrets from that time in my life. It was chock full of bad decisions, but the bad decisions are part of what got me here, today. And I like it, mostly. I grew up, got a career, started a family. As we do.

My longest drives now are four-hour endurance runs back home to see my folks and the few friends who might be available for a quick visit. The best part of the drive is a two-lane back road that connects two highways, half an hour from one end to the other. Lots of fields and hills; an oddly placed Army Cobra helicopter; a roadside farmer's market. I have the greatest little sidekick who already seems at home on the road. In between "are we there yets," he looks out the window thoughtfully. Sometimes he asks for rock 'n' roll.

MY UTERUS DID NOT WANDER
Tamara Miles

1.

I had a poem about my uterus,
but it was taken out, traded for my tonsils
I guess, which I kept, along with my ovaries,
although they have almost retired
from egg farming.

The fact is, my ovaries
are as confused as my hormones;
they live together but never really talk,
as they are both anticipatory; they don't deliver,
or they show up unannounced, moody.

2.

My uterus never wandered; it wondered.
Where did those two babies go? How
did I get so lucky to have the one who stayed?

My uterus was enlarged. Of course it was,
what the hell? It wanted to take over;

it wanted to be bigger than life.

3.

My uterus lay awake at night wondering
what I did wrong, to be able to bring to life only
one perfect human being. I laughed because
my uterus was apparently an imbecile.

That's not nice. My uterus was differently
abled. It cried in blood, in fibrous longings,
too much, too often. It hurt me,
and I felt like it did so on purpose. I deeply
resented my uterus for its selfishness,
its cruelty.

4.

My uterus apparently felt that I had done
it some injustice, or that it had done me one,
and between us there was always this
reckoning.

I was glad when it was over.

5.

The doctor gave me a photo of my uterus.

It was strange,
but I showed it to other people, as if
(my god) anyone wanted to see it
this way—on the outside, exiled.

6.

My father's mother had a uterus.

She kept him in it although it was uncomfortable.
Not for him, not for a long time anyway,
and he wasn't quite sure he wanted out,
especially when he saw, like Jesus,
that he had no crib for his bed, and frankly,
no father in the flesh/only in the sky
somewhere and always. His mother
saw him looking up and called the adoption agency.

7.

He got a father later, a man whose
wife had an argumentative uterus. They picked
him out at the Kansas City Cradle. He called
that woman 'mother' for a while. She took her uterus
to California. He never saw it again.

Today we looked at the original uterus, the first
– it smiled shyly at us from dark eyes in a 1941 high
school yearbook, thanks to Ancestry DNA,
which had kept it like a secret poem.

NEVER LOOK AT THEIR FACES AND OTHER UNWRITTEN RULES
Sonya M. Hamrick

Standing on the parade field alongside other Sailors and Marines was nothing new to me. There were award ceremonies, retirements, inspections and at this particular moment, there were deployments. This would make my third to what I liked to call the sandy place that God had forgotten about. We were not the only ones standing there. Friends and family were also with us. Many of these families had done this same thing on numerous occasions. I liked to call it a game of 'hurry up and wait.' This is exactly what we all did. We would hurry ourselves along, packing gear, preparing our families and then get to the parade field only to find ourselves waiting.

This particular deployment certainly felt different though. I did not know the people that I would be deploying with. I would be leaving my battalion and going off to the deserts of Iraq with an advanced party of Marines where I would be part of a Combat Logistics Regiment. This worried me a little. I am not a shy person by any means but what would I say during that eighteen hour plane ride with a group of strangers that I had never met? At the moment though, that would have to wait. My daughters, Taylor and Ali needed me and not only that, but my husband Reuben needed me too. He was about to be left behind for nine months with two teenage daughters. He had no idea what he was getting himself into, but he was the spouse of a Sailor and a Hospital Corpsman whose job at this particular moment was to go and work for nine months with a group of other Sailors and Marines.

Reuben knew that my job was important but I was also the mother of his children. These two girls were not ordinary children though; they were the daughters of Petty Officer First Class (FMF) Sonya Hamrick, also known as Hambone. I had taught them to be strong, the Navy and Marine Corps had taught them to be even stronger. We were all one tough family. As I hugged them all and waved goodbye, I blew them what we called our signature kiss. It always ended with us all holding up a peace sign. Deep inside we all wanted this war to end. Taylor, my youngest, once asked me if I was going to die. My answer was, I cannot promise you that I will not die but what I can promise you is that I will do my very best to come back home alive and well. Was I scared? Hell yes I was scared, and if you were one of us that said you were not then you were a damned liar.

I must have slept the majority of the bus trip to the airport. I did not want to talk to anyone and I damned sure did not want to let a group of strange men see me cry. It was not going to happen. Tears were saved for when I was alone in my bunk at night. After the bus trip came the long wait for the plane ride to Iraq, which was the most boring part. I sat and ate pasta salad that my friend had prepared for me and smoked cigarettes. The funny thing about smoking is that I only did it while I was deployed. The moment that I came back home I could drop the habit like it was nothing. It was at this very moment that I was approached by a Colonel and his Gunnery Sergeant. Are you a real Doc, which was what the Marines affectionately called us, or are you an admin Doc? An admin Doc, they could not be serious! Of course I am a real Doc. Charlie Company had made sure of that. The other male Corpsmen in my unit had taught me to shoot and clean my weapon, they had taught me how to properly dawn a gas mask under the pressure of an impending gas attack and on previous deployments we had learned to care for many different types of trauma. I was trained to work in Shock and Surgical Trauma Platoon. Of course I was a real Doc. Why must Marines assume that a female Corpsman does nothing but administrative work?

The plane ride to Kuwait went by fairly quickly with numerous stops along the way. I have always said that I have seen the world from airport windows because we were never allowed outside the terminals due to potential terrorists threats. The countries that I landed in appeared to be very beautiful and I would always think I would love to visit them once I retired. Staring out those windows would keep me occupied. Once we arrived in Kuwait I felt as if I were at home. I spoke up and said to one Marine, "It will not be long now." The trip from the airport to base is very short. He just smiled. The funny thing about being on that particular base was that I had just left there last year after spending nine months. The local contractors recognized me and most were wondering why I was back so soon. The sight of familiar faces made me feel comfortable, but it was for just a brief period. We would head into Iraq the next day.

Once arriving in Iraq, the meetings began. You know the type; the meet and greets, the rules would be read that we must follow and then we would be given a tour. Shortly after one of these particular meetings, about three hours after I had arrived, there was a very large explosion! This explosion rocked the building that I and a group of Marines were sitting in. I immediately dropped to the ground, put on my Kevlar helmet and flak jacket then quickly crawled under the largest table that I could find. When it was all over, which was just a matter of seconds the Colonel began to yell, "Doc!" No one yells doc unless some one was hurt but in this case no one was. He wanted to make sure that I was ok. The Marines that I was there to mend if injured were protecting me from whatever was going on outside. I was strong, I was independent and I was underneath a table. The Marines found this to be hilarious! They invited me to go outside with them so that they could try to figure out where the explosion had happened.

I found that to be silly. Why would anyone want to go outside when you could simply just look out one of the many windows that was now broken. Just yell if you need me Colonel. That would be the last time that I would see the Colonel and that group of Marines for the next several weeks. I was being moved to the other side of the compound; the side no Marine wanted to find him or herself visiting. I was headed out to work at the Surgical Shock Trauma Platoon, also known as the SSTP. This would be the beginning of what would later lead to my condition known as Post Traumatic Stress Disorder but I did not know it at the time.

The Corpsman on the other side of the compound welcomed me with open arms. My arrival meant that they would soon be headed back to the United States. They were eager to get me settled in and orientated to my surroundings and I was eager to get started. The date was August 18, 2005. It was five days before my thirty-sixth birthday and I was going to celebrate it alone and without the people that I loved, but the event turned out to be very exciting. We were mortared that day; as a matter of fact we were mortared quite often. One specific day comes to mind. I was in my wooden hut and was beginning to unpack my things when once again I heard a very loud explosion much like the one that I had heard on the day I arrived. I grabbed my Kevlar helmet and flak jacket hurrying to put it on when

I noticed a nurse that was simply just walking around. What in the world was she doing and why was she not putting on her gear. She looked over at me and said, "You need comfort food and warm tea." There was a microwave inside our hut and she was making me a bowl of macaroni and cheese. I did not know what to think other than I really could use a bite to eat. She then began to explain to me that the mortars would get closer at times and that this one was something that I really did not need to worry about. Everyone would soon need to head to the SSTP so that the Chief could do a head count and that I needed to hurry up and finish my meal.

This nurse that I had met turned out to be very helpful to me during my first few days on that third tour to Iraq. She hooked me up with a ride to the local store so that I could purchase a blanket and other comfort items. She sold me her microwave, television and radio but one of the most important things that she did was teach me the unwritten rules of the compound. One particular rule was that I should never look a patient in the face. Do your job, do not personalize with them and move on to the next patient. I asked her if she had followed that rule and her response was simply 'no.' I found that I too would break this rule. I was a mother and a strong and compassionate woman. How could I possibly not look at these young men and women as the they lay there injured?

My first experience with breaking this rule was when a Soldier had come in who had been electrocuted and he was in the process of getting CPR. I had taken over compressions and I looked into his eyes. Oh, how I wanted to bring life back into those beautiful grey eyes. This would not happen. I often question if I had performed the procedure right and was I part of the reason that he is no longer with us. He was a handsome young man who was surrounded by many of his friends. I saw their faces as well. In their faces I saw hope, fear, sadness and anger. How I wish that we could have saved him. He would be the first of many patients whose images I still carry with me.

One of the first unwritten rules that I did learn to follow was to tell the patient that they would be ok. No matter how bad it appeared, if the patient was talking, then they would be okay. This was often a lie. I found myself playing the role of a mother. If my child had injured themselves to the point of needing an emergency room visit, I would always tell them that they were going to be okay. I would hold their hand, talk to them through the bad stuff and then bring them home. It was no different in this case. I would hold their hand and tell them that they would be okay, even as I watched the life leave their eyes. A part of my very soul would always exit with them.

Sometimes looking into the faces of these young men and women was a happy occasion. It meant that they would live to see another day and that they would be headed back home. Minor gunshot wounds always came with a story and often times the story involved a sniper. A patient would claim that the sniper missed killing him by just inches to which I would always reply, "Well, thank God the sniper was not wearing his glasses today." That would always make the patient laugh. I loved spending time with these young men and women; they reminded me of the daughters that I had left at home. I could only imagine how worried that their mothers would be after hearing the news that their child had been injured. I would be in full panic mode until I saw my child and kissed their face if it was me.

There was an ongoing discussion between the SSTP staff and the Morgue about who had the worst job. The staff at the morgue felt our job was and I did not get that until I began to sit with those patients who were dying. This was a difficult job but I did not want them to die alone, of course others would be present such as the Chaplain and other members of our team, but I found myself wanting to sit with them. I needed to hold their hand, I needed to wash their faces, talk to them and pray over them. Is that not what a mother would do for any child? On one particular occasion, I recall sitting with someone who had squeezed my hand as I spoke to him. The doctors would tell me that that this happened often times due to involuntary muscle movement but I did not believe it. He knew that I was with him and now he is still with me. I can feel him squeezing my hand while I write this.

The days on deployment came and went fairly quickly; mainly because we stayed busy taking care of numerous patients and before I knew it, I was on my way home. The advanced party had arrived and I was ready to go! I looked forward to seeing my family and friends who had spent many days praying and wishing for my safe return. I remember kissing the ground the moment that I landed on American soil. It was a very emotional experience but little did I know that I had left a part of me back in Iraq, a part of me that I have still not gotten back and I never will.

The first night home was crazy, I had very little sleep coming back on the plane ride, the girls and Reuben were anxious to have me home. We had dinner, friends came by to say hello and hours later when I had just settled into bed I realized that there was someone in the bed with me. I was terrified! Who could this be? I wanted to scream out to the others in my hut that there was an intruder and that he was in my rack but it turned out that this was not the case. I was at home now and the intruder was my husband. I had a lot of adjusting to do, but no one would know about this incident. I would simply just blow it off. As the days went on I began to have other things that would occur such as nightmares and hallucinations. Certain smells would bring about horrible memories and loud noises would send me diving onto the floor. I chose to ignore all these things, but it was the anger that my family could not ignore.

I had become such an angry and bitter person. I mean honestly, how could the citizens of this country walk around and act as if nothing was happening overseas? How could these people possibly go to the mall or dinner or anything without thinking about the war that was going on in Iraq? I just did not get how people could be so happy. I began to scream at my children for no apparent reason, I was always mad at my husband and my co-workers were beginning to notice a huge change in me. I finally broke down and admitted to Reuben that I needed help. This strong independent woman needed to see what the Marines called 'the wizard' also known as the psychiatrist.

It is really strange to wake up in a daily blur due to an overload of medication that is meant to keep you from being depressed and prevent nightmares and hallucinations. All I wanted to do was eat and sleep. So that is exactly what I did when I was not working. I had lost a few friends who just decided to stay away from me once I admitted to being ill. Post Traumatic Stress Disorder is not contagious but they acted as if it were. Now that I think about it, maybe they were avoiding me in order to avoid their own symptoms. I did not like the medication that was given to me; I had the right to feel emotional! Why was it fair for everyone else to be angry, but when I became angry or upset I was asked if I had taken my medicine? This combination of pills had taken the place of my emotions and I was not going to allow that to happen. One by one I began to stop taking the pills. I was going to reclaim the mother in me, I was going to become that strong independent woman that had went to Iraq and I was going to make friends with the monsters that now lived in my mind. If they were going to reside there then I might as well acknowledge them This strategy would prove to work. I remember a time when one Officer decided to ask me daily if I was feeling okay, and when I got tired of hearing it I replied with " I am fine but the little guy that sits on my shoulder has a cold." Needless to say, the officer no longer asked me if I was okay.

I was beginning to take control of my life and my emotions and did not care who it pissed off. I was going to be in charge of me from now on. No doctor and no pill was going to bring back what I had missed for so long and that was my personality. Working on myself has been a struggle, I have had my ups and downs but with the help of my family, my Sisters and Brothers who served with me and my spirituality I have regained that part of me. I am now a very happy woman. I am a loving wife, grandmother and mother. I have rediscovered myself and for that I am grateful.

TRAVELING THE CROW ROAD WITH MY DAUGHTER
Sheri A. Barker

From the moment I knew you were an addict
I faced every aspect of your disease head-on.
I did not shy away from confrontation with you or the people in your life who hurt you.
I was staring down dealers and other criminals long before I owned a gun.
I took you out of parties and flop houses, any time day or night that you called me, crying,
asking for my help, even when my only backup was 800 miles away.

I did not shy away from holding you when you were sick,
Brushing your hair, washing your face, washing your hands.
I fought nurses who tried to treat you like your illness made you less than human.
I fought dealers at my door, the magistrate, APD, BCSD, your addict friends, your abusive boyfriend, your father…and you.
Always you.

You fought back harder than any of them,
Only rarely able to believe that we were on the same side.
You and I together, as we had been from the first stirring of life in my womb.

When I finally had someone to fight by my side for you,
Team Beth accomplished things I never thought possible, including
Getting you into safe space.
But as always, your November storms were the most fierce and
You disappeared over and over again.

There were days that the skies were gray when I woke, and
When I rose from my bed they would reach for me.
I opened my arms to slip effortlessly into them,
Putting on my mourning robe.

That is how it was to live in mourning for someone who was not dead.
Someone who was so far gone that I could not touch her;
Someone who was so lost in the shadows of her own mind
That communication only happened through the veil between the worlds.
The phone became a Ouija board and I could not understand the messages you were sending.
The planchette moved in endless, random circles.
Spirit, can you hear me? Is anybody there?

Then the long dreaded phone call came, and my head-on confrontations
Left me no corner in which to hide.

Years ago I faced the reality of the likelihood of your death.

I made hard decisions and careful plans, only some of which worked out

After the day I can only think of as Monday.

Part of my plan was to wash and brush your hair for you.

To wash your face and hands.

Those simple tasks are a mother's most basic expression of love,

Yet the circumstances of your death deprived us both of those moments together.

I cried and breathed my way through the pain of your leaving in the same way

I cried and breathed my way through the pain of your first arrival.

Five days after Monday, when I was finally able to see you,

I had to see you by myself before I would allow anyone else in.

Wasn't that the way it was when you were born to me?

I had long wondered if I could do it, but that long wondering gave me space to prepare myself.

Head held high, shoulders back, I walked to you, steady on my feet and

Steady in my heart, bringing you gifts of comfort for your journey.

Honoring the vessel for your precious spirit was important to me.

I am grateful we had that time together,

and like everything about you, I faced it head on

Because I love you too much to sweep your truths away like inconsequential dust.

Since that Monday, I have faced your absence in the

same way I faced your illness.

I do not think of you as gone, only away, traveling the Crow Road.

You are simply journeying without me until we can be together again.

When you visit me in dreams now, it is with your head held high and your shoulders back.

You are steady on your feet.

Smiling.

Those magical blue eyes are clear.

You communicate with ease, by words or graceful gestures.

And we are steady in our hearts, together.

FREEDOM TO MOVE AROUND THE CABIN
Angela Kunschmann

My childhood, as I recall, was a constant moving about. My father was a military man and when I was 6 months old, we moved to Germany. We stayed there until I was 3 and then moved to Fort Knox. At age 5 we moved back to Maryland. Until I was about 17, we moved quite a bit within the state. My parents loved to explore areas and we often did day long road trips. Living in Maryland meant you could be in Virginia, Delaware, New Jersey, or Pennsylvania within a couple of hours. I used to complain about those road trips a lot because I was trapped in a hot car with people that I wasn't necessarily getting along with. But we still went. I used to tell myself I would never travel anywhere when I grew up and left home.

However, in elementary school we took a lot of field trips. Being so close to Washington, DC, we often went there for our educational trips. I used to get excited about these because I was transported to another world. I saw my first mummy in 5th grade when we went to the Smithsonian. I watched a play about Harriet Tubman in 7th grade and I wanted to be just like her. I spent many years cooing over the monkeys at the National Zoo. When I saw the permission slips for field trips, I became a giddy and happy child who would count down the days to those trips to get away and have a new experience.

Around the time I started high school, I began to dread the bus rides because once again I was trapped in a vehicle with people I didn't much care for. I had occasionally walked to school in my elementary years, a little secret that my father still does not know. It wasn't a short walk, took me an hour every morning. The same happened when I started walking to my high school. It allowed me the opportunity to have peace. I wasn't being bombarded with everyone else's drama or emotions. I could even talk to myself if I wanted.

I left home early at the age of 16. I didn't have a car and that meant a combination of hitchhiking and walking to my friend's home that was about 30 min away by a car ride. It was 1991 and the idea of a young 16-year-old girl hitchhiking gives me the chills in my spine. At the time, I knew I was okay. I had a destination I wanted to get to and by all that was holy, I was going to get there! As scary as the hitchhiking sounds, I met some kind and sweet people. Once I got to my friend's home, I became quite the nomad. I relied on my feet to take me everywhere and there was a real sense of freedom in doing so. I walked through some dangerous parts of Baltimore and yet there was something so reassuring about it, knowing that I could get to wherever I wanted whenever I wanted.

Unfortunately, I ended up in a drug rehabilitation center not too long after. Yes, it was a good thing to happen to me. The unfortunate part of the story was that sense of being trapped again. That I couldn't just go walk and clear my mind. I couldn't just pick up and go wherever I wanted. I had big healing to do and I was confined.

I moved to North Carolina a couple of years later

when my rehabilitation had been completed. My parents and sister were moving there and I joined them. Unlike the freedom I had in Baltimore, I was in an area that had very little in the way of sidewalks, city planning, or public transportation. I still felt trapped and would routinely take walks on dangerous country roads just to get away. Eventually my family decided to move back to Baltimore where they could live easier. I chose to stay and moved to a place that had better public transportation, albeit still not what I was accustomed to in Baltimore. By now I had become so addicted to walking that if I suffered insomnia at 3 am, I took a walk.

A few more years passed and I found myself pregnant. I decided to go home to my family and try to rebuild my life and bring my child into a world that I thought was better. It wasn't. A few months later I was in my car and driving back to North Carolina. Although it wasn't Baltimore, I had grown fond of North Carolina and wanted to be there. The trip back was one which solidified my need to be alone when I traveled. I took the roads I wanted. My father had made sure I knew how to read a map as a child and there was no GPS in my car at that time. I didn't even have a cell phone! But there I was, driving to North Carolina all by myself. I could sing as loud as I wanted. I could listen to the music I liked. I could stop and eat when I was hungry. I could stop and pee (often since I was pregnant) without anyone complaining about my making the trip take too long. I felt free. I wanted to experience different areas so I purposely took odd side roads and stopped at tiny roadside dinners.

In 2000, when that baby was barely 11 months old, I had the opportunity to go to Houston to see my Great-Grandmother (or GG as I called her). It was her birthday and I gave her the first of her Great-Great-Grandchildren. I am terrified of heights which is why walking and driving everywhere was my thing. This time

I flew, so that I wouldn't lose my job for taking too long on my trip. Although I was scared to death to take my precious baby onto the flying death trap, I did it. And I felt free. The stewardess allowed me to move to a less populated section of the plane so that I could free myself from others' emotions. My baby could crawl all over the seats and peer out the airplane window.

Stepping into Houston was like stepping into a new world for me. Although I had been living in the south for 7 years, Houston is not the same type of south I had grown accustomed to. I had an opportunity for an adult night out with family so I could experience the best of what Houston had to offer: horse racing. When we arrived, I was overwhelmed and intrigued by the betting areas. I wanted to experience everything fully, so I figured out how to place a bet and picked one that had my baby's name in it. That horse won. I remember how thrilling it felt and thought, "well, this is pretty cool." Then we left and I heard some country music that made me cringe. I apologize now to my country music loving friends, it's just not a type of music I am fond of. But I experienced it and will remember the sounds and smells of the horse racing.

By the time I had more children who were coming of an age for day long trips, I had the urge to move on. Unfortunately, I was partnered with someone who wasn't fond of day trips anywhere. I had somehow lost touch with that part of myself that loved those day trips enough to leave his sorry ass behind. Instead I stayed and coddled him. The only time we really traveled was for his family trips when they insisted he needed to be there. He was an unpleasant travel companion and I became the person who once again disliked traveling anywhere.

In 2013, I left that partnership and began to rediscover myself. It started with returning to my daily walks. I held a job downtown and on my short 15 min breaks, I would take a quick walk around with some headphones in. I could get lost in the music in my ears and enjoy the movement. In 2014, I began to run. I started slow and would combine walking with jogging. I started entering in 5Ks so that I could keep myself motivated. There was something about running that made me feel like I was in control. I was the pilot and I could decide which street to turn down and where to avoid those big Dobermans who aren't fond of runners. I was alone with my thoughts and my music. I would feel that rise and fall of my chest as I kept my breath in check and I would feel the tightness of my calf muscles.

In 2015, I began traveling again. I drove along the parkway and visiting little towns just outside of my city in North Carolina. Sometimes I just drove for the sake of driving and listening to music. I found hiking trails to take my children on so that I could introduce them to the love of walking and feeling free.

By 2016, the camping bug had hit me once again. I had gone before when I was partnered but would go without him so that I could enjoy it. Now I was off and doing it on my own. I started with a single travel companion and it was wonderful. I then moved to some festivals with tent camping sites available so that I could be with my tribe and enjoy the travel to somewhere else. To sit in the driver's seat with my vehicle loaded up with gear, to know that no man would be there to tell me which direction to go in or how to properly set up the tent. It was just me and whomever I deemed worthy to ride in the passenger seat (often a female companion). This was also the year that I started traveling to Tennessee, which is only about 45 minutes from my home. It's not much different than North Carolina but it's new to me. It's full of places I haven't been offering me experiences I hadn't had yet. I met my current partner there and he is one of those people that is ready to have an adventure with me if I ask him to. Although he doesn't like to call it an adventure. If I say I hadn't been in a particular store or tried a particular nightlife venue, he is more than willing to join me, something I had not experienced outside of my parents! On our very first date, we went roller skating together because I hadn't done it in forever and I wanted to. We had a fantastic evening and it left an incredible mark in my brain.

On Dec 30, 2016, I fell and broke my leg. I was bed-ridden the first four days since I was in a splint. The once mobile and freedom loving woman was now stuck in a bed with her new man taking care of her, a very uncomfortable place for her to be. No more walks to clear her head. No way to really move and feel independent. I couldn't go to the bathroom or even shower without some help. Or could I? I became determined that I would find that freedom and the independence to move about. Once I got the cast on, I set about to tackling those tiny tasks that suddenly seemed important. I learned to go to the bathroom by myself, to dress myself, and to shower on my own. I was on pain meds and the doctor warned me that I could not drive while on them, my left leg was broken so driving wasn't an issue outside of the pain medications. I wanted nothing more than to be able to drive so that I could feel that freedom once again.

Although I love my sweetheart dearly, the relationship was too new for all this one on one contact. My sanity needed that driving capability. He worried about me tremendously but it was my top priority.

That first day I drove was the best day I had in a long time. I felt like I could go anywhere and see whatever I wanted. I couldn't go to a store to buy groceries alone, I had to have help filling my gas tank, but once I was behind the wheel I was no longer incapacitated. I drove to North Carolina with the biggest smile on my face and ready to hug my children tightly. Then we drove some more and we caught up one another on all the tiny details of our lives.

I continued to grow and adjust to my disability. I

found comfort in going to Walmart for my social interaction for the day. I could just cruise around the store in one of their motorized carts for hours and feel like I was a part of society. I continued to drive whenever I got frustrated. It's been 6 months and my bone has healed but I am now re-learning to walk. I am outfitted with a boot and occasionally need a crutch for assistance. My sweetheart got a short-term job in South Carolina so I took it upon myself to drive down and see him. I had never been to Columbia before, I had only driven through it. My sweetheart could not wait to share with me all that the city had to offer. Shortly after I arrived, after 3 hours in my vehicle, we got into his car and he drove me through the town. He had gone to college in Columbia so he showed me what he knew was there and we found other great spots by accident. On another day, we chose to go to a minor league baseball game and it was one of the best games I had been to in a long time. I routinely go to games in North Carolina but I hadn't realized how white-washed those games were until I went to the game in Columbia. We sat in one of the most diverse groups I had ever sat in. I grew up in diversity but I had been away from it for so long. I loved watching all these different folks talking to one another and enjoying the game. I was somewhere else and it filled me with such harmony and joy. I didn't want to leave. But I did leave just a few days later.

Since that trip I have thought a lot about the joy that movement brings me. I am slowly building up my ability to walk. As difficult as it gets on some days, I still try so that I can feel that sense of freedom within me. I don't drive as much right now for sheer economic reasons, but I am planning some trips soon. I am going to Atlanta for a conference and the thought of traveling for it sends a thrill up and down my spine. I have a female companion for that trip and I can't wait to indulge in that feeling of somewhere else and experience what Atlanta will offer. I have only been twice but for an amusement park. This time I will be in town! I am also planning a trip in October, one that will take me back to Washington DC. I already have my hotel roommates lined up and I am considering flying this time. Although I love to drive and feel free, this time I want to fly for the sake of saving some time and immersing myself in culture. I haven't flown since 2000 and it wouldn't hurt me to embrace that experience once again.

In all my trips, I see that common theme. The feeling of freedom, the sense of independence, and the joy of immersing myself in a new experience. It doesn't take very much to make me feel giddy and happy inside. Traveling provides plenty and I want more of it. I want to hop into the car and head to a beach so I can feel the sun hug my shoulders and the ocean kiss my toes. I want to drive somewhere I haven't been and see how those people live. I want to hear different languages be spoken. I want to see the diverse types of dress. I want to hop on a cruise ship and go somewhere tropical so I can swim with a dolphin. I want to hop on a jet and fly to a country in which they don't speak any English. I want to be challenged in communication so that I can better understand that human experience. I want to visit Germany and see the graves of my ancestors. I want to wake up in England and have a cup of proper tea. I want to go to Egypt and see the ancient pyramids and the hieroglyphs that line the walls. I want to hike the Jotun mountains and watch the aurora borealis in Iceland. I want to visit Belgium and taste the best in chocolates that the world could offer. I want to go to the Maldives so that I can eat inside of an aquarium and swim in the ocean. I want to feel my community abroad. I want to see what makes them feel so alive and special. I want them to show me what makes their little town so special. I want to discover all the wide ranges of beauty that our planet has to offer. I no longer want to be stuck in my own tiny bubble. I want to be immersed, to learn, to appreciate, and to see the value in each human. I want that freedom to move about the cabin of my life and get the absolute most out of it. Isn't that the point of travel? To pilot our own lives and move about freely? To discover new foods and odd traditions? To understand our neighbours better so that we can treat them better?

I firmly believe it's when women travel that we unite the world. Men have used to travel for dividing and conquering but every woman I have ever talked to about traveling has said something similar, that we learn more. That we find innovative ways to bridge our worlds together and find common ground. There is no need for us to force others to see our way. It's about sharing compassion and empathy to all we meet. And when women do it alone, they declare themselves as their own authority figure. We show the world that our needs are met on our own and that we own our power. More women should be encouraged to travel. Will you help us encourage them?

THE ANNIVERSARY TRAIN
Catherine Nurmepuu

[content caution: sexual abuse]

My feet are still dripping of the Shenandoah as I hurry uphill to the Harpers Ferry rail station. River grit slides between my heel and sole: sand, shell, grassling bits--all the collected fortunes of a professional wader. Had I far to go in these shoes I would surely blister, but I am unconcerned. I am content to slop along between bearers of suitcases. I have a bit of joy in my sodden step. I weave between anxious travelers—proud, cocky, my chin cast upward to meet the mountain before me; for I know that I need no bag and no clean shoe and no dry foot, as I am not come to this rail station like every other passenger to be whisked away again. I am on another mission: not to begin a journey, but to end it.

Today is our anniversary—this train and I.

And I am getting off.

November sun glistens on the rail. A plaintive child asks her mother when the train will be here, when will it come, why won't it hurry up?

Careful what you wish for, girl.

***

"This man is going to watch out for you," my mother promised that day, smiling beside the conductor on the Chicago platform. He never promised much himself. Still, I thanked him as he helped me up the little stool into the car.

I marched like a princess down the aisle to an empty seat. I was free, I told myself; free of my mother, of the ghastly factory town she'd dragged me to, of the cold gray world of government cheese and Salvation Army pantries and neighbors with needles that I had been forced to endure. I was free—at least for a week.

I was sixteen.

The conductor came by once, to get my ticket; twice, to offer me a magazine. The third and fourth times, he just smiled. On pass number five, he invited me to come try the steak cooking in the dining car.

"I can't afford— "

"It's on me," he said, winking. "Come on—you can't starve yourself. It's a long way to Washington."

This man is going to watch out for you.

. . .

The Harpers Ferry passengers all craned their necks to catch the first glimpse of the train. My eyes wander upward to the great craggy face of the mountain I love; it is golden now, glowing as if from within. Though I know it is only an effect of the sunset, I also know that if I could stand there against its blessed stones right now, my flesh would also glow as if from within. I have climbed it often enough to know this is true. And whatever science is in that, there is surely also some magic: light, mountain, woman, soul, weaving together in a glorious pattern of a moment. I am never so strong, I think, as I am on that rock; never so grounded, so free, so absolutely safe.

...

There were white tablecloths on the dining car tables. The train swayed, sometimes softly, sometimes roughly, causing my spoon to clink now and then against my china plate. It was a pleasant sound.

"You don't talk much."

The conductor was resting across the table from me, watching me enjoy my dinner. I smiled, mumbled, fell to a coughing that brought tears to my eyes. He swept over to my side and patted my back. I felt the hot sting of embarrassment on my cheeks as I thanked him. My mouth was full of food. I'd never had steak before, not the sort that hadn't been ground up first and mixed with filler. I didn't know how to cut it.

...

The stationmaster announces that my train will arrive soon. I sigh, clutch my stomach, lean against the rich red siding of the new old train station. I try to count its incarnations, its deaths and resurrections through war and flood. Historical facts of this railroad float through my head:

The desperate abolitionist who captured a train here and let it go again, to his own doom;

The general who stood like a stone wall, but complained the trains were too noisy and shut them down;

The soldiers who rebuilt the river crossing eight times;

The flood; the flood again; and ever again, the flood;

And then, its role in my life. The last seems so small, so dreadfully insignificant, and yet it has controlled my world for twenty years.

So much death, so much destruction--and yet here I still am, with a train to wait upon.

...

"May I ask you something?"

He had a kind voice.

I paused from my game of solitaire, the Ace of Hearts half-overturned, and glanced up at the conductor. He had given me the playing cards this morning—along with a breakfast of cinnamon rolls and two types of juice, orange and apple. He was handsome, I thought. And he had been so nice to me throughout the whole trip.

"Of course," I agreed.

"Are you a virgin?"

I nearly dropped the playing cards he'd given me. This wasn't the question I had expected. It wasn't the sort of question men asked high school girls; was it?

He laughed at me, leaned closer. I could see a miniscule cut on his chin, supposedly where he had shaved. He smelled of lemon and mint and underneath that, cigarettes. "I think you are."

...

I feel the train before I hear it: the earth of Harpers Ferry quakes just slightly, with a rumble that moves up through my knees. I begin to feel sick inside. I close my eyes, then force them open again. I will witness this; I will bear witness to every moment of it.

I have been controlled by this day for twenty years, but today I am ending it.

"I am off the train," I half-whisper, half-croak to myself. "I am off the train, I am off the train, I AM OFF THE TRAIN."

...

The window was an uncomfortable thing to be clinging to; the glass was cold, the emergency exit handle was pressing into my shoulder. The conductor sat next to me on the bench seat of the lounge; he had shut this part of the car off to other passengers, explaining in his gentle way that he "just wanted to talk."

But he was very close, and coming closer; he smelled more of cigarettes now than lemon and mint.

...

I stand on the platform, the window of the lounge car dead center in front of me. Shadows move inside, just enough to be human, but all details lost. I speak to that window, to the window of twenty years earlier, to my teenage self inside.

"Get off the train," I beg. "You are safe here."

Of course, she does not listen. And I know that when this train rolls away with her, things are going to be very rough for her for quite some time. This is the moment, the pivot point, the tick in time where her fate shifts, where the predator sinks his fangs into her soul; and what a quest she will have, to root him out and set things straight again.

Twenty years.

"I am going to hold your heart," I tell that teenage girl; "I am going to hold it right here, in this mountain for you. And you come back, and you come find it. You must believe, child, that you are going to get off the train."

I realize I am the voice of my own saving.

...

The train eased to a stop; my eyes wandered instinctively outside, to see where we were. My breath caught—not from nervousness this time, but because I was looking at the most beautiful sight my nature-starved eyes had seen in some time: a little village of twinkling lights wandering up a hillside, a towering mountain emblazoned in the fiery colours of autumn, a river sparkling silver over the rocks, and a mist—a mist that belonged not entirely to the mountain or the river but seemed to have an identity of its own, its tendrils catching on trees and roofs and ruins of—of what?— something in the river, something with a story I did not know but surely must be fascinating.

I fell in love with the place before I knew its name.

He gave it to me.

"Harpers Ferry," he laughed, and it was really more of a scoff. He tugged at my elbow, wanting my attention. My stomach twisted; my eyes devoured the scene with more intensity.

"There is nothing there," he muttered.

But I knew this was wrong, and what's more, I swear something called to me. Something in the back of my mind, perhaps the part that knew what this man was, the part that was raising a ruckus in my gut, reached up and whispered something preposterous:

'Get off the train. Here. Now. Climb over the table and get out the door and run up that hill. You'll be all right. GET OFF THE TRAIN.'

I did not.

...

The train is pulling away, slowly; and I am not on it. I repeat this to myself over and over again, this grand declaration of independence: I am off the train; I am off the train; I AM OFF THE TRAIN.

I shall not be ruled by this day anymore; I shall not let it pull me away from my own path; I shall not ignore the wisdom of my own heart; I shall not be bound away in fear and shame.

I watch the train go, tears rolling down my face; it disappears into the gaping mouth of a mountain tunnel, and is gone from view. I think of my girl self, gone twenty years ago: and mourn her, and love her, and forgive her.

In my sloshing shoes, I head home through the gathering mist, casting my arms wide to trace the fog and all its secrets. Joy lives in my heart, and a sense of reunion.

We are off the train, dear; we are safe, and we are home.

THE BEAUTY OF LANGUAGE AND THE INADEQUACIES OF STANDARD DICTIONARIES
Ellen Sandberg

Over the years, I have had many adventures as I traveled about the world either on my own or with friends. Some good, some not so good. But perhaps there is a kind of magic in the first time you do something.

Many years ago, some time after the dinosaurs roamed the earth but before the advent of cell phones, I arrived in Europe. I was in my twenties and it was my first major trip on my own. In fact, it was a new beginning because I was moving to London and would start my studies at London University in the autumn. I felt confident and free. Perhaps even a little daring because I had left the safety of my home and family in the USA. I knew a little French and less German, but I was armed with my standard foreign language dictionaries. And as I said I was brimming with confidence. I decided to spend a few weeks exploring Europe before starting my stay in the United Kingdom.

My first stop was Paris. Who does not dream of visiting romantic Paris? The Louvre, the Art Nouveau

Metro entrances, the food, the wine. It could make one dizzy with delight.

My attempts at French allowed me to get around quite well even though the natives who tried to interpret those attempts couldn't hide their winces at my pronunciation. The kind ones did anyway. Some showed open disdain or just acted as if they didn't know what language I was attempting to speak. Still, I was not discourage or intimidated. I suppose I possessed a certain arrogance in my youth that let me overcome minor rejections. I loved the city. It was beautiful and exciting. Fresh croissants and coffee in the morning: I was in Paris!

There was even a glorious moment, one I have treasured to this day. At the Arc de Triomphe I received the most wonderful compliment I could image. I was about to take a photo of the structure. My family had complained that I usually snapped pictures of ducks, flowers, squirrels, etc. that might have been taken anywhere. I would come home from family trips with lots of wildlife photos without any idea if that was a New Jersey swan or one from Massachusetts. It was even worse after a school trip to Europe. Was this picture from Switzerland or Italy or Greece? And was I alone, since there were never any people in them, let alone recognizable buildings? I had to start taking images that proved I was actually in a foreign country. Just as I was going to take the picture of the Arch de Triomphe, a man stepped in front of me. He excused himself and then stared at me. He said in English, for he seemed to know I was American at a glance, that I looked like a faerie princess--the kind of woman every boy dreams of falling in love with when he grows up. I think my mouth fell open. He then seemed very embarrassed and added that he was not trying to pick me up. He gave me a smile and raced off. It was so fast, I did not have time to tell him to wait, to go have coffee or wine with him, that I would not have minded being getting to know him better. But he was gone. Who knows what it might have become if he had stayed? On the other hand, it has lived as a perfect moment. I remember him as being very tall and handsome. In truth, he was probably rather ordinary. My memory has created him not as how he was, but how he made me feel.

I was still walking on air when I decide to take the train to Versailles. It was magnificent. A faerie princess needed a palace and I would not mind having that one. I could see myself in beautiful gowns and jewels. I would, of course, avoid Marie Antoinette's fate. In fact, I would avoid the whole French revolution since it was all rather bloody. But my daydreaming was interrupted because the tour was about to start. I asked if would be in English. The woman nodded and motioned the group to follow.

It was not in English. It was in French. I understood I was in France and I should not be surprised that they spoke French. However, this was a tourist site and I would have thought it made allowances for the different nationalities visiting there. I was very good at reading French and if the French was spoken rather slowly and carefully I could understand at least part of the meaning. The guide spoke at such a rapid speed that I might not have understood her even if she had been speaking English. Two other women about my age looked as confused as me. We started talking. They were from Greece, but spoke excellent English. So we tended to lag behind the group and shared our knowledge and our comments. This apparently was not permitted. Our guide who would have made a perfect prison guard, snapped her fingers to move us along. When we tried to tell her we didn't understand her, she ignored us. Then another tour passed by. The guide was speaking in English. The three of us moved closer to him. He saw us and guessed what had happened. He motioned us to follow his group. When our guide saw this she walked over to the other guide. They had a heated discussion in French. Perhaps it was against the rules to switch guides in the middle of a tour. Our guide pointed to us and made it clear we were to stay with her. She just assumed we would obey. She was very frightening. As soon as she went to the front of the group, the other guide whispered to us to quickly follow him into the next room. We did. The rest of the tour was not only informative, it was a lot of fun. The two Greek students and I took the train back to Paris. We had a good laugh about the whole experience. The three of wished our French had been up to the first tour, but we were glad the other guide rescued us. Back in Paris, we went out for some wine and dinner. Then we parted company and wished each other safe and wonderful travels.

I left Paris. I did leave a part of my heart there. I took the train to Switzerland. As we crossed the border, our passports and tickets were checked. One of the officials studied each document as if he were able to decipher some hidden message which advised to detain and arrest the holder of that document. We were all under suspicion. His eyes watched for the slightest sign of guilt. But he could find nothing, so we crossed the border into Switzerland.

I was not planning to spend a long time in Zurich. My destination was farther east. When I had traveled in the area with my fellow students a few years before, we had stopped at a lovely town in Austria near the borders of Switzerland and Germany. One of my friends had studied there and we had a wonderful time and ate too much chocolate. That was a surprise at the time because I didn't think you could eat too much chocolate. I was looking forward to another visit.

I did like my short stay in Zurich. I only had time for a quick look around but I managed to fit in a two hour boat tour. It was totally relaxing and gave me a desire to come back and see more of the city.

Leaving Zurich, I took another train to that small,

picturesque town in Austria. Bregenz was as lovely as I remembered. It was situated on a beautiful lake. There was a quality about the town that seemed frozen in time. I am sure during the annual music festival it was much less peaceful. The crowds would have been a little overpowering. But now, it was quiet and magical. I fell in love with it all over again. After all, this time I felt that I was a faerie princess and this looked like a faerie tale village. The buildings were a soft cream colour and the roofs were shades of grey and terra cotta-like soft red. The tranquil lake stretched out like a blue mirror in front of the town. Behind the town, the hills rose up high and were covered with dark green forests. The town was set like a jewel between them.

Best of all were the Konditoreien. There was one on almost every corner stocked with sinful assortment of cakes and pastries that would tempt a saint. Just looking at the varieties could make one swoon. A dozen or more creations in chocolate. Cakes and tortes covered in fruits and nuts. Whipped cream. Whipped cream everywhere. Pink cakes, yellow cakes, white cakes, strudels, meringues, cookies, and so much more. I felt like I was a child in a candy shop but with the spending power of an adult. I had the restraint of a child as well. One could get dizzy trying to estimate the amount of sugar used in even one of these shops. Although the dizziness probably could be attributed to the amounts I was consuming rather than the amounts I pretended to calculate.

In the evenings, I walked along the lake. On one occasion, the setting sun turned the sky and water a magical shade of lavender. A bevy of swans flew by me. I held my breath. Their wings turned gold catching the last of the light as they landed gracefully in the lake. It was all so perfect. It was another memory to lock away and revisit when I needed a moment of beauty.

I lingered by the lake as the stars began to appear in the sky. I might have been tempted to stay there all night, but I was getting hungry. I stopped at a small restaurant near the water so I could still watch the stars which now were also reflected in the lake. The dinner was wonderful. I don't remember all of it and I am sure the setting had something to do with my enjoyment. I do remember how I ended the meal. Despite my pastry indulgences during the day, I simply could not resist a slice of rich chocolate cake covered in cream. Then I headed to my pension a few blocks away. I fell into the comfortable bed that awaited me there and had very pleasant dreams.

Taking stock of my travels so far, I was getting along just famously. With my limited language skills, my dictionary, my maps, and my clever pointer finger, I was able to order food, pastries, tourist items, get on and off trains, and book hotel rooms. There was that semi-unpleasant experience in Versailles and I still believed that official on the train was disappointed he couldn't arrest me, but those were small incidents. I was able to communicate with the people I met. My encounters with nature and the beauty of my surroundings needed no words since the feelings were untranslatable in any case. So I was covered for any travel need.

Then it happened. The cloud that threatened to rain on my parade—to upset all my carefully thought out plans. At the time, it seemed like a major crisis. I would learn in my future adventures that as far as possible travel disasters went, it was a rather small cloud. But I was so upset. My menstrual period. A whole week early. My periods were accompanied with cramps, nausea, and headaches. When I was being more theatrical, which unfortunately was not that rare an occasion, I moaned I must be hemorrhaging; that this could not be normal. My doctor told me it was just a fact of life and I just had to live with it. He was, of course, a man and never had a period, normal or otherwise. At those times, I wished men would have menstrual periods and get pregnant for just one year. If that were to happen, I was sure there would suddenly be a slew of products to handle the pain of those facts of life. I tried not to be bitter. It was years before I discovered the miracle of chasteberry and found some relief. But that did not matter at the time. I was in a small town in Austria and naturally, I was unprepared. Still, the town was not that small and much of its population was made up of women, so the necessary products had to be available.

I made my way to the nearest chemist / drugstore / pharmacy. It was very well stocked. I glanced around. It looked very much like similar stores in my country. There were shampoos, band aids, vitamins, and many other products I did not need at the moment. I made several turns around the store. I saw nothing that looked like either tampons or sanitary napkins or anything that I thought I could use. Of course, I did not know the name of any of the local companies that might offer what I needed.

But I had my dictionary. I searched for possible words that would help me. I could not find anything.

The woman who ran the shop had looked up at me several times. She was a large woman neatly dressed in a white blouse and a brown skirt. Her hair was grey at the temples and she wore it back in a tight, but not severe bun. Her cheeks were very red, but it was natural and not blush. It was obvious she smiled a lot and it was a warm smile. Her eyes were kind. She observed me wandering around. Probably my growing look of concern alerted her to the fact that I might need some assistance. She came over and asked if I needed any help. It did not take long to establish that she did not speak any English and my German was insufficient to explain what I needed.

I explored the book in my hand frantically turning the pages. I would stop when I thought I might have found the word. Then I would shake my head and continue. She waited patiently although her smile was becoming a bit strained. However, she was not annoyed at me. I could imagine she had grandchildren and she was showing me the patience she had with a child. She wanted to help me and was frustrated she did not know what I wanted. After a few almost unintelligible attempts, I finally gave up trying to find an exact translation. I would just piece together what I could and ignore grammar and reason.

I looked up some words. Stringing them together I said, 'Ich haben meine monthly flugen.'

I am not sure why I had not looked up the word "monthly," but I was beginning to panic and was not thinking clearly. I didn't want to find out how long the toilet paper I stuffed in my underwear would save me from public mortification. I did know enough to understand I had basically told the women I had my monthly flowing river. Well, as I had mentioned, my periods were pretty heavy and uncomfortable. Still, what I had just said was rather ridiculous.

The woman looked at me as if I was demented, or perhaps that I was experiencing an unnatural phenomenon.

'Ich haben meine monthly flugen? Monthly flugen? Monthy flugen?' She repeated it over and over. Finally, I could see in her eyes the minute the penny dropped and she understood my request. Her eyes lit up with joy. 'AH! AH! AH!'

She took me over and showed me where the products was kept. I quickly purchased a supply, thanked the woman, and headed back to my pension. I later went back for aspirin and she knew right away what I wanted. But I was lucky that this time, my period gave me only minor discomfort. I attributed that to all the chocolate I had been devouring.

In fact, I was feeling well enough to take a walk in the woods. I needed the exercise after all the sugary delights I had sampled. I did not climb to the top of any of the hills, but I did walk rather far. Although the sun was shining as soon as I entered the forest, it seemed more like twilight that midday. Although this was not the Black Forest, I could see how places like this could be called that. It was dark and mysterious. It certainly was another aspect to my faerie tale trip. I was not afraid. I did not meet any wolves, or goblins, or elves. No old woman offered me an apple. I didn't get lost. Well, only once and for a very short time. So I managed to walk in my enchanted forest and come back safely.

When I left the shadow of the trees, the light almost blinded me. It took me a few moments for my eyes to adjust. When they did, I saw a man staring at me. He approached and ask me to come for a drink of wine with him. He said it in German, but I did understand him especially since he made drinking motions with his hand.

I replied politely, 'Ich trinke nicht.' Although I think that meant I did not drink anything.

He must have assumed that I didn't know enough German to know what I was actually saying, because he asked me to go out with him for various other beverages. I turned to my trusty dictionary while shaking my head in a negative fashion and muttering 'nein' over and over again. But I couldn't find the right phrase to make it clear I wasn't interested. "Go away" did not work. I kept searching. I wished the dictionary had more slang in it. I needed something stronger.

He persisted. He then asked me to come to his house. My page turning became more rapid. But then he took out his wallet and started handing me money. He either misjudged my profession or he was trying to show me he could pay for the drinks. I gave up with the dictionary and tossed it in my bag.

I looked him straight in the eye and yelled very loudly, 'Police. Polizei! Do you understand Polizei?'

That did get his attention. He looked startled and just ran off. I went back to town and had a very big piece of chocolate cake.

So my trip began and ended with encounters with

strange men. One very lovely that has brought me smiles over the year and one rather horrid that gets me angry even now. In both cases the man disappeared as suddenly as he appeared.

I packed and started my journey back to London and my university. I thought it would be wonderful to have a travel dictionary that dealt with all the things a single woman traveling on her own would need. Perhaps I would write one. So far I haven't even tried. I relaxed on my flight back to London. I had nothing to worry about in London. There would be no problem interpreting what was said. After all, we spoke the same language.

Was I in for a surprise! But that, my friends, is another story.

MY WANDERING FREEDOM
Lisa Wagoner

I have wandered since I was a toddler, taken over the Atlantic Ocean to visit the homelands of Germany and Austria several times. Indeed, when I was five and we moved to New York City, I cried because the Staten Island Ferry did not drop me off in Europe. It was documented. The love of wandering is deep within my bones. I am my mother's daughter and my grandfather's favorite, both restless wanderers.

When I was around twelve, my family moved from Little Italy in New York City to the Irish neighborhood of Woodside, Queens. It was there I became Honorary Irish, drank my first Irish whiskey, sang Irish songs and learned the history of my people. I say my people when at the time I didn't think I had a drop of Irish blood within me. I was, at best, a wild mixture of German, Austrian, Portuguese, with a smattering of a Hawaiian childhood on my father's side. Yet the Irish called to me the way living amongst Italians in Little Italy did not. I became friends with the Colleens, the Kierans, and the Siobhans. My first boyfriend was Irish, and he charmed me with family tales from the Emerald Isle. Once we all were in different high schools, my neighborhood friends

303

made me Honorary Irish in Donovan's Pub, the local watering hole for the families. Impressed with my mimicking of an Irish accent, my quick memorization of Irish history facts, and the way I could drink whisky neatly and efficiently, they dubbed me Irish with much love and laughter.

My wanderlust was fostered throughout my childhood, but my freedom was curtailed within my matriarchal family. I lived a dichotomy of rootless wandering with some extremely strict rules. I chafed at the restrictions and used my agile mind to circumvent most of them. I longed for complete freedom.

Ireland was sealed in my heart, locked away when I moved down South after high school, to begin a life of college, working, marriage and raising a family. I looked longingly at pictures of Ireland, but it registered no more to me than any other foreign place just out of my reach. I worked, my marriage ended, and my children reached adulthood. I visited many places, but never Ireland.

Then, a few years ago, Anthony Bourdain posted a response to a question he was asked about what he would drink in his fantasy bar. His answer? To be in Belfast, in the afternoon, listening to the Pogues, dust motes dancing in the afternoon light in a wood paneled bar. I posted that on Facebook, charmed by this answer, and filed it away. I didn't realize it at the time, but I had manifested a desire to experience the same thing.

The years went on, and I moved away to the mountains of North Carolina. My sons were independent and I felt restless. The mountains called to me and I wanted to experience somewhere new. Contrary to my own childhood wanderlust, I had stayed in one place for decades, so that my children wouldn't be subjected to moving and upheaval. To be honest, I missed it. I was eager to live somewhere else.

And oh, how my wanderlust returned. The mountains had called to me and I returned to many of my childhood touchstones: the Blue Ridge Parkway, the little towns, the different roadways. I even had the word "wanderlust" tattooed on my arm, in honor of my mom.

Without my quite knowing how, stepping stones for a pilgrimage to Ireland began to appear. I joined a local film society and it introduced me to the film *Good Vibrations*. It was the story of a prominent figure in the Belfast punk scene, Terri Hooley. I had always loved punk music and was enchanted with the story and some of the music I'd missed. Soon after, I met someone online from Belfast, Northern Ireland. We began chatting daily, and I listened with utter delight to his Northern Irish accent. We both shared a love of history, and he was impressed with my knowledge of the Easter Uprising of 1916. The names rolled off my tongue: James Connolly, Joseph Plunkett, Patrick Pearse, Seàn MacDermott, and Thomas MacDonagh among many others. Those brave men fought for freedom and some were executed soon after their capture. The love story of Grace Gifford and Joseph Plunkett reminded me of the stories I had heard long ago in Woodside, Queens. My eyes teared up as I heard the lovely song "Grace" about their brief, hours-long marriage before Joseph was executed. Soon, encouraged by my Irish connection, I began to watch documentaries, learning more and more about Irish history and their quest for freedom. I read the Proclamation of the Republic often, and was stirred by the words.

Indeed, something was stirring in me. The familiar Irish world in which I briefly lived in my youth returned to my present day. I had always gravitated towards Irish beer, music and literature, and they became part of my life again, I kept Dublin time on my world clock and lived simultaneously in two time zones. It was easy. My body was in North Carolina, and my heart was in Ireland. I managed to thrive in both places simultaneously.

Months went by and our friendship deepened. Soon,

we began talking about my traveling there.

And, as the Universe is wont to do, things fell into place.

I was on my way to Dublin, Ireland! The details are not important of how it worked out. Bolstered no doubt by my original manifestation of Anthony Bourdain's dream bar, my connection with my Belfast beloved, the pull of my Irish knowledge? My years in Woodside certainly came to the forefront as I discussed and revisited Irish history. The Universe, as it is so often does, materialized the means and the time to go on this trip. Amazing things happen when I get out of my own way, as evidenced by my easy time of arranging this trip.

In the early part of September, I began my journey. My heart sang as I flew across the ocean. It had been a few years since I had been in Europe, and I couldn't wait to have a new stamp in my passport. Even my flight over was exciting, with a drunken passenger causing an uproar and delaying our exit off the plane. I barely slept, and the hours melted away as we flew into an Irish morning.

I was in Ireland! The land was green, the air was different, the accents were intoxicating. As always with a soul connection, I met my Irish friend, we felt like we knew each other forever, and we began to explore Dublin. Ah, Dublin. The streets seemed familiar and on top of the open air tour buses, I kept commenting, "This looks like Queens!" over and over. No doubt to the consternation of my fellow passengers. In a way, it did feel like home, my original Irish home in Woodside.

Here I must pause to give a paean to the Irish Breakfast. It was my first meal in the country and to say I fell in love with a plate of food is quite the understatement. Nothing matches the beauty or the taste of all the different components, in a mild variation here and there at various places. Comprised of eggs, sausage, bacon, beans, tomatoes, mushrooms and blood sausage, it is a feast that sustains and satisfies. It is one of my favorite memories. If you can miss food, I certainly miss that meal.

One of our first tourist stops was to the General Post Office (GPO) in Dublin. I saw it from afar as we walked towards it in the busy streets. This was where the Easter Rising happened, yet in the present day, it was calm and quiet, a regular post office—ornate, to be sure, but a functioning, old-fashioned post office. As I stepped on the street where it stood, I felt different. I felt the shadows of history as we walked towards the front doors. This was the spot of the Easter Rising of 1916, where more than 1,500 Irish men and women fought with members of the British army as they staged an insurrection. I felt the columns with my hands, wanting to feel some remnant of the history that took place there. My soul was stirred reading the posted Proclamation of the Irish Republic, discussing freedom for women.

My mind went back to my days in my Irish neighborhood. I had heard the history and the names of the men who fought and died for freedom. I felt my own constraints of the teen years, chafing against restrictions, many that seemed arbitrary. Freedom I could taste on my tongue and when I felt free, I was my happiest. That surge of happiness welled up in me as I wandered through the GPO. People fought for freedom here, and I felt it singing in my veins. I touched the marble, the wood, all the trappings of the past. I felt it in the air, the dim echo of the shouts of the past. I was in the same place as those brave people a century ago. I was home.

Our journey continued with a visit to Glasnevin Cemetery. My first stop was to visit Michael Collins' grave. Tears welled up and poured over in an unending stream as I stood in front of his resting place. Surrounded by flowers, his grave stood right in front of the new café opened up just outside the gift shop. My tears covered my fury as cutlery clanked and people chattered. There was no barrier between the diners and his grave. I wept for the indignity of it. This man meant so much to me, as through the years I had read so much about his life, and his beliefs. I owned the movie with Liam Neeson and could recite entire passages from scenes. I had learned of a woman in France who sent flowers to his grave regularly, until the flower shop closed. I had tried to find that woman to see if I could join her in again sending those tributes, but no luck. There are a few people in history that I admire, and Michael Collins is one of them. He passed away in 1922, yet he is still beloved, as evidenced by the masses of flowers at his grave. That gave me a bit of joy, and I found it hard to tear myself away.

Cemeteries are so full of history and quiet beauty, and Glasnevin was no different. We wandered among the graves, and familiar names appeared. It was like greeting an old friend here and there, just being in the same spot with them. A man in WWI era clothing appeared and led a group to a grave. He began to read a letter from the Easter Rebellion as part of his tour. He was quite dramatic and clear, and engaged his audience. Off to the side, another man in uniform stood. I'm not sure what possessed me at this point, but I went up to him and asked if he knew where Grace Plunkett's grave was located. He led me straight to her very plain grave.

Ah, Grace. The love story of Grace Gifford and Joseph Plunkett touched my heart very deeply. Joseph was part of the Rising and he was executed soon after. The night before he died, he wed Grace in the jail chapel and they spent a total of ten minutes together. Not alone. The song "Grace" has the most beautiful lyrics: *Oh Grace just hold me in your arms and let this moment linger/They'll take me out at dawn and I will die/With all my love I place this wedding ring upon your finger/There won't be time to share our love for we must say goodbye.*

The song is played at Celtic soccer games, and is a standard at the Irish pubs. Grace never married again, and died Joseph's widow. To be at her grave and pay her tribute felt right. I had known of her and Joseph's story since I was a teenager. My first love was Irish and he told me the story. To stand at her grave was to come full circle.

Next stop in our journey was Kilmainham Gaol, the prison where many of the pivotal members of the Rebellion were imprisoned, and where they were executed. Grace Plunkett herself was imprisoned there, and she painted a beautiful mural on the wall of her jail cell. I saw it through a peep hole, and the colors were still vivid. I tried to imagine her wedding to Joseph as we sat in the chapel, seemingly untouched from their wedding day. I held hands with my Irish love and tried to imagine the devotion of a woman to marry a man she knew was going to be executed. While the guide spoke, I wanted to somehow experience her feelings in those moments, even for a brief millisecond. I feel as if I did, a brief tingle was felt in my hands, as I gazed upon the setting of their wedding. To fight for independence, to give up your life, to stand for your principles. My heart swelled with even more love and admiration for the couple. Grace continued to honor Joseph's memory, and their devotion reaches through time and gets caught up in your throat as you try to imagine that happening in present times. Would I be so brave? Would I be so determined? I would like to think that yes, I would.

Our final stop in Dublin was the visit to the Arbour Hill Cemetery. It is a serene, stark place, behind the Arbour church. It is the final resting place of fourteen of the executed leaders of the Easter Rising in 1916. Among those buried there are Patrick Pearse, James Connolly, and Major John McBride. The gravesite is surrounded by a limestone wall in which their names are inscribed in Irish and English. I walked around that wall and read each name out loud, so that they would be remembered. I wish there were words that could adequately describe the mélange of feelings I had. I had traveled the journey of the Easter Rising to its beginning, to the imprisonment and execution, to final resting places. I was moved to tears so often, because I could feel the strain of wanting freedom in the very air of the places I visited. They deserve to be remembered, and they are, in beautiful and severe ways. Gravesites, plaques, their names stated over and over, like a mantra. The words of the Proclamation are carved on huge walls overlooking their final resting place, both in Irish and English. I read the Proclamation aloud, so that the words would be uttered and remain in the air that surrounded them. It may seem strange that a woman from North Carolina would feel that it mattered so much, but I felt the need deep inside me. I am connected to these people, somehow. I feel it and know it, as I know my own reflection in a mirror.

My journey then continued on to Belfast, and I fell in love. Dublin was lively and frenetic, a bit boisterous and joyous. Belfast was a bit ornate, a little bit more serious, but with an air of resilience. It became a new home for my heart. I visited the site where the Titanic was built (another story for another time, another piece of my heart). And then I asked to see the murals: The Peace Wall. Colorful murals with messages of peace and hope. Words for freedom. Honors for Mandela. Words for peace in present day troubles. The air in that part of Belfast is troubled, as apt as the time referred to as The Troubles. It is feisty and resistant. I felt myself feel feisty and ready to fight anyone who would try to take my freedom away. I come full circle from my days longing for freedom as a teenager. I was there, neither Protestant nor Catholic and I still felt ready to fight. Fight who or what? I did not know.

I saw the murals on the buildings, including the huge portrait of Bobby Sands. I knew Bobby Sands from living through that moment in history, vaguely aware of his hunger strike. I saw the movie *Hunger* that told the story of the Hunger Strike. I felt sorry for him at the time, with no true idea of what he stood for or why he did it. Yet there he was before me, larger than life, smiling for eternity in colorful paint. Next stop was the visit to the cemetery to visit his gravesite, where I knelt and took in his grave among so many other 'volunteers.' There is a long row of those who died in the Troubles. Their pain is palpable in that spot. So is the sense of defiance. Never have the green, white and orange been so very vivid as on that day when I paid homage. The sky was overcast but the colors were so very bright. I can still feel the gravel under my shoes as I walked among them. I felt pride. I felt sorrow. I felt the fierceness of my independence and freedom. I am free, as much as I can be in this regulated world. Visiting these places confirmed my original ties to the Irish people and their history. Maybe all I felt was an admiration for a people, with no real connection. Funnily enough, my new Irish friends in the pub would often ask, "Are you sure you aren't Irish? You seem very Irish to us!" I took that as a badge of honor.

As trips do, this one ended. My Irish story did not end there, however. My wandering took me back to another visit a few months later, yet right before my second trip, I went to a concert.

It was a concert I had waited many years to see, of an artist I discovered through one of my Irish friends in Alabama. Loreena McKennitt came to the city where I lived, and I was beside myself with excitement. She usually toured in Europe or out West, and I never thought I would get the chance to see her perform. The night was magical. I was surrounded by friends, and she was on stage, surrounded by candles and a few fellow musicians. In between songs, she would tell little stories or discuss her research, and one mention in particular caught my attention. Her music is ethereal and full of Celtic melodies, and much of her research takes place in Ireland and Scotland. She mentioned how the Celts had wandered throughout Europe, and were not confined to just Ireland or Scotland. Then her next words stunned me: the Celts had settled in various European countries, such as present day Germany and Austria.

My maternal family comes from Germany and Austria, several generations back. The Celts had settled there! I was very likely connected to the Celts! The mystery had been solved, and I knew deep in my heart this was true. This was the connection I had been seeking all this time. No more would I wonder why Ireland felt so much like home. It is in my DNA most likely, possibly even a small part. As the Universe did with the Anthony Bourdain response that I had stored away (and experienced myself in just that exact way in Belfast), so did it provide an answer when I most needed it. "Full Circle" is a song by Loreena that she sang that night at the concert, and the lyrics resonated so beautifully with that revelation: I had indeed come full circle. From living in an Irish neighborhood, to becoming Honorary Irish, to being a teenager determined to always be free, to wandering to Ireland to follow my heart, to connecting with those who fought for freedom for their country, and back to the land where my family probably originated. I had come full circle, with my wandering, my freedom, my heart. My wandering had led to learning so much about myself in relation to a people and a country. My wandering freedom had led me to a new home. Ireland is in my heart and a home I will return to again one day.

WALKING VEILED THROUGH KHAN-EL-KALILI: PRESENTATION PERSONA AND PAGANISM IN MODERN EGYPT
Cynthia Talbot

Traveling as a single woman and a member of a minority religion is always challenging. Traveling to a part of the world where the language, religion, and culture is so very different from one's own is an adventure. Learning to live in the day-to-day world of city and village life in a modern Muslim country takes determination, a very open mind, and a lot of bravery or stupidity depending on your point of view. Learning which train cars are open to women, how to shop for everything from clothing to meat in the sprawling labyrinth of the suk, plus navigating women's rituals, specialty markets, and parts of the mosque: each day brings a change in viewpoint and a new way of looking at old habits. When can blending in be freedom and when can standing out be an advantage? Walk through modern Egypt with the eyes of a modern western, pagan woman Return to the land where the wandering womb was first recorded and see it through the lens of the new millennium.

I love Egypt. I love the people, the amazing history, the smell of the markets, the crash of the Mediterranean along the Corniche in Alexandria. I love the Metro in Cairo. I even love the bustle of Cairo. I abhor the traffic. I am a big city girl, born in Los Angeles and raised within the Loop in Chicago. But Cairo—oh, Cairo!—is an altogether different creature. I arrived with a friend in May of 1997. Two women traveling alone from Dallas to New York to London to Cairo, we were young, and brave, and we were going to be spending the next 6 weeks meeting with the people we'd be working with in the coming fall.

You don't deplane down an air-conditioned walkway. Instead you walk down a set of stairs rolled up to the door and right on to the tarmac. What hit me first was how very dry the air was. The wind was blowing, and it felt as if all the moisture was immediately pulled out of my body. The shuttle bus that takes you to the terminal had a cooler inside and as we boarded they gave each of us a water.

I learned my first word in Arabic. *Izzazat Maya*, which means bottled water. It's sold everywhere. And I learned to drink a lot of it.

The first few days remain a blur. I remember my hotel. I remember the very nice desk staff. And I recall the movie theater next door because it had air-conditioning. And tickets were four pounds Egyptian. That was about a dollar at the time.

Sue and I explored a lot. We took taxis, we took the bus, and we tried the Metro. The Cairo subway system is surprisingly wonderful and clean. It's also one of the only non-smoking areas in the country. The first two cars of every train are only for women and their children. I come from a city where the trains are a necessary evil you take because you want to get somewhere. I could spend all day riding the Metro.

I remember the first time Sue and I bought our tickets and headed down the stairs. A Muslim woman in the most amazing full niqab and abayah in bright canary yellow walked with us and explained in perfect Oxford English how the train car system worked. "The first two cars are for women only," she said.

I was just young and militant enough to think to hell with that, I'm riding in whatever car I want. But I tried to stifle my reaction. Sue, who was not as good at keeping quiet said. "Why can't I ride with them?" And indicated the men standing waiting for the train.

"You could. Many women ride with their husbands or family. But why would you want to if you don't have to? Men are loud and they reek of smoke and they never stop talking. Women only in the first two cars. We can talk about shopping and where you work and not worry about men," said our new guide. She glanced about. "Also, some foolish boys will try to get fresh. They think all American and English women are easy. Too much American television. They are not allowed in the first two cars. So come ride with us."

It was my first lesson in navigating the role of women in Egypt. They look after each other because by and large they do not think men (young men specifically) have manners. They aren't wrong. The young men's driving, mostly of motor-scooters, is enough to convince me of that!

I learned a lot about my misconceptions of Muslim women and men. I learned wonderful lessons on how to make the most of inhospitable climates, scant resources, and few modern luxuries.

In my first year in Egypt, I learned to navigate Cairo, al-Qahirah as the locals call it. I learned that if I hailed a taxi in Arabic, I didn't get charged tourist prices. I learned that if I went to the market with friends and we each spent a little, I got better prices than if I shopped alone. I learned how to grind grain for bread, how to pluck chickens, how to make yogurt, and how to milk a goat. I did not, however, learn how to kill the chickens *well*. My chickens were fit only for soup. So I stopped trying because wasting a recourse as valuable as food is a sin, both in the Muslim religion and in my own.

I helped slaughter and prepare the sheep for Eid al Fatir, the feast to end Ramadan. And I learned that the slaughter had to be done so that the animal did not suffer and was not afraid. That the slaughtering was done on a sacrifice stone down by the river that still bore the ancient hieroglyphics for AmmunRa and Hapi, the deity of the Nile, was an inside joke in the village. "It has been done this way since the pyramids were new," I was told. "Why would we now do differently? If it has always worked, do not try to fix it." As a worshiper of those ancient gods, I was considered odd, and more than one person thought I was a bit mad—or perhaps just not very bright. But no one minded that I poured my water to AmmunRa and Anpu and Auset and not to Allah. It did no harm to anyone and I was willing to do the work of making the feast and cleaning up afterward.

I learned what it was like to live in a place where my skin tone was the oddity. Where my language was ne people learned second, or third, or seventh. I bargained in Japanese in Alexandria, and pulled out my very rusty German in Luxor. And I learned Arabic quickly.

I was welcomed to people's homes to share meals, when all they had was a couple of mangoes, flat bread, and mint tea, and where we had to sit on the floor because there was only one chair and grandma was too old to get up and down anymore.

I learned dirty jokes that women shared while getting sugar waxes and how to use real kohl for eyeliner. I learned where the women's markets were in Cairo, and Aswan and Alexandria. And relearned my first lesson about Egyptian women. They are fiercely proud of their places. Women may go to any market, but men may not come to theirs. There may be hours of the day set aside for only women to use a public pool, so that we could all swim in western bathing suits, without them having to worry about me and without having to worry about how we looked to men. Let me tell you, as an American woman, not having to care if I'd shaved my legs that day and going swimming anyway was wonderful! I learned when to wear a hijab and why. According to Egyptian women, and this is by no means the way it is in other parts of the Middle East, or the wider Muslim world, certainly, you wear hijab or niqab or your choice of headscarf for a few reasons: Because you are going to mosque obviously, because you are visiting conservative family members, because you are trying to look professional for an interview or a bank loan or some such, because your friends are wearing theirs and you don't want to stand out—you'll likely have to barter down from tourist prices as well, if you are the only one not wearing a scarf. Also because you feel like it, and occasionally because you just don't want to bother fixing your hair. I fell most often into those last two categories. My hair is very long and a pain to deal with on good weather days. Putting it up and only having to throw a headscarf on was often a wonderful thing!

Walking through Khan el Khalili in slacks, a loose cotton shirt, and a simple hijab, was the most fun way to shop. I got much better prices, especially from the shops run by other women. I got invited to sit for tea while bothersome teenage boys were sent for what I wanted. "It will keep them out of our way while we talk," I was told. I had to actually argue with a stall owner to be allowed to pay for my goods when he saw that I had only enough money for the purchase and would not be able to take a taxi home. I had enough change for a bus ride I explained (I love the Metro, the buses in Cairo I abhor with a passion. They reek of cigarette smoke.) No, I was told, he would get a friend to give me a ride if I insisted on paying. So I agreed, and we had tea and falafel while we waited for the friend to come.

I learned that no one expected Americans to have manners. No one expected me to try to speak Arabic. It was assumed I was Christian—and that I was looking for a husband. It was assumed that I would want to stay in fancy American or European hotels, and that I would not like to go to mosque. I did my best to disprove all those assumptions and expectations. In return I learned not to assume that Egyptians were uneducated just because they were farmers or tour guides. I met lawyers and teachers who had decided to do both. I learned that women were not second-class citizens, that they could and did hold jobs, own property, practice law, and run businesses. I learned that much of what I thought was Muslim was actually culturally Saudi, or Urdu, or even Sudanese. Egypt is as different from Saudi Arabia, despite both being Arabic-speaking countries with a Muslim over-culture. In the same way that Texas is very different from the Orkney Islands, despite both having English as a first language, and belonging to the same Christian over-culture of history.

I learned to tell time by the sun and not a clock. I learned to be patient, that sometimes things can not happen when we want just because we want them, another virtue my faith and that of my Muslim hosts. I learned old skills, from baking in a wood oven to washing clothes by hand. I learned to shamelessly take advantage of the fact that no one understood what being pagan was, so I could make up religious reasons not to do things I didn't like and no one questioned it. I do not eat carp: I hate it! Therefore, no river fish were allowed in my religion—and still aren't! I learned to be part of a community I was not born to.

What I learned most was that traveling as a woman in a very foreign land was worth the risk. It was frightening, and sometimes very hard, dirty, and heartrending. But I learned that hospitality is found in distant places and that I can be a good and gracious guest. I am stronger and more knowledgeable for the travel. I learned to set aside my own prejudices, at least some of them, and let people tell me who and what they were—and not to expect them to fit into my preconceived notions of who they would be. I hope the women and men I met and worked with, did business with, and traveled with have a better understanding of Americans, or at least odd American women with odd religions and open minds. Traveling makes us no longer strangers in a strange land, but fellow pilgrims on the road to knowing more. That is the greatest gift of the time I spent in Egypt.

HOTEL SHEETS
(SONG LYRIC)
Victoria Squid

White sheets
    In another city
Nights long
    And mornings pretty
In a hotel room
    With nothing to do:
Nothing belongs to me—
    Not even you.

White sheets, starry nights
Your laugh and sweet delights
No story, no reason, no rhyme
'Why don't you come up and see me sometime?'

Stolen kisses
    Always taste sweet
Stolen lovers
    Now a *fait accompli*
In a hotel room
    With so much to do
Just a short time to know
    All about you

MY WANDERING UTERUS

White sheets, starry nights
Your laugh and sweet delights
No logic, no reason, no rhyme
'Why don't you come up and see me sometime?'

Final morning
    Last goodbyes
Smiles on our lips
    And tears in our eyes
In the hotel room
    We make our farewells
The ribbons that bind us
    Weave a bright spell

White sheets, starry nights
Your laugh and sweet delights
No story, no reason, no rhyme
'Why don't you come up and see me sometime?'

ACROSS THE CERULEAN SEA:
WOMAN ON WATER?
Jane Toswell

I take freighters. For fun. And for work.

First, there is my own personal interpretation of Virginia Woolf's room to herself: I have a large room with two windows (one to starboard, one to stern), my own personal bathroom, a single bed, a desk, lots of books, a separate bench built into the corner with a fixed table, and an entrance which you can only find on purpose, heading down the corridor from the captain's quarters and round the corner. Technically, it is 'cleaned' every day, but in the real world the steward arrives once a week to change the bedding and clean the room. Once a month it gets a serious deep clean.

Every day, I can turn up for breakfast between 7:30 and 8, lunch between 11:30 and 12:15, and dinner between 5:30 and 6. The food is cooked by a Georgian chef who wants to please the captain so we're getting a lot of fish (the captain is Romanian, his predecessor Russian, so we had a lot of beef and pork then), and served by the Filipino steward. Lunch is three courses, breakfast and supper one course each. There isn't a lot of choice, but the food is tasty. If I want food, I turn up on time. If not, there is a refrigerator in each room, and bottled water is hauled in whenever I ask. If we are at sea, the first officer will fill the tiny swimming pool on request (well, the cadets do the work, as they occupy the lowest rung on the ladder towards officer-ship), though it's best not to request too often.

Life on a freighter is a very delicate balance of competing interests and workloads. But mostly I can spend my days working. I can sit at my desk, look out either of my portholes, listen to some of the music I brought with me on the miniature speaker my brother provided, and read or write. I have some of those massive tomes that we always plan to read and never quite get to, and I've decided to translate a monograph on medieval Germanic literature written by Jorge Luis Borges, and I want to retranslate *Beowulf*, and I have an introduction to write to a collection of essays – well, the usual academic collection of tasks, minus anything that would need connection to the internet or a lot of books and research.

So I work, read, take a break walking on the pilot deck looking for other ships, whales, or airplanes (the latter so I can feel superior and slow-moving), and occasionally visit the bridge to find out what the news of the day might be and how far we've traveled since my last check. If the crew isn't working in the front holds (and on some ships even if they are), I can head out to the bow, sit on a relatively uncomfortable steel deck, or on a hatch or bollard (sometimes there is a spare deck chair but mostly someone forgets to tie these down so they get blown away). Or I can do the *Titanic* thing and sit right out at the bow. Sometimes there are flying fish out there, sometimes dolphins, more often porpoises, and occasionally (for me just in northern waters) killer whales. If we're in a busy shipping lane, or a fishing area (or in many places both at once) there is a lot more to watch. Plus, if I time it right I am literally almost a thousand feet away from the next human being (back on the superstructure, and forward it could be several thousand miles to the next human). I like that. Actually, I like that feeling of solitude so much it's a bit worrisome.

The sun is blazing hot, especially on the steel structure. A slightly hazy day is a good one for the bow. But if it's windy or the waves are up, not a good idea. In the rain the steel can be infernally slippery. Add wind, gusty wind, and you could miss your footing very easily. The officer of the watch might forbid the trek to the bow, and worse, if you're out there and it becomes windy or rainy, someone might be sent (taken away from real work) to get you back. It's never good to be the passenger who interferes with the working of the ship, no matter how polite the guys are about it. At least, that's my view. But I adore the utter silence at the bow, with the occasional creaking of the ship as it slices through the waves, the sense of flying since the bow itself is well above the waves. The bulbous down below is actually out in front and cutting through the water so it's not even slapping against the ship much these days. It's a marvelous feeling. And a nice way to take a bit of time off from all that work I brought.

Second, though, there are the complications. One of the reasons I take freighters is that I am completely out of touch, except when in port. It's really expensive and complex to send and receive emails, or to make phone calls. For ten US dollars, I can buy a card that will give me about twenty minutes on the satellite phone, and either I have to pick a time when no one else wants to use it (3 a.m. is good) or I have to stand in line for a while. The sailors all try to push me to the front of the line, but their need is as great as mine, and I'm only a passenger. Being cut off like this can be good, but you have to be used to being isolated and alone. That's an odd thing to say when the ship will have 26-30 people on it, all moving about the superstructure, eating either in the officer's mess or the crew mess. But, save for the passengers, they all have work to do and shifts in which to get it done. They might get bored when off shift, but a good first officer will ensure that they have a work plan and plenty to occupy them. An oceangoing vessel has to be painted with astonishing frequency, every single bit of it including the cranes. The salt water degrades everything, including steel hawsers. If it's a container ship, there is work to be done checking the struts and locking mechanisms holding the containers in their rows, and the refrigerated containers need daily checking as well. If it's a general cargo ship with mixed load, that takes more checking. There is always something to fix or jury-rig on a ship. So, work is going on all around me, and it helps me to work. The crew's work, though, is mostly physical. Even the chief engineer is in the engine room whacking things as necessary. They all pass fitness tests as they come aboard and are approved for duty. I'm not fit. But six decks' worth of stairs down to the main deck for meals and back up to my quarters helps.

On my first ship it was possible to walk all the way around on the main deck, without clambering up companion-ways or jumping over anchors. Since then the ships have gotten less and less passenger-friendly, including smaller staterooms, less convenient corners of the ship for the passengers, a lounge with films but no DVD player or vice versa, no additional funding for food, less access to the bridge especially when on the pilot which is the most fun time as you're coming into a port. On the second and fourth ships (across the Atlantic to the Mediterranean and across the Pacific to China and back) it was possible to climb one companionway and clamber across the stern jumping over bulkheads every six feet, and to walk most of the rest of the way. But not on the newer ships. So getting some exercise requires thought and some foreknowledge. The electrical current is erratic so exercise bikes break down, as do treadmills, when they are to be found on the ship. The crew has a weight room, but as a woman alone I'm not going to use the grungy-looking free weights in there. I brought a skip-rope once. Not good. A freighter at sea is constantly shuddering and juddering. The steel deck is never quite in the same place, and every time you come down the deck is in a slightly different spot. And it's steel. No give to it at all. And the deck above is too close to swing the rope properly. Going outside where you could at least swing the rope will bring you lots of watchers, and a few comments at the next meal. Also not good. On the other hand, it does open up some conversational opportunities. Those can be fun.

Everyone on a freighter has to have functional English as that's the language of the sea. So, as an expert in English I can expect to have some of the guys looking to improve their English if only to be able to take the Able Seaman or Officer's examinations. Or, they just want someone to talk to. Ships are very hierarchical and very organized, so if over time you don't want to chat with the first officer every day after he finishes his morning watch from 4-8 a.m., you can just eat breakfast and leave before 8. Or, if you enjoy the chance to talk with the electrician and carpenters at the end of their workday, be on the pilot deck with a couple of spare beers at 6 p.m. and they're likely to appear. Every sailor I've met knows someone, often a relative, who is in Canada, so I spend a lot of time looking at pictures and talking about Winnipeg or Thunder Bay or Leamington (someday I'll see a picture on a fancy iPhone of someone I actually know). On the other hand, I also get to learn about life in the Philippines, in Sri Lanka, in China, in Romania and elsewhere. And I pick up some tips on ports, which can be really handy.

Often, I've been the only woman on the ship. At first, this felt very uncomfortable. The superstitions haven't really died. Sailing is for men only. Even in military forces, the slowest to accept women serving seem to be the navies. It is changing, though. Sailing up the east coast of China a few years ago, I was called to the bridge one afternoon by the second officer, so that I could listen to the corresponding second officer on a ship coming south as we travelled north. Our second officer wanted me to hear that his counterpart was a woman. It was a nice moment. He did assure me that there were more women coming into the officers' corps on freighters. But this was the first one he had heard. So that's a complication too. But really the principal complication is the same as the principal benefit: it provides large quantities of solitude.

The Day on a Freighter, at sea and on shore:

A day at sea offers a pretty straightforward structure. The freighter moves at around 17 knots, sometimes if the captain is in a hurry around 20 knots. This isn't fast. Cruise ships run a lot faster. The freighter chugs across the ocean. It's noisy too, a kind of underlying background hum. Ideally the ocean is pretty calm, so the freighter just trundles along. If it's got a slight swell, you can feel it but it's pretty easy to get used to. The Atlantic, being a small ocean squashed between two continents (see how your perspective changes?), can be choppy and even quite cool and windy. Then, of course, there can be storms which trap you inside. And what's called a 'following sea' which rolls through the ship stern to bow, causing it to pitch. Worst of all can be a sea that causes the ship both to pitch (forward and back) and to roll (side to side). You have to figure out how to jam yourself into your bunk, and if the rolling is the worst of it, move to sleep starboard/port, but if the pitching is the worst of it, sleep bow/stern. It can be far more exhausting that those 'three all-nighters-in-a-row' that we all recall from school. You subsist on toast. And sips of water.

If you decide to try out a short freighter leg, my advice would be a ten- or fourteen-day run around the

Caribbean, albeit not during tornado season. It would give you a better sense of the pattern of the days, and would have enough stops to be more interesting. Generally, a freighter works its way up a coast loading up, then charges across the ocean, then works its way through two or three ports to unload. So at sea the day is pretty quiet. The seamen work from 8-4 or thereabouts, and the officers stand their two four-hour watches and then do other jobs. The first officer stands watch 4-8 a.m., supervises the work of the crew during the day—especially work on the ship and on the cargo holds—and stands a second watch from 4-8 p.m.. The captain, more commonly at sea called the master, works however many hours it takes to clear all the paperwork, supervise all the ship's work, pop up here and there looking wise and helpful, and plan for the next port. The second and third officers are in charge of navigation and safety respectively, so it's the third officer who appears in the passenger's quarters to discuss lifeboats, rescue suits and drills. There are lots of drills on a well-organized ship. One sign of a badly disorganized ship is a total lack of drills. The days can blend into one another in this pattern, so a good captain ensures that there is some variety. Sometimes this means a ship party, with barbecue and (sadly) vast quantities of karaoke, and a somewhat modulated amount of drink. Sometimes it means launching the lifeboat in the Sea of Japan and circling the ship trying to avoid the multitudinous numbers of jellyfish (which are mucky to remove from the hull). But mostly, for those freighters that have them, variety means the passengers.

For sheer entertainment value, passengers are very handy. A grumpy or irascible master plus a demanding passenger provides the entire ship with huge delight and amusement. Stories of wacko passengers enrich the tale-telling of sailors for decades. A bosun (boatswain, the real boss of the ordinary and able seamen) once told me a tale that went back thirty years to a passenger getting stuck in a hold and no one noticing because the passenger should not have been anywhere near the midships holds. Problems: Requests for fancy food. Demands for the master to call a taxi. Constant demands for the master to send and receive emails. Demands that the liquor stores be opened inside the required international distance away from the shore because the passenger really needs a drink. Falling down while drunk and threatening to sue because the companionway was too steep. Demanding that the chef serve only fish that had been moving about in a school and killed ethically (I heard, and in fact, translated, this request by a French passenger unable to eat anything that had once had a higher-level brain). Demanding a different cabin. Demanding two mattresses to cushion the delicate passenger against the travails of the ship's motion. Demanding ten pillows. Sunbathing nude at the bow, and having the pants fly overboard in a gust of wind (saw that one). Heaving a lawn chair overboard in a fit of pique, then demanding the captain turn the ship around in order to rescue said chair, the last one on board (saw that one, too). Asking to pilot the ship because of having previously piloted a twenty-foot yacht. Setting up on the bridge with binoculars, GPS, maps and shortwave radio to "help" with the navigation. Oh, the passengers are a treat. My own bizarre interest in reading was a pretty minor entertainment. At least I could be counted on to have a bizarre adventure ashore, which would cheer up the next couple of days.

A day alongside or navigating into a port is a wholly different tale. When the pilot arrives, at a set distance from the port, all the crew is generally mobilized, with the possible exception of the first officer. The master goes to the bridge and stays there for the duration of the piloting. Sometimes this can take ten minutes, sometimes three or four hours, sometimes ten or twelve hours. It depends on where the port is and how many obstacles are to be navigated on the way in. Often, the piloting takes all night. The Houston port is twenty or so miles inland from Galveston, past all the oil refineries lit up like Christmas trees, and it's a tricky navigation job as there are also tugs and local ferries of cargo and people crossing back and forth. Louisiana is worse, as the channel at the mouth of the Mississippi into the port winds back and forth so that you can literally see the ship in front of you three hundred yards away going in the other direction (and twenty minutes later, you're both heading forward but in the opposite direction). Shanghai at the mouth of the Yangtze is busy beyond belief. And in Asian ports there are mad fisher-boats "shooting the dragon," blasting past the bow as close as they can manage in order to gain good luck for the day's harvest. As one second officer laconically pointed out when I was holding my breath on the bridge, "mostly, they want to live." The men have to stand by the anchors and lines, one crew with the second officer at the bow, and another with the third officer at the stern (and the boatswain with whichever officer might need help).

Once the ship is tied up after extensive manoeuvring, all kinds of complex engagements begin. There are various kinds of inspections, passport control, the port agent, and eventually the start of the cargo operations. The first officer or chief mate oversees these, pretty much around the clock until they are complete. The men now work six hours on and six hours off. It's astonishingly exhausting stuff but hypnotically interesting to watch. Mostly the longshoremen and longshorewomen (I've seen some) sit in cranes on the edge of the dock or positioned directly over the ship, and unload containers, and then reload. It's best to do so in a balanced way, so the ship does not heel over. Other functions remain the same, including meals and suchlike, but the hatches are often secured, and the cadets (the young guys learning to be officers) stand watch at the gangway. The focus of all activity is the main deck, where the chief mate has an office and oversees all the cargo operations. If the shore cranes break down or never worked or do not exist, the ship's crew activate the onboard cranes. The operations can be astonishing delicate. I once watched two nuclear reactors loaded in Shimonoseki, Japan, and off-loaded in Louisiana, all from barges, and all by the ship's cranes (the two biggest cranes working together, and just barely being sufficient for the weight). A yacht was easier, as one crane swung it to the oceanside and dropped it in the water, one of the electricians having worked all night to get the yacht up and running. At Shanghai, once, the ship made port at 3 a.m., unloaded its entire cargo (a full load, seven or eight hundred containers) and loaded up a full complement of containers, weighing anchor just about twenty-five hours later. Since I had to pass "face control," bringing my face to the immigration officers rather than having my passport stamped as part of the collection the captain presented to the visiting officer, and there was no port agent free to take me there until after 10 a.m., my visit to Shanghai consisted of just about twelve hours. It was fun; luckily the port agent drove me to Pudong, opposite the old city of Shanghai on the Huangpu River. I could walk under the river, visit the city, watch the gorgeous tour and restaurant boats, and return to shop in the modern mall–and then enjoy a truly strange taxi ride back to the port (I had the address written by the port agent in Chinese characters, but apparently it wasn't entirely clear as we stopped several times on mysterious corners featuring guys surrounding a fire in an oil barrel and cooking their dinners on spikes). Shore leave ended at 10:30 for departure overnight, and I barely made it, tossing every renminbi I had in the general direction of my confused but happy taxi driver. He'd clearly never taken a passenger deep into the docks before. It was fun. And I was not late back to the ship.

Woman Afloat (Alone?)

Physiologically speaking, taking freighters is hard work. The average age of passengers on a freighter is about 69. Over 75 is not supposed to happen, but my clear impression is that as long as the passenger can move about comfortably and climb those stairs, it does habitually. So most women passengers on a freighter would be post-menopausal. And that would be a good thing. I took my first freighter when heading off to England for my first sabbatical. It seemed like the thing to do. I was one of four single female passengers (two were friends but travelling separately, I think), and one single male passenger. I was the youngest by thirty years. That was 1995 and the freighter I took was across the Atlantic, with Italian officers and a mixed south Asian crew. The captain even had two young women on board for cleaning and food prep (I don't think the chef allowed them to do any cooking, except perhaps for breakfast). The ship was gleaming, and we were all pretty comfortable. All of the women were readers and we traded books, and played a couple of games of Uno every afternoon. The one man was the most excited about being on a freighter, but least adapted for the job. He wandered the ship chatting to the crew and the officers, and we were all banned from the bridge a couple of days in because he was lonely and thought that the officers of the watch needed company. On the third or fourth day out on the crossing itself (we had done a few days up and down the U.S. east coast), the chief engineer invited us all to visit his engines. This visit, I realized on later trips, was a standard piece of good manners. It was also enlightening. Chief engineers like their engines, and even in the deafening noise of the deepest part of the ship, right beside the massive engines, they will be attempting to talk and explain. Which is fun. But that's where I realized that everything on a ship (save for the food scraps thrown off the stern) gets recycled or saved up to be taken ashore—and very little is saved up to be taken ashore, mostly just plastic and non-biodegradable materials). But sewage is broken down and recycled. There was a massive glass tank of sewage in the engine-room. Rolling about in it I could see tampons. Mine. Ick. They were not, from the look of it, degrading as quickly as they should have. Probably because ships are not made to deal with these issues.

On that occasion, it was too late to do anything about the tampons. I remember flushing with embarrassment. I was young enough not to look around to see if anyone was watching me. And it was only a one-month trip so the problem would not arise again. Looking back, I realize I should have asked the young women who were cleaning on the ship.

But for the next freighter I was prepared, sort of. Wrapped heavily in opaque black plastic (and so unavailable for tossing off the stern), I put the used tampons in the bathroom garbage bin. I was lucky, as I had an eager young steward, probably more embarrassed by the situation than I was. And that was my practice for the next couple of freighters, since it had worked. Working upon me, though, was the charming thought of rats and mice. They're always a problem on ships (I'm a medievalist; I teach the Black Plague), and attracting them five or six decks up in the superstructure with the smell of blood just seemed like a bad idea. And if the rubbish bin in my quarters didn't get emptied every day or two, and its contents placed in the large metal bin on the stern, with a big heavy lock and weight on top of it, I would be attracting rats. A ship is essentially a really big steel can (decks, bulkheads, doors, everything) with sometimes a bit of fake wood pasted onto the lounge walls or the mess—and yet the modern rodent still finds its way through. So when I found myself on a ship without daily service to my room, which happened about my fourth or fifth freighter, I used stealth tactics. Try to picture this: one companionway up the centre of the superstructure (that's a staircase for the landlubber), and a set of steeper ladders (again, we'd still call them stairs), generally offset, around the outside of the superstructure. If I try to sneak down the outside set, I'm crossing back and forth. Also, at night most of the hatches are secured, so I have to go all the way down to the main deck, search for a rubbish bin in the galley or mess areas (the ones sure to be emptied), and especially make sure I find the one whose contents will go into the metal bin outside, since I don't want to be responsible for dumping plastic into the ocean, but I also don't want to dump tampons covered by a bit of Kleenex into a garbage bin, as someone on the ship will notice blood and wonder if there is an unreported injury. And who wants to have that conversation with the master? So the stealth tactics can be tricky, and harder yet if I have cramps. Also, once I've sneaked my way back up to my own deck, I sometimes find the hatch secured from the inside, which requires climbing back down to the main deck and up the central companionway (and I'm sure to meet some curious soul) or up to the bridge, to knock upon the windows of the nerve centre of the ship and interrupt the officer of the watch to beg to be let back in. The best solution is the most brazen: carry them below at mealtimes in a discreet paper bag, and drop in the rubbish on the way into dinner. Best of all, of course, is to be able to take them off the ship, in my bag, when in port. This was my go-to solution, until the utterly hilarious day in Korea when I left the ship and discovered that the port security there required the scanning of my bags. So my purse was scanned, while I stood by with a rictus grin on my face. Nothing was said. I decided, for my own peace of mind, that nothing was noticed. Roll on menopause, when I wouldn't have to worry about this anymore.

And, since I'm shifting onto that topic, let me point out, in passing, another advantage of ship travel. The air conditioning is cranked right up in the superstructure.

It's cold in there. I've been on ships when the heating system was needed, and it works just fine. But the a/c is *outstanding*. Fabulous for dealing with hot flashes. Sometimes the contrast is shocking: steel decks heat up a lot, so when it's hot outside, you can see the heat waves shimmering off the deck. If you happen to be going through the Suez Canal and the sailors are sandbagging the bridge, it's horrifyingly hot, and you need a litre of water every couple of hours. And your sinuses clog up the second you step back inside. That's better than the alternative of not having a/c.

If something goes wrong with the engines, and you're becalmed for several hours, you discover lots of new facts. A becalmed ship is at the mercy of the ocean currents: it spins slowly and distractingly around. It climbs up and down the waves. You get seasick. And that's bizarre as you're not actually moving. It gets warm inside. Very very warm inside. The chef probably has one stove that is not on the mains, or possibly he'll break out the rust-ridden barbecues that you thought were scrap metal. Now, through your open porthole you can smell the fish grilling, and watch the showers of sparks rise up and twinkle in the curtains on your porthole. Okay, maybe it's time to close the porthole and dump water on the curtains. Fire is not really a good thing on a ship. Especially a becalmed ship without any power to send to the hoses. If something goes wrong with the engine on a freighter, you can feel the tension everywhere. A smart chief engineer comes to every meal, and says firmly but calmly to the captain (usually late to meals but on these occasions sitting there firmly and calmly eating his grilled fish and daikon radish salad) that he expects to resolve the problem very soon. A smart captain nods approvingly and comments on the weather. Not all captains are smart. Nor all chief engineers.

This takes me to the problem that most people think is the big one for a woman alone on a ship. Getting propositioned, to put it tactfully. I have to say, this is just not really a problem. The longest stretch for a modern ship is about twenty days, for example from San Francisco to Shanghai. From Los Angeles to Auckland is twenty-five days at fourteen knots, but a speed of sixteen or seventeen knots is more likely for a cargo freighter which would have some time-sensitive material on board. So that's about three weeks at most. I know the ordinary seamen and able seamen tend to be around 20-30 years old, and the officers maybe 27-40. Masters might be older, and the chief and first engineer might be in their 40's or 50's. The last time I took a ship I was older than all the crew save for the master (though every single other passenger was significantly older than I was, so I still felt comparatively young). On age, then, it never was seemly behavior to respond to an advance. (Not that it happened very often.) Moreover, it's just not polite to get involved with one of the ship's complement. A ship is a very delicately functioning mechanism, and any changes to the workings of that mechanism are highly scrutinized. A seaman with a crush on a passenger, or even just one who enjoys chatting with a passenger, will be teased unmercifully. It's important to be equally engaged with all members of the ship's crew, and not to play favourites if that's possible. Once, I was on a ship with a woman who was knitting socks for every single member of the crew. They received these socks with absolute and utter delight. She worked through the list by seniority, to ensure that she knitted and handed out the socks correctly. And they really appreciated the thought. After she left the ship, a dozen of the sailors in turn cornered me to gift me with the socks (she did specialize in rather lurid shades), and eventually we all agreed that donating the socks to the seaman's mission in the next port was the solution. They all received the gifts with tremendous courtesy and kindness, and none of them wanted the socks. Those seafarers reminded me about the fundamental kindness of most human beings.

On only one ship was this kindness and sense of courtesy utterly lost. It was a dying cargo line, and the ship, in mid-journey, received orders to mothball itself, to offload crew, cargo, passenger, and officers, and to leave the ship empty and anchored off Barcelona (most ports have such ships anchored offshore, as that's a cheaper way to store a disused ship that might be needed again than to put them in drydock, and much cheaper than tied up to a dock). Not only was the line collapsing, but the ship was doing so with a very bad crew, headed by an astonishingly lazy master. He spent his days borrowing my books on medieval history and reading them in his quarters, before taking long naps. He was never seen anywhere on the ship; the steward even took his meals to his stateroom. The first officer, a surly soul, ran everything on the ship but in a wholly uninterested way. The second engineer played the movie *Titanic* in the officer's lounge right next to my cabin every night for the first three weeks of the passage. I refused to go watch, but the air conditioning did not work in my cabin so I had to leave my door open to stay cool; I think I am perhaps the only person on the planet who has heard Leonardo DiCaprio go down to a watery grave well over two dozen times, but never seen it. It was a bizarre choice of film. The second engineer told me that he was afraid of the sea and playing the movie was a way to fight the fear. Okay. Maybe. Or maybe it was his idea of clever fun with the passenger. My phone started ringing on about the third night out from Cuba, initially just with propositions of the "Hey, you wanna party?" variety. This was only my second freighter so I was not sure what to do when this did not stop. I went to speak with the first officer, as the master was clearly disengaged, and also I didn't want to get someone fired if that could be avoided. The first officer told me not to answer the phone. I buried it in towels. Didn't work. I unplugged it. Two days later the third officer (in charge of safety, and he should have been on this earlier) appeared at my door. He got an earful. He disappeared. Then knocks started on my door.

I finally stopped the harassment by putting a large poster on the door pointing out just how offensive this behavior was, how it would stop or I would provide the full log of it to the freighter line head office including details of people I had seen and photographed. And I headed out on deck with my camera and took a lot of pictures. Some guys, strangely, tried to dodge me. I came up with a number of creative threats to their continued employment. I also took down several of the lists of the ship's complement and hoarded them in my room, to make sure that they all knew I had their names. And I closed my door and opened the porthole to get cooler air (not supposed to be done especially in the evenings as it bleeds light outwards and can affect night vision for the sailors). The first officer turned up a couple of days later to try to insist that I take the sign down and stop my harassment of his men. He got a serious earful. A couple of members of the ship's complement apologized when I ran across them out on deck during this period, but did so when they were sure that others could not hear. That was a seriously damaged crew. Certainly there were problems with the employer, and with the agent who was hiring the crew, but the real problem on that ship was a bad master and a worse chief mate. On the upside, I got very good food as the chef and steward were desperately unhappy about the situation, and there was a very nice selection of books on the ship, gorgeous weather, and a very easy passage across the Atlantic. I disembarked in Valencia, a couple of days earlier than my contract required, and I was happy to leave. It did not put me off freighters, but after that I evaluated the ship's officers as quickly as possible. And when they changed over (officers are supposed to change every four months, crew every six or eight months), I was right on hand to assess the new guy.

Woman Ashore (Alone)

Going ashore is tricky for a woman travelling alone, especially a North American woman. I have to be rich, and therefore am a target to be fleeced. This means creative thinking. Freighter ports are not like cruise line ports. They're at the seamy end of every town. I could often walk to the seamen's mission, and call for a cab from there, or offer to pay for a cab to take several sailors into town (some wanted the mall, some wanted Walmart and Best Buy, some wanted to see the sights) and arrange to meet to go back. If there were other passengers we could sometimes book a trip with a port agent, if the price sounded reasonable, or at least get a taxi into the city and work from there. Rarely, it was possible to walk right into the main part of the city. Qingdao (known in North America more as Tsing Tao, the place where the Germans established a brewery in the nineteenth century and proceeded to make lager) is a Chinese resort town, and the ship docked less than a mile from the city centre: that was quite lovely, as every day we could disembark, walk in, explore, eat a meal in town if we felt like it, and get back for supper (or stay for a beer). The worst ports for overcharging passengers were in the Middle East and northern Europe (Antwerp, where I paid sixty euros for a trip of a few miles, and got dropped off at passport control where I waited four hours for the taxi driver to come back to collect me, at which point the passport officer, who had steadfastly refused to stamp my passport, seized it and mashed his stamp on it in one second flat–to get back I headed to the seaman's mission and hopped the free bus for sailors). In Dubai, the port agent suddenly announced that there was a landing fee of a hundred bucks and I needed to pay it to him personally, in U.S. dollars. It's important to keep a sense of humour about these issues.

In the Dominican Republic once, the two passengers

from Texas and I walked over to the trailer that served for customs and passport control. It was very informal. I was inclined to think the couple in the trailer were making up their rules on the spot. I was charged five bucks port fee, and the Texans ten bucks each: I spoke Spanish, they didn't. I insisted that we all pay the same amount. And then we walked out through the chainlink fence and wandered about on our own. In Korea, the guard at the gate waved down a cab for me and chased after me to write down the number of Korean won I should be paying for the taxi. It wasn't an area for English speakers. Later that day I perused a menu, tried all my languages, listened to a sequence of other languages I did not recognise, and eventually the nice waitress and I just pointed at one offering. I got six courses of glorious food for about twenty-five bucks; the only problem was that I ate all of the first three, thinking that I must be nearly at the end of the meal when I was just at the beginning. The family children came out of the kitchen and played hide and seek with me. We traded a few American cultural references— Superman and Pocahontas are all I remember—and they pointed me at a tea shop so that I could buy the right thing on my way back to the ship. On another occasion, also in Korea but a different port, I walked round the harbour into town, exchanging money in a bank (very complicated procedure in small Asian cities), buying some nifty kitchen gadgets I still use, taking pictures of the ferocious carved figureheads on the prows of fishing boats (and the blue eye right behind), and eating–sad to say–a hamburger before running into some of the deckhands and paying for our taxi back to the ship (they were back on duty, and I was heading for my bunk). It was my first junk food in months. Tasted good.

I never had any particular difficulty navigating or negotiating my way into the port. Well, except San Diego. You were supposed to wait for the "guy" who would drive you the five hundred yards to the gate and charge ten bucks. The bosun at the gangway that day told me just to walk it, and I did. Apparently the "guy" was from Homeland Security and he later stood at the gangway demanding to know who I was and asking for a fine of a thousand dollars. None of the guys admitted knowing the mysterious person who had left the ship (the only woman in the whole port, and they didn't know me at all). When I came back to the port, I got even luckier as my return coincided with a bunch of the crew coming back for their shift in cargo operations, and they slowed the taxi on the way in to grab me. I never paid the fine. But, I had used up my quota of luck, so I did not go ashore again to use the ticket I had bought for the San Diego Padres game that evening. I found ports surprisingly safe, and the folks working there usually very helpful. Even in America I learned that discussing sports with the security guys offers a solid way into tips and plans, and out of the gate. Once, the pilot arranged for a tugboat to take me across the sound from Oakland to San Francisco, as he'd decided his goal for the day was getting me to a Giants game. That was my most innovative exit from the ship. And the baseball game was wonderful. I had a great seat close to third base, and all the beer and food I wanted served directly to the seat. They don't offer that in Toronto for the Blue Jays, certainly not for that price. I felt the most at risk in American ports (the night-time ride through the Houston port when to confound terrorists they had turned all the lights off, and I had only minutes to make my ship—that was truly hair-raising) and in Middle Eastern ports. Once out of the ports, the usual caution and intelligent common sense applied. Inside the ports, I learned to avoid the local security if I could, and ask crew members—even from another ship—for help if I needed it. And they would always help. The confraternity of seafarers at work.

My best moments

One: The ship sailed into Ha Long Bay in northern Vietnam, passing among hundreds of small limestone islands on a glorious blue day in August. Once we anchored (the ship was too big to contemplate tying up at a dock), I encountered a port agent who was neither a rapscallion nor an extortionist. Yes, he could arrange a trip that afternoon, on his brother-in-law's small fishing boat, to the limestone caves and to other islands of note in the area. The captain and the first engineer came too, as neither had had the opportunity to visit this UNESCO-designated heritage site. The fishing boat came with a family who lived on board; the little girl led me through the caves, which she clearly knew well, and the wife toured with the men. I had seen limestone caves before, but these are massive and spectacular. They've been lit beautifully, different sections in different colors, the stalactites and the stalagmites shimmering blue and green and yellow. It was a really wonderful afternoon, on the fishing boat with the curious Vietnamese family, and then ashore just wandering about (and then we found a place where we could check email, always critical). A leisurely, lovely place.

Two: The ship arrived at Gibraltar at dawn, with porpoises escorting us to our anchorage for the day, where we collected fuel and offloaded cargo and people through the day. Speeding past us were some of the most astonishing yachts. The guys told me about each one, the engines, the shapes, sometimes the owners. We left in the evening so I got to watch the sunset over Gibraltar as well as the sunrise. A stunning place, with huge geographical significance, but also stark beauty.

Three: One night in the Pacific. I'd been writing, drafting some important article or other, and kept working long past midnight. My brain was still buzzing, so I headed out to the deck. And looked up at the sky. Before that I had not seen a blue velvet sky filled with stars. And when I looked to port, there was a long line of fishing boats with their bow lights on. Velvety blue darkness, thousands of stars and constellations lighting up the sky, and a string of lights like pearls across the horizon.

Four: The Suez Canal. Ships walking across the desert, on channels so narrow that from a half-mile away they look like they are sailing on the sand.

Five: The Panama Canal. From the bow, a full day of shifting up in lock after lock, sailing across Lago Gatún in a sudden summer downpour, followed by steaming sun that dried the deck while I sat all alone at the bow to read my book and keep my feet high enough that the crocodiles would not be interested as the ship sauntered past; and then precipitously downwards through the locks on the Atlantic side.

Six: Haiti, destroyed by a tornado, from a ship that had reprovisioned in order to be the first to arrive at Port-au-Prince. This was long before the truly devastating earthquakes that Haiti has suffered; for this one, people were just digging into the rubble and rebuilding their houses, though they were grateful for the supplies and water that we had brought. At breakfast the next day the Polish captain asked me if I thought the crew and other passengers might like "shrimps." I said yes. Lunch that day was as much fresh shrimp as you could eat. Fresh-caught. Shrimp, garlic, salt, lemon, olive oil. We disgraced ourselves, stacking up mounds of shells. The chef didn't even bother to prepare a vegetable. Everybody ate shrimps. And we contributed to the Haitian economy, which needed the boost.

Seven: Sunsets all over the world. So stunning out to sea, without the bleeding of light caused by all that conurbation. And sunrises.

Eight: Just watching the wake from the stern. Hypnotic. All that foaming water, gradually smoothing out farther away. Our vanishing track in the ocean surface.

Nine: So much more. So many best moments. I take freighters.

For fun. For work. For sanity. For remembering my independence. For remembering my dependence.

I take freighters.

So could you.

COLOPHON: THE METRICAL EPILOGUE CCCC MS 41
K. A. Laity (translator)

Bidde ic eac æghwylcne mann,
brego, rices weard, þe þas boc ræde
and þa bredu befo, fira aldor,
þæt gefyrðrige þone writre wynsum cræfte
þe ðas boc awrat bam handum twam,
þæt he mote manega gyt mundum synum
geendigan, his aldre to willan,
and him þæs geunne se ðe ah ealles
                                    geweald,

rodera waldend, þæt he on riht mote
oð his daga ende drihten herigan.
Amen. Geweorþe þæt.

MY WANDERING UTERUS

I beg also the ruler—protector of the realm—
Inspire any person who reads this book
Who takes up these covers during their lifetime
May they wish pleasant work upon the writers here,
Those who wrote this book with their two hands
Though they may not have much in those hands.
In the end, wish them a good life
And grant them that they have all the power
Of the everlasting heavens and that they may
Until their days' end praise the gods.
Amen. So mote it be.

MY WANDERING UTERUS

THE WOMEN'S LEAGUE
OF ALE DRINKERS
Purveyors of Superior Entertainment

Follow the adventures of Dundee's finest
supernatural detective!

Airships & Alchemy

from the author of The Mangrove Legacy

Kit Marlowe

Helen Rochester has a dream: unveiling her airship at the Paris Exposition of 1867. It's sure to make a splash. Her interfering father wants to chaperone the journey even though he's afraid of going up on the sky. Besides, she has doubts about the alchemist. He's promised her a revolutionary new fuel, but does he really need a winged Venetian lion?

How to be
DULL

Basil Morley, Esq.

"ONE OF THE FUNNIEST BOOKS
I'VE READ!"

"THE DULL REVOLUTION HAS BEGUN."

"BEST SATIRE I'VE READ IN YEARS!"

CPSIA information can be obtained
at www.ICGtesting.com
Printed in the USA
LVHW031652140223
739491LV00001B/149

9 781986 379014